THE STRUCTURE AND PERFORMANCE
OF THE AEROSPACE INDUSTRY

PUBLICATIONS OF THE INSTITUTE OF
BUSINESS AND ECONOMIC RESEARCH
UNIVERSITY OF CALIFORNIA

THE STRUCTURE AND PERFORMANCE OF THE AEROSPACE INDUSTRY

by Herman O. Stekler

UNIVERSITY OF CALIFORNIA PRESS 1965

BERKELEY AND LOS ANGELES

UNIVERSITY OF CALIFORNIA PRESS
BERKELEY AND LOS ANGELES, CALIFORNIA

CAMBRIDGE UNIVERSITY
LONDON, ENGLAND

MANUFACTURED IN THE UNITED STATES OF AMERICA

Institute of Business and Economic Research
University of California, Berkeley

The opinions expressed in this study are those of the author. The functions of the Institute of Business and Economic Research are confined to facilitating the prosecution of independent scholarly research by members of the faculty.

TO JOAN

PREFACE

This study presents an analysis of the structure and performance of the aerospace industry, in particular, of the relationship between the government and the private firms. The aerospace industry has been selected for our investigation because of its enormous importance to our economy. Second, although previous studies, such as those by Peck and Scherer, have focused on the entire weapons-acquisition process, they have not attempted to isolate the economic factors working in a particular market segment of the defense industries. This, then, is an industry study which tries to relate the performance of an industry to its structure.

The scope of the entire research effort was limited by the un-availability of much relevant data. At the onset it was decided to use only published data. Thus, the major sources of information for this study were the published documents of the government's procurement agencies, Congressional hearings, and the trade journals. Since this industry has devoted a large percentage of its resources to defense work, it is highly probable that a large amount of significant data could not be used because of military security classifications. The absence of these data may have resulted in the conclusions being somewhat weaker than some observers may find desirable, yet it is unlikely that the major findings would be altered were the remaining data available, for outside observers who have had access to these data have not disputed the findings.

In order to determine the market relationships which prevail in this industry and affect the behavior of the firms, an analysis of the structure of the industry must be undertaken. This structure can then be compared with the performance of the industry and inferences drawn about the relationship between these two variables. However, before that analysis is begun it is appropriate to trace the historical development of the aircraft industry. This perspective is provided in the opening chapter. Several aspects of the importance of research and development to industry and government are likewise introduced. In Chapter 2 a theoretical framework for the study is presented, developing a definition of the aerospace industry and attempting to measure the impact of the industry on the economy.

In Chapter 3 the number of firms in the industry is determined, and the role played by each type of firm is discussed. In other words, the activities of each type of seller are examined. The government's role as a buyer or group of buyers is also analyzed at this stage. Since the relationship between the buyers and sellers operating within this market is the crucial element, it is necessary to analyze the competitive practices which prevail in this industry and the degree of competition which exists. These topics are discussed in Chapter 4, along with an examination of institutional arrangements that the government has introduced in order to encourage efficient performance.

The type of contract which is awarded to a firm bears upon the risk which the firm accepts and may also, in turn, affect the firm's performance. It is for this reason that the contractual forms used in this industry are discussed in the first half of Chapter 5. The remainder of that chapter deals with the risks imposed by these contracts, the overall risks borne by the aerospace firms, and an estimate of the opportunity costs of the aerospace firms. This last datum is then compared with the level of fees which prevail in the industry.

It has been argued that the aerospace industry has experienced several fundamental structural changes. These are examined in Chapter 6 with the primary emphasis upon entry into and exit from the industry. Chapter 7 then presents estimates of the barriers to entry which prevail in two segments of the industry.

Given this structure, the final step in this study is to determine the performance of the aerospace industry. This is done in Chapter 8, but it must be noted that the traditional measures for judging an industry's performance are inapplicable in this case. Thus, several new measures are developed in order to obtain sufficient data

from which inferences may be drawn. The structure and performance of the industry are then related to each other in the conclud-
ing remarks.

Throughout this book frequent recourse has been made to the
trade journal known at various times as *Aviation Week, Aviation
Week Including Space Technology,* and *Aviation Week and Space
Technology.* For purposes of simplification, all references to the
three stages of this publication are standardized as *Aviation Week,*
the title used most commonly in library references.

The research for this study was supported in part by the National
Aeronautics and Space Administration under General Grant No.
NSG-243-62 to the University of California, Berkeley. The grant
has been administered by the Space Sciences Laboratory of the
University. I wish to express my gratitude to NASA for providing
the funds necessary to undertake and complete this research. Edi-
torial assistance and typing was provided by the Institute of Business and Economic Research on the Berkeley campus of the University of California.

In addition, I wish to thank Professor Samuel Silver, Director of
the Space Sciences Laboratory, and Professors C. West Churchman,
Joseph Garbarino, Lee Preston, and John Wheeler, who have been
leaders of the Social Studies Project of the Space Sciences Laboratory, for the active encouragement they provided. This study has
benefited from the comments and criticism of Lee Preston, Albert
Rubenstein, C. West Churchman, Merton J. Peck, Murray L.
Weidenbaum, and also from innumerable participants in the Social
Studies Project. Any remaining errors are, however, solely the responsibility of the author.

H. O. S.

Berkeley,
December, 1964

CONTENTS

TABLES

1.

DEVELOPMENT OF THE U. S. AEROSPACE INDUSTRY, 1903-1963

Introduction

Before beginning the analysis of the structure and performance of the aerospace industry, it is appropriate to consider the manner in which the industry reached its present stage of development. The transition from aircraft industry to aerospace industry was more than a mere change of names. To see this transition in perspective a brief history of the industry's development is presented first. A short discussion of the relationship between the aircraft-aerospace firms and the government follows, for several questions on the financing both of research and development projects and of physical plant and equipment must be analyzed. This relationship is examined in detail in Chapter 3.

In addition, our attention in this chapter is focused on the changing product mix of the industry—not only the mix between government and commercial production, but also the distribution of output and type of activity undertaken for the government (i.e., aircraft versus missiles and rockets, and research and development vis-à-vis production).

Moreover, in the course of the transition from the aircraft industry to the aerospace industry the functions of firms engaged in the industry also changed, and the scope of the industry's activities was enlarged to encompass firms not originally included in the aircraft industry.

1

HISTORICAL DEVELOPMENT

INITIAL DEVELOPMENT—1903-1914

By 1900 all components necessary for man's first flight, including the internal-combustion engine, were under development, but it was not until 1903 that the first successful flight was made.[1] The discovery of abundant reserves of oil provided the energy to power airplanes as well as automobiles and undoubtedly contributed to development of the industry. However, the political instability in Europe, the armaments race of the early twentieth century, and World War I, all created a market for airplanes and were the major factors causing an expansion of the industry.

Before World War I no real aircraft "industry" as one would commonly define an industry existed. Rather a type of "backyard" production process existed.[2] Furthermore, data for this pre-1914 period are virtually nonexistent.[3] The available figures (Tables 1

TABLE 1
U. S. AIRCRAFT PRODUCTION, 1909-1913

Year	Number of aircraft		
	Total	Military	Civil
1909	...	1	...
1910	...	...	...
1911	...	11	...
1912	45	16	29
1913	43	14	29

SOURCE: *Aerospace Facts and Figures, 1962* (Washington: American Aviation Publications, 1962), p. 6, and *Aviation Facts and Figures, 1945* (New York: McGraw-Hill, 1945), p. 7.

and 2) indicate the relative unimportance of both military and civilian airplane production and the lack of attention paid to military aviation as reflected by the size of the military appropriation for this purpose.

---

[1] Aircraft Industries Association, *Aviation Facts and Figures, 1945* (New York: McGraw-Hill, 1945), p. 6. Also published in various years as *Aerospace Facts and Figures*.

[2] *Ibid.*, p. 36.

[3] In 1914 the Census Bureau reported on aircraft production for the first time. Until 1925 the aircraft and engine production data are reliable only to the extent that they reflect production trend.

WORLD WAR I AND INTERWAR PERIOD—1914-1939

World War I provided the United States aircraft industry with a major impetus. Between 1914 and 1916 annual production expanded from 49 to 411 airplanes, mainly as the result of increased exports (Tables 3 and 4). With our entry into the war, production

TABLE 2
APPROPRIATIONS FOR U. S. ARMY AIR CORPS
AND NAVAL AVIATION, 1909-1913
(in dollars)

Year	Army Air Corps	Naval aviation
1909	30,000a	. . .
1910	. . .	. . .
1911	25,000	. . .
1912b	100,000	25,000
1913	100,000	10,000

SOURCE: *Aviation Facts and Figures, 1945,* p. 53, and *Aerospace Facts and Figures, 1960,* p. 27.

a Allotted to pay for Wright airplane which completed tests in 1909.
b The personnel of the Army Air Corps consisted of 751 men.

increased to 2,148 in 1917 and 14,020 in 1918, but dropped drastically with the end of the war. The development of these airplanes and the facilities in which production took place were privately financed, with the manufacturers actively competing for these sales.[4]

The industry had sharply expanded its productive capacity to meet this war demand, but in 1919 the government not only curtailed its aircraft purchasing, but also placed its surplus on sale in the open market.[5] These factors, coupled with the inadequate financial resources of the aircraft manufacturers, forced many into major reorganization or bankruptcy in the early twenties. In this period the four major companies which had produced 75 percent of the airplanes and engines for the Army during the war either left the industry or reorganized. Curtiss Aeroplane and Motor Company and Wright-Martin Company reorganized; Dayton-Wright Company stopped making airplanes; and Standard Aviation Company

[4] *Aviation Facts and Figures, 1945,* pp. 36-42. On the other hand, engines were financed by the military services. R. Schlaifer, *Development of Aircraft Engines* (Cambridge, Mass.: School of Business Administration, Harvard University, 1950), pp. 15, 31, 41, 61-66, and 160.
[5] *Aviation Facts and Figures, 1945,* p. 36.

went out of business.[6] Despite this shakedown, twenty-five aircraft companies, including the reorganized ones, remained in the industry in 1925.[7]

TABLE 3
U. S. AIRCRAFT PRODUCTION, 1914-1939

Year	Aircraft		
	Total	Military	Civil[a]
1914	49	15	34
1915	178	26	152
1916	411	142	269
1917	2,148	2,013	135
1918	14,020	13,991	29
1919	780	682	98
1920	328	256	72
1921	437	389	48
1922	263	226	37
1923	743	687	56
1924	377	317	60
1925	789	447	342
1926	1,186	532	654
1927	1,995	621	1,374
1928	4,346	1,219	3,127
1929	6,193	677	5,516
1930	3,437	747	2,690
1931	2,800	812	1,988
1932	1,396	593	803
1933	1,324	466	858
1934	1,615	437	1,178
1935	1,710	459	1,251
1936	3,010	1,141	1,869
1937	3,773	949	2,824
1938	3,623	1,800	1,823
1939	5,856	2,195	3,661

SOURCE: *Aerospace Facts and Figures, 1962*, pp. 6-7.

a These figures include aircraft production for export and for domestic consumption. See *Aviation Facts and Figures, 1953*, p. 25.

Although military sales declined precipitously, it was not until the late twenties that sales of civilian aircraft exceeded military sales. At first, civil air transportation was limited to carrying mail, but in 1927 the first airline to carry passengers was formed. The creation of the airlines provided a new market for the aircraft manu-

---

[6] *Ibid.*, p. 37.

[7] *Aircraft Year Book, 1926* (New York: Aeronautical Chamber of Commerce of America, 1926), pp. 191-205. Twenty-four of these companies were listed as airplane manufacturers. There were five engine manufacturers, including four which were also listed as airplane manufacturers. The other company was the Packard Motor Car Co.

facturers. Sales in this market soon exceeded military purchases. The success or failure of the airplane manufacturers clearly depended on their ability to compete for commercial sales. Many man-

TABLE 4
AIRPLANE DELIVERIES AND EXPORTS, 1914-1919a

Year	Number of airplanes delivered and acceptedb by:			Exportedc	Total
	Army	Navy	Post Office		
1914	11	4	...	34	49
1915	20	6	...	152	178
1916	83	59	...	269	411
1917	1,807	206	...	135	2,148
1918	11,916	2,075	9	20	14,020
1919	409	273	13	85	780
TOTAL	14,274	2,637	22	753	17,686

SOURCE: *Aviation Facts and Figures, 1945*, p. 7.

a Excludes deliveries to users other than the government.
b Excludes spares delivered, remodeling jobs, and intergovernment deliveries.
c Fiscal years 1914-1918, calendar years thereafter. Forty-one airplanes delivered or exported in the period July-December, 1918, are included in 1919.

ufacturers had legal ties with some of the early airlines. Boeing, Douglas, and North American Aviation were among the firms that had such connections.[8] In 1930 there was no plane or company which seemed to dominate the market, for the airlines were using forty-one different airplane models of nineteen separate manufacturers.[9] The Ford and Fokker trimotors were extensively used,[10] but neither of these companies advanced the state of technological development. In 1931-1932 the Ford and Fokker trimotors were re-

---

[8] John H. Frederick, *Commercial Air Transportation*, rev. ed. (Chicago: Richard D. Irwin, 1946), p. 9.

[9] According to the Department of Commerce, there were 215 companies manufacturing airplanes in the United States in the middle of 1930. Of these 215, only 79 firms had manufactured planes which held approved type certificates. *Aircraft Year Book, 1931* (New York: D. Van Nostrand Co., 1931), p. 117, hereafter cited as *Aircraft Year Book* for specific years. Fifty-four companies were considered important enough for this publication to list them and the airplane models which they produced. In addition several other companies were listed even though they were divisions of either Curtiss-Wright or United Aircraft and Transportation Co. Four duplicate divisions were eliminated from the list of nineteen manufacturers whose models were used by the air-transport companies. We may then conclude that in 1930 the air-transport companies were using models of fifteen aircraft manufacturers which were independent at that time. The models of the four other companies may have been bought at an earlier time when these companies too were independent.

[10] Frederick, *op. cit.*, p. 421.

placed by Curtiss-Wright's B-18 and T-32 Condors.[11] By 1935 the number of different models used by the airlines had been reduced to twenty-six representing the output of twelve manufacturers.[12] At this point Douglas and Lockheed were emerging as the leading firms in the industry. Douglas' DC-2, used in 1934-1935, and DC-3, introduced in 1936-1937, eventually resulted in the company's becoming the leader in the industry. Lockheed and Boeing were both able to compete, but the extent to which Douglas dominated the industry can be seen from Table 5. Douglas emerged as the industry leader because of the technical superiority of the DC-3.

TABLE 5
AIRCRAFT IN SERVICE, U. S. SCHEDULED DOMESTIC AND INTERNATIONAL AIRLINES, 1938 AND 1941

Number of aircraft in service					
December 31, 1938a			December 31, 1941		
Manufacturer	By model	By firm	Manufacturer	By model	By firm
Boeing		39	Boeing		43
247-D	39		247-D	27	
			B-307	8	
			B-304	8	
Douglas		143	Douglas		328
DST	30		DST	45	
DC-2	46		DC-2	16	
DC-3	67		DC-3	267	
Lockheed		45	Lockheed		34
Electra	33		Electra	18	
12-A	3		Lodestar	16	
14-H	9				
Sikorsky		5			
Others		6	Others		6
TOTAL		238	TOTAL		411

SOURCE: U. S., Civil Aeronautics Board, Economic Bureau, Rates and Audit Division, *Annual Airline Statistics, Domestic Carriers, Calendar Years 1938-1942* (1944), p. 134, and *Aerospace Facts and Figures, 1962*, p. 110.

a Data for 1938 do not include the planes used by the international airlines.

The industry's growth in this period can be noted in several dimensions. The dollar sales of the industry increased from less than

---

11 *Ibid.* General Motors obtained working control of Fokker Aircraft in 1929.

12 *Aircraft Year Book, 1936*, pp. 315-338. By this time, the number of aircraft manufacturers had been reduced to 30 with an additional 8 firms engaged in the production of aircraft engines.

one million to close to a quarter of a billion (Table 6), with the value added, generated by this industry, showing a corresponding increase.[13] Moreover, 63,994 people were employed in the industry

TABLE 6

VALUE OF AIRCRAFT AND PARTS PRODUCED, 1914-1939
(in thousands of dollars)

Year	Value added by manufacture[a]	Value of products[b]
1914	656	790
1919	7,246	14,373
1921	4,235	6,642
1923	9,116	12,945
1925	9,655	12,525
1927	13,645	21,162
1929	43,785	71,153
1931	27,177	40,278
1933	18,503	26,460
1935	30,986	45,347
1937	93,144c	149,700c
1937	67,763	106,568
1939	183,247c	279,497c

SOURCE: U. S., Bureau of the Census, *Sixteenth Census of the U. S.: 1940 Manufactures, 1939*, Vol. II, P. 2, *Reports by Industries*, Groups 11 to 20 (1942), pp. 540-541.

a Values of products less cost of materials, supplies, fuel, purchased electric energy, and contract work.

b 1914-1929: Total selling values at plant. 1931-1933: Values of aircraft less values of engines installed. 1935: Includes values of instruments and accessories, but not the value of engines, propellers, and power-plant accessories installed.

c 1937 and 1939: As 1935, but includes value of aircraft *engines*.

by 1939 as compared with 222 in 1914 (Table 7). However, the industry was still small when compared with all manufacturing industries, for in 1939 the aircraft and parts industry accounted for only 0.6 percent of all manufacturing employment and 0.7 percent of total value added by manufacturing.[14] Despite this growth the in-

---

13 Sales for the 1935-1937 period can be divided into four major categories: the military services took 40 percent of the sales; exports accounted for 27 percent; airlines for 23 percent; and small civilian planes for 10 percent. T. Lilley, P. Hunt, J. K. Butters, F. F. Gilmore and P. F. Lander, *Problems of Accelerating Aircraft Production During World War II* (Cambridge, Mass.: Harvard University, Division of Research, Graduate School of Business Administration, 1946), p. 5.

14 Total manufacturing employment and value added in 1939 were $9,722 million and $24,683 million, respectively. U.S., Bureau of the Census, *Sixteenth Census of the U.S.: 1940 Manufactures, 1939*, Pt. 2, *Reports by Industries*, Groups 11 to 20 (Washington, D. C.: U.S. Government Printing Office, 1942), pp. 540, 541. Hereafter citations of government publications will not contain place of publication and publisher unless they are not Washington, D. C.: U.S. Government Printing Office.

dustry was not in a strong condition before the outbreak of World War II. Two of the seven major firms had plants that had either a very small backlog or were virtually empty.[15]

WORLD WAR II—1939-1945

With the outbreak of World War II, the American aviation industry expanded rapidly. From a 1939 production level of 5,856 airplanes, the industry increased its output to the wartime peak of

TABLE 7

EMPLOYMENT IN THE AIRCRAFT INDUSTRY, 1914-1939

Year	Wage earners (average for year)	Salaried officers and employees[a]	Total
1914	168	54	222
1919	3,638	659	4,202
1921	1,395	557	1,952
1925	2,701	...	...
1927	4,422	1,064	5,486
1929	14,710	3,910	18,620
1931	9,870	...	...
1933	7,816	1,810	9,626
1935	11,384	3,547	14,931
1937	24,003	7,917	31,920
1937[b]	30,384	...	...
1939[b]	48,638	15,233	63,994

SOURCES:
  A: U. S., Bureau of the Census, *Biennial Census of Manufactures.*
    1914-21, Census of 1921 (1924), p. 1080.
    1923, Census of 1923 (1926), p. 1019.
    1925, Census of 1925 (1928), p. 1087.
    1927, Census of 1927 (1930), p. 1125.
    1931-35, Census of 1935 (1938), p. 1129.
    1937, Census of 1937, Part 1 (1939), p. 1182.
  B: U. S., Bureau of the Census, *Census of the U. S. Manufactures.*
    1929, Fifteenth Census: 1929, Vol. II, Reports by Industries (1933), p. 1191.
    1939, Sixteenth Census: 1940 (1942), p. 54.

  a Includes proprietors and firm members (this is the word used—no explanation of meaning) in earlier years.
  b Aircraft and parts, including aircraft engines. Engines not included in other data.

---

15 The seven major firms were: Boeing, Consolidated, Curtiss, Douglas, Lockheed, Martin and North American Aviation. U.S., Senate, Committee on Military Affairs, *Hearings on S2868, Procurement of Aircraft,* 1939, p. 8. Despite a conscious effort by the government to expand the capability of the industry, several plants were empty. Consolidated's was almost empty, and Martin had no government orders. U.S., House, Committee on Military Affairs, *Hearings on An Adequate National Defense as Outlined by the Message of the President of the United States,* 76th Cong., 1st Sess., January 17-February 3, 1939, p. 10.

96,318 in 1944 (Table 8). This vast expansion required the construction of new facilities, for in 1940 the industry had the capacity of manufacturing only 17,000 planes.[16] These plants were mainly financed by the federal government because the industry did not have the financial resources. The gross value of the additional capacity created between July, 1940, and July, 1945, for the production of aircraft, engines, parts, and accessories was $3,894 million[17]

TABLE 8
U. S. AIRCRAFT PRODUCTION, MILITARY AND CIVILIAN,
1940-1945

Year	Total	Military	Civilian
1940	12,804	6,019b	6,785c
1941	26,277a	19,433b	6,844c
1942	47,836a	47,836b	d
1943	85,898a	85,898b	d
1944	96,318a	96,318b	d
1945	49,961a	47,714b	2,047

SOURCE: U. S., Civil Aeronautics Administration, *U. S. Military Aircraft Acceptances, 1940-1945* (1946), pp. 2-3.

a Includes U. S.-financed aircraft manufacturing in Canada.
b Includes military aircraft for Lend-Lease.
c Includes domestic civil output only.
d No production other than military.

(Table 9). This must be compared with a figure of $114 million, the value placed on all facilities available in 1939 for the production of the mentioned products.[18] Data are available (Table 10) for twenty-four major firms, showing the extent of the difference between private and federal financing of these new facilities, with the largest part coming from government funds.

A large increase in the capacity of the industry was also achieved by utilizing the existing assembly plants of the automobile com-

---

16 U.S., Senate, *Hearings on Senate Resolution 244, The Purchase of Implements of War by Foreign Governments*, 76th Cong., 3d Sess., 1940, p. 9. Much of this capacity had been created by foreign orders mainly from Britain and France. Some of these orders included in the terms of the contract a payment to the company for expanding its plant. *Ibid.*, p. 8, and Lilley, Hunt, *et al., op. cit.*, p. 15. For instance, the experimental and development, and tooling costs of the P-40 had been paid for by foreign orders.

17 See Table 8. Of this amount approximately 10 percent was privately financed.

18 U.S. War Production Board, "Facilities Expansion, July 1940-June 1944," *Facts for Industry*, Series 50-4-1, pp. 6, 17.

panies and converting them into aircraft-assembly plants.[19] Moreover, the expanded use of subcontracts enabled an increase of production without an even larger increase in the capacity of the

TABLE 9

Cost of Emergency Facilities Expansion in the Aircraft Industry
1940-1945
(in millions of dollars)

Type of expansion	Total	Privately financed	Federally financed
Total expansion 1940-1945a	3,894	420	3,474
Structures 1940-1945a	1,556	212	1,344
Equipment 1940-1945a	2,338	208	2,130

SOURCE: U. S., Civilian Production Administration, Industrial Statistics Division, "Wartime Manufacturing Plant Expansion, Privately Financed, 1940-1945" (March 15, 1946).

a Cost of manufacturing facilities authorized July, 1940-June, 1945.

aircraft industry.[20] It has been estimated that near the end of the war about 30 to 35 percent of the assembled airplane weight was being produced by subcontractors.[21]

Moreover, all facilities were utilized more intensively with the result that employment in the aircraft and parts industry rose to 7.6 percent of all manufacturing employment by 1943 (Table 11).

---

[19] In 1943, aviation items accounted for more than 40 percent of the dollar volume of General Motors. General Motors Corporation, *35th Annual Report*, for year ending December 31, 1943, p. 6. However, in converting to the manufacture of aviation products, the specialized nature of automobile tools required that at least new tools, and in some instances new plants, were required. The Willow Run plant was built for the government but was operated by the Ford Motor Co. "What Uncle Sam Expects of the Automobile Industry," *Automotive Industries*, LXXXVI, No. 2 (January 15, 1942), pp. 17-52; Lilley, Hunt, *et al., op. cit.*, p. 71. According to one observer, the number of prime aviation contractors increased from 28 in 1939 to 81 in 1943. See W. G. Cunningham, *The Aircraft Industry, A Study in Industrial Location* (Los Angeles: Lorrin L. Morrison, 1951), p. 97.

[20] Before the war, some aircraft manufacturers were subcontracting portions of their work. The firms which subcontracted were generally the smaller firms in the industry. U.S., Senate, Committee on Military Affairs, *Hearings on S. 2868, Procurement of Aircraft*, 76th Cong., 1st Sess. 1939, p. 8. For a discussion of the role of subcontracting in this industry, see Neil E. Harlan, *Management Control in Airplane Subcontracting* (Boston: Division of Research, Graduate School of Business Administration, Harvard University, 1956); and John S. Day, *Subcontracting Policy in the Airplane Industry* (Boston: Division of Research, Graduate School of Business Administration, Harvard University, 1956).

[21] Day, *op. cit.*, p. 16, and Lilley, Hunt, *et al., op. cit.*, p. 36, U.S., War Production Board, *Historical Reports on War Administration*, Special Study 21: "Aircraft Production Policies under the National Defense Advisory Commission and Office of Production Management, May 1940-December 1941," May 30, 1946, p. 102.

This figure actually understates the wartime importance of the industry, for a considerable part of the manufacturing activity was subcontracted. If an estimate of total employment in this activity is added to the other employment data, in January, 1944, the aircraft

TABLE 10

SOURCE OF FUNDS FOR AIRCRAFT, ENGINE, AND ACCESSORY FACILITIES
EXPANSION, 1940-1944a
(in millions of dollars)

Name of company	Federally financed	Privately financed
Bell Aircraft Corporation	92.9	5.8
Bendix Aviation Corporation	110.5	10.8
Boeing Airplane Company	71.1	5.4
Chrysler Corporation	197.6	0.8
Consolidated Vultee Aircraft Corporation	142.4	27.5
Continental Motor Corporation	87.8	2.1
Curtiss-Wright Corporation	425.2	46.3
Douglas Aircraft Company, Inc.	196.9	15.1
Fairchild Engine & Airplane Corporation	41.6	1.4
Ford Motor Company	223.6	11.3
General Electric Company	49.6	3.1
General Motors Corporation	501.3	33.7
Hughes Tool Company	. . .	. . .
Lockheed Aircraft Corporation	29.8	25.1
The Glenn L. Martin Company	77.4	3.9
McDonnell Aircraft Corporation	. . .	. . .
Nash-Kelvinator Corporation	71.5	0.1
North American Aviation, Inc.	78.7	5.0
Packard Motor Car Company	93.1	0.3
Republic Aviation Corporation	45.1	0.6
The Sperry Corporation	44.9	1.0
Studebaker Corporation	92.9	0.5
Thompson Products, Inc.	30.5	4.0
United Aircraft Corporation	206.8	36.9

SOURCE: U. S., Surplus Property Administration, Report to Congress, *Aircraft Plants and Facilities* (January 14, 1946), p. 40.

a Value of facilities authorized.

industry accounted for 12.4 percent of total manufacturing employment.[22] The total sales of the industry rose to more than $16 billion, including the value of products which were exported or given to our allies through the lend-lease program.[23]

---

[22] This figure is an overestimate, since the total employment of *all establishments having aircraft subcontracts* was included even when aircraft and parts were not the primary activity. U.S., Department of Labor, *Monthly Labor Review*, "Wartime Developments in the Aircraft Industry," LIX, No. 5, November 1944, pp. 911-912, and U.S., Manpower Commission, *Manpower Statistics*, June 1945, p. 15.

[23] In 1944, the value of exports of aeronautic products (including lend-lease) was more than $2.8 billion or more than 15 percent of the total sales volume of all aeronautic products.

One further development should not go unnoticed. The war period saw a sharp rise in government-financed research and development expenditures for aircraft. Expenditures by the National Advisory Committee for Aeronautics (N.A.C.A.) rose from $2.2 million in 1940 to $24.1 million in 1945.[24] Likewise, the research and development expenditures of the military services rose from $26.4 million to $513 million in 1945. However, only a part of these

TABLE 11

EMPLOYMENT: AIRCRAFT AND PARTS INDUSTRY, AND
TOTAL MANUFACTURING, 1940-1945

Year	(1) Employees in aircraft and parts industry[a] (000)	(2) Employees in all manufacturing (000)	Percentage of (2) in (1)
1940	148.6	10,985	1.3
1941	347.1	13,192	2.6
1942	831.7	15,280	5.4
1943	1,345.6	17,602	7.6
1944	1,296.6	17,328	7.4
1945	788.1	15,524	5.0

SOURCE: U. S., Bureau of Labor Statistics, *Employment and Earnings Statistics for the United States, 1909-1960*, Bulletin No. 1312 (1961), pp. 29-30, 215.

a Includes engines.

military expenditures were for aircraft, engines, and parts. Finally, the newly created Office of Scientific Research and Development was spending $114.5 million by 1945.[25]

POSTWAR PERIOD—1945-1963

With the end of the war, the industry's sales declined as fast as they had expanded, falling from the wartime peak of $16 billion to about $1 billion by 1947.[26] Not the entire burden of this decline was borne by the aviation industry, for the wartime sales figures had included the armaments carried by the airplanes, and the loss of these sales did not affect the industry. Moreover, the automobile firms ceased playing an important role in the industry. The aircraft industry did experience excess capacity, but the largest portion of

24 National Science Foundation, *Federal Funds for Science: III, The Federal Research and Development Budget, 1953, 1954 and 1955*, 1955, p. 41.
25 *Ibid.*
26 *Aviation Week*, February 23, 1948, p. 35.

the wartime expansion had been financed by the government, which owned the plants. Consequently these government-owned facilities imposed no financial burden on the firms. However, firms which had been subcontractors during the war did experience financial difficulties.[27] There is also some evidence indicating that the military services were protecting the existing aircraft firms by spreading the work among them. The purpose was to preserve the industry's skills and capacity and assure the survival of this vital defense industry in case of another war.[28]

It had been expected that the demand for commercial aircraft would be a factor to compensate for the decline in military-aircraft sales. Only 1,417 military aircraft were produced in 1946, whereas 35,000 civil aircraft were manufactured.[29] Part of this civilian demand was the result of the expansion of domestic and international airline service. However, this stimulus quickly disappeared, for the level of civil-airplane production showed a steady decline from the 1946 postwar peak (Table 12). In fact, North American Aviation, which had started manufacturing a family-type plane, called it a failure and discontinued its production.[30]

Douglas was able to regain its prewar dominance in the airline market with its DC-4's and DC-6's, but by 1948 the domestic commercial market for aircraft had become saturated.[31] Lockheed, Consolidated Vultee, Boeing, and Martin also produced aircraft, but these companies were not as successful as Douglas.[32] In 1950, Doug-

---

[27] Day, *op. cit.*, p. 26. However, many firms also experienced deficits in the immediate postwar period.

[28] Merton J. Peck and F. M. Scherer, *The Weapons Acquisition Process: An Economic Analysis* (Cambridge: Harvard University Press, Division of Research, 1962), pp. 355 and 375. *Survival in the Air Age,* A Report by the President's Air Policy Commission, 1948, p. 60. *National Aviation Policy*, Report of the Congressional Aviation Policy Board. Congress of the U.S., March 1, 1948, Senate Report No. 949, Pursuant to Public Law 287, 80th Cong., 2d Sess. to establish a Temporary Congressional Aviation Policy Board.

[29] *Aerospace Facts and Figures, 1962*, p. 7. However, many of these airplanes were very small. To manufacture one of these, not as much labor was required as was needed to assemble a large military bomber.

[30] North American Aviation, *Annual Report, 1947*, p. 1.

[31] Douglas Aircraft Co., *Annual Report, 1948*, p. 1.

[32] Lockheed started, canceled, and then restarted its Constellation project. In developing the plane it received financial assistance from TWA similar to the aid given by five airlines to Douglas when it was developing its DC-4. F. Taylor, *High Horizons —The United Airlines Story* (New York: McGraw-Hill, 1958), pp. 113-115, and 150. Richard Caves, *Air Transport and Its Regulation* (Cambridge: Harvard University Press, 1962), p. 100.

las aircraft still dominated the air-transport market (Table 13).

Between 2,100 and 2,500 airplanes were built for the military in each of the years 1947 to 1949. This low level of military production, coupled with the less-than-expected growth of commercial

TABLE 12

U. S. Aircraft Production, 1946-1961

Year	Total	Military	Civilian
1946	36,418	1,417	35,001
1947	17,739	2,122	15,617
1948	9,838	2,536	7,302
1949	6,137	2,592	3,545
1950	6,200	2,680	3,520
1951	7,532	5,055	2,477
1952	10,640	7,131	3,509
1953	13,112	8,978	4,134
1954	11,478	8,089	3,389
1955	11,484	6,664	4,820
1956	12,408	5,203	7,205
1957	11,943	5,198	6,745
1958	10,938	4,078	6,860
1959	11,076	2,834	8,242
1960	10,237	2,056	8,181
1961	9,472a	2,000a	7,472
1962	9,333a	2,000a	7,333

SOURCE: *Aerospace Facts and Figures, 1963*, p. 7.

a Estimate.

TABLE 13

Aircraft in Service: U. S. Scheduled Domestic and
International Airlines, 1950 and 1955

	Aircraft in service	
	1950	1955
Beechcraft	10	
Bell	6	
Boeing	50	36
Cessna	14	
Convair	119	221
Curtiss	2	
Douglas	758	779
Lockheed	123	177
Martin	33	119
Sikorsky	5	12
Vickers (English)		8
TOTAL	1,120	1,352

SOURCE: U. S., Civil Aeronautics Administration, *Statistical Handbook of Civil Aviation 1956* (1956), pp. 69 and 87.

sales gave rise to fears about the survival of the aircraft industry.[33] The extent by which sales declined in this period can be seen from Table 14.

TABLE 14
ANNUAL SALES OF A SELECT NUMBER OF AIRFRAME MANUFACTURERS,
1945-1949
(in millions of dollars)

Company	Year				
	1945	1946	1947	1948	1949
Boeing	421.0	14.0	21.7	126.9	286.8
Consolidated Vultee	644.0	13.7	47.4	112.4	196.8
Douglas	244.0	106.7	128.5	118.6	117.0
Grumman	236.8	37.6	24.2	41.0	59.8
Lockheed	418.0	113.6	134.4	125.6	117.7
Martin	356.2	37.6	23.4	72.7	52.0
North American	400.4	55.8	19.8	94.8	124.7
Northrop	86.4	26.4	28.8	26.0	28.2

SOURCE: Annual reports of the companies.

The drop in employment in the aviation industry is further evidence of the decline in importance of the industry. From a wartime peak of more than a million employees, employment fell to a postwar low in May, 1948. Both aircraft production and employment had begun to rise even before the Korean War in 1950, but that conflict greatly accelerated the process.

The Korean War required expanded aircraft production, but the stand-by facilities created during World War II were now partly obsolete. As a consequence, new facilities were once again required, and again the government provided the largest portion of the financing. In this period, however, the industry contributed 34 percent of the expansion cost as compared with the 10 percent it had financed during World War II (Table 15). Even after the Korean War, aircraft production remained at the high level reached during this conflict. The postwar employment peak of 909,100 occurred in

---

[33] See *National Aviation Policy* and *Survival in the Air Age*, especially pp. 38 and 51. There were 15 airframe companies in existence at that time, but more than 75 percent of all Air Force funds for airframe procurement were concentrated in three firms. Boeing, which was developing several big bombers, had a policy of subcontracting 50 percent of its work to other airframe manufacturers. Boeing Airplane Co., *Annual Report, 1947*, p. 1, and *Annual Report, 1948*, p. 3. The Martin Company was then actively engaged in subcontract work on major aircraft components. See its *Annual Report, 1949*, p. 10.

April, 1957,[34] but the production of military aircraft declined steadily thereafter as missiles achieved an important role in our deterrent force.

The successful development of the hydrogen bomb enabled the Air Force to place part of its deterrent strength in ballistic missiles. Some aviation companies had been working on guided missile projects since the close of the war,[35] but the year ending June 30, 1951,

TABLE 15

AIRCRAFT INDUSTRY EMERGENCY-FACILITIES EXPANSION:
COST AND FUND SOURCES, WORLD WAR II AND KOREAN WAR
(in millions of dollars)

Type of expansion	Source of funds		
	Total	Private	Federal
Total expansion			
1940-45a	3,894	420	3,474
1950-53	3,528b	1,204c	2,324b
Structures			
1940-45a	1,556	212	1,344
1950-53	1,085b	805d	280b
Epuipment			
1940-45a	2,338	208	2,130
1950-53	2,483b	339e	2,044b

SOURCE: *Aviation Facts and Figures, 1953,* p. 11; U. S., Civilian Production Administration, Industrial Statistics Division, *Wartime Manufacturing Plant Expansion, Privately Financed, 1940-1945* (March 15, 1946).

a Cost of manufacturing facilities authorized July, 1940-June, 1945.

b Estimate.

c Total is that procured by Aircraft Division of National Production Authority to 1953.

d Total is that procured by Aircraft Division of National Production Authority, March 1, 1953.

e Total is that procured by Aircraft Division of National Production Authority, March 1, 1953.

must be considered the one in which the missile began to come into its own.[36] In that year, the funds made available for missile development and production increased nearly 500 percent over the previous year's level (Tables 16 and 17). However, the funds expended on the longer-range ballistic missiles were increased only after the suc-

34 U.S., Bureau of Labor Statistics, *Employment and Earnings,* July 1957, IV, No. 1, 1957.

35 Between 1946 and 1949, North American Aviation and Douglas had noted in their annual reports that they had some guided missile contracts.

36 In 1952, the Navy announced that it was developing three guided missiles, the Terrier, the Regulus, and the Sparrow.

cessful development of the hydrogen bomb. Thereafter, the defense expenditures devoted to the procurement of missiles increased enormously. The missile and the airplane, therefore, became, in part, substitutes, which could perform similar missions. Normally, one

TABLE 16

DEPARTMENT OF DEFENSE EXPENDITURES: FOR TOTAL DEVELOPMENT AND PRODUCTION, AND FOR GUIDED-MISSILE DEVELOPMENT AND PRODUCTION, 1951-1964

Fiscal year	Total development and production (in millions of dollars)	Guided missiles (in millions of dollars)	Guided missiles as percentage of total
1951	3,976	21	0.5
1952	11,478	169	1.5
1953	17,297	245	1.4
1954	15,957	417	2.6
1955	12,838	604	4.7
1956	12,227	1,005	8.2
1957	13,488	1,855	13.8
1958	14,083	2,434	17.3
1959	14,409	3,337	23.2
1960	13,334	3,027	22.7
1961	13,095	2,972	22.7
1962	14,532	3,442	23.7
1963a	16,632	3,817	22.9
1964a	16,337	3,506	21.5

SOURCE: *Aerospace Facts and Figures, 1963,* p. 23. U. S., Department of Defense, *Order of Magnitude Data on Comparative Expenditures by Functional Title as if FY 1965 Budget Structure had been Adopted Circa 1948,* FAD-397 (January 21, 1964). The data note that "amounts include estimated comparability adjustment not supportable by accounting records." Other data which support the trend of these data though not their numerical accuracy appear in U. S., Senate, Subcommittee of the Select Committee on Small Business, *Hearings, The Role of Small Business in Government Procurement,* 87th Cong. 1st Sess., April 25-26, 1961, p. 42. For fiscal years 1952-1959 those percentages are 1.5, 1.7, 3.2, 5.5, 9.6, 15.3, 20.9, and 24.5.

a Estimate.

would expect that such a shift in final demand would cause the industry whose demand fell, to decline, while an entirely new industry grew. In this case, however, the aviation industry did not decline, for many airframe manufacturers became missile manufacturers.[37]

---

[37] In all segments of the defense industry, firms to keep their relative standing had to shift successfully with changing defense requirements. See Peck and Scherer, *op. cit.,* pp. 126-128. Lockheed might be cited as an example of the way the aircraft firms adjusted. In 1955, aircraft accounted for 94 percent of the company's sales. This was down to 43 percent by 1960, with missiles and space projects now accounting for more than 50 percent of the company's business. *Missiles and Rockets,* January 9, 1961, p. 38. Also see *American Aviation,* July 1, 1957, p. 21, where it was argued that the airframe companies would become the missile-system contractors because the Air Force wanted to assist the companies in counteracting the impact of reduced aircraft procurement.

The introduction of the missile speeded two developments which affected the structure of the industry. First, research and development expenditures became a larger percentage of the total cost of all weapon systems. Second, there had been an increase in the use of electronic components within airplanes, but the development of the missile caused an even larger demand for these components. As

TABLE 17

DEPARTMENT OF DEFENSE FUNDS AVAILABLE FOR MISSILE DEVELOPMENT
AND PRODUCTION, 1946-1961
(in millions of dollars)

Fiscal year	All missile programs	Intermediate and intercontinental ballistic missiles
1946 and prior	72	2
1947	58	. . .
1948	81	. . .
1949	98	. . .
1950	134	. . .
1951	784	1
1952	1,058	1
1953	1,166	3
1954	1,067	14
1955	1,468	159
1956	2,281	526
1957	4,506	1,401
1958	5,180	2,150
1959	6,900	2,946
1960	6,718	3,216
1961	8,292	5,458

SOURCE: *Aerospace Facts and Figures, 1962*, p. 20.

a result the electronics industry began contributing a larger percentage of the value added of successive generations of weapon systems.

The increased importance of research and development can be seen from Table 18, where the aerospace systems are ranked within each category from the earliest postwar model to the latest system. In every case, the introduction of new models is associated with research and development costs which have risen relative to total system costs. Part of this increase may be attributable to smaller production runs, for the fixed research and development costs are thus spread over a smaller number of airplanes.[38] However, there

---

[38] In World War II, 3,700 B-29's were produced, but there were only 2,000 B-47's, and 600 B-52's. Peck and Scherer, *op. cit.*, p. 161.

has been a genuine increase in the complexity of the newer weapon systems. This is indicated by the number of electronic components on board our bombers. The B-17's and B-29's, which were used during World War II, had only several thousand electronic components. The B-47 carried 20,000; the B-52 has 50,000; the B-58 carries 95,000, and the B-70, if it is developed, will carry more than the B-58.[39]

For additional evidence of the growing importance of research and development for all defense sectors, one need only consult

TABLE 18

RESEARCH AND DEVELOPMENT EXPENDITURES AS A PERCENTAGE OF TOTAL SYSTEM COST FOR SOME AEROSPACE SYSTEMS

System	Percentage [a]
Bombers	
B-36	2
B-47	3
B-52	5
B-58	18
B-70 (small fleet)	30
B-70 (large fleet)	12
Fighters	
F-86	1
F-100	3
F-105	21
F-108	23
Other Systems	
Atlas-Titan	20
DynaSoar	19

SOURCE: Peck and Scherer, *op. cit.*, p. 315.

a These data, in some cases, are estimates.

Tables 19 and 20. Table 19 presents research, development, test, and evaluation expenditures. These data are not strictly comparable from year to year because the present budget structure upon which these data are based was not adopted until 1961. Thus, Table 20, which presents total federal expenditures for all phases of research and development, is more meaningful in indicating the trend of federal research and development expenditures, for the figures include not only the research, development, test, and evalua-

---

39 *Aviation Week,* August 17, 1959, p. 77. It has also been estimated that 60 percent of the total cost of an ICBM is attributable to research and development expenses. *Missiles and Rockets,* February 8, 1960, p. 11. This does not contradict Peck and Scherer's data, for their data refer to total system cost and not to the cost of a single missile.

tion funds listed in Table 19 but also funds attributable to research
and development which are identifiable from the procurement accounts. In addition, amounts directly in support of research, development, test, and evaluation included in military construction,
shipbuilding, and military personnel appropriations, and funds

TABLE 19

DEPARTMENT OF DEFENSE EXPENDITURES ON RESEARCH, DEVELOPMENT, TEST, AND
EVALUATION, AS IF FY 1965 BUDGET STRUCTURE HAD BEEN ADOPTED CIRCA 1948
(in millions of dollars)

Fiscal year	Expenditures
1953	2,148
1954	2,187
1955	2,261
1956	2,101
1957	2,406
1958	2,504
1959	2,866
1960	4,710
1961	6,131
1962	6,319
1963	6,376
1964a	6,943

SOURCE: *Aerospace Facts and Figures, 1963*, p. 23. U. S., Department of Defense, *Order
of Magnitude Data on Comparative Expenditures by Functional Title as if FY 1965
Budget Structure had been Adopted circa 1948*, FAD-397 (January 21, 1964). The data
note that "amounts include estimated comparability adjustment not supportable by
accounting records." Other data which support the trend of these data though not
their numerical accuracy appear in U. S., Senate, Subcommittee of the Select Committee on Small Business, *Hearings, The Role of Small Business in Government Procurement*, 87th Cong., 1st Sess., April 25-26, 1961, p. 42. For fiscal years 1952-1959 those
percentages are 1.5, 1.7, 3.2, 5.5, 9.6, 15.3, 20.9, and 24.5.

a Estimate.

available for the construction of research and development facilities, are also included in these data.

The trend of federal research and development expenditures is
obviously upward. However, the data for the earlier years may be
understated since a considerable part of the earlier research and development activity may not be identifiable from the procurement
accounts.

The increased importance of research and development expenditures meant that firms had to change their attitude toward research
and development contracts. Previously firms sought such contracts
only if they promised future production contracts.[40] The industry

---

[40] Peck and Scherer, *op. cit.,* p. 406, and Schlaifer, *op. cit.,* p. 64.

was geared toward production contracts not only because their profit rates were higher, but because firms naturally sought those contracts which would utilize their idle capacity. However, research

TABLE 20

FEDERAL EXPENDITURES FOR RESEARCH AND DEVELOPMENT, 1946-1963
(in millions of dollars)

	Federal research and development expenditures	
Fiscal year	Total	For major national security
1946	918	784
1947	898	768
1948	853	698
1949	1,080	889
1950	1,080	871
1951	1,298	1,063
1952	1,815	1,565
1953	3,101	2,832
1954	3,148	2,868
1955	3,308	2,979
1956	3,446	3,104
1957	4,462	4,027
1958	4,990	4,463
1959	5,803	5,048
1960	7,738	6,639
1961	9,728	7,719
1962	10,195	7,820a
1963a	12,337	8,572a

SOURCE: *Aerospace Facts and Figures, 1962*, p. 48. National Science Foundation, *Federal Funds for Science, Fiscal Years 1961, 1962, and 1963*, NSF 63-11, January 1963, p. 49.

a Estimate.

and development became a basic operation in the industry, and the aviation firms were able to adjust to this change.[41] This period also

41 Whereas during the Korean War 90 percent of General Electric's defense work was in production, by 1959 this was reduced to 50 percent, and the remainder was in research and development. U.S., Senate, Subcommittee of the Select Committee on Small Business, *Hearings, Small Business Participation in Defense Subcontracting*, 86th Cong., 1st Sess., April 22-24, 1959, p. 185. This is not atypical, for by the early sixties, 71 percent of North American Aviation's sales were billed from research-and-development-type contracts. Herbert Solow, "North American: A Corporation Deeply Committed." *Fortune*, June 1962, p. 147. It is important to note that the ratio of research and development to industry sales is 31 percent for the aerospace industry, 20 percent for the weapons industries in general, but only 3 percent for all industries. *Report to the President on Government Contractors for Research, and Development*, prepared by the Bureau of the Budget, and referred to the Committee on Government Operations, U.S. Senate. Senate Document No. 94, 87th Cong., 2d Sess., May 17, 1962, p. 2.

However, the required reorientation toward research was not anticipated by the

saw the emergence of firms *primarily* engaged in research and development.

It has been noted previously that electronic components accounted for a bigger percentage of the value added of each succeeding weapon system. This assertion can be easily substantiated. Where electronic equipment including controls accounted for 13 to 20 percent of the cost of an aircraft, it was estimated that electronic equipment accounted for as much as 50 percent of the cost of a missile.[42] Part of the growth in the importance of electronics is attributable to the increasing use of special-purpose test and measuring equipment and other ground-support equipment.[43] Moreover, the guidance and control systems accounted for a significant if not the major part of the cost of each missile.[44] The implication of this development was that the airframe manufacturers, which previously had not attained expertise in electronics, would have to develop such a capability in order to be able to compete for military contracts. In Chapter 6, we shall focus on the methods used by the aircraft firms to obtain this capability.

A significant development affecting the industry was the rapid transition into the space age. The first announcement of an impending satellite launching was made in August, 1955; but the spage age actually began when the Russians successfully orbited two Sputniks in the fall of 1957. Since that time more satellites have been placed in orbit by both nations, including scientific, communications, and

---

aviation companies and may have necessitated a difficult transitional process. For instance, the Atlas Scientific Advisory Committee headed by Von Neumann reported in 1953-1954 that no aircraft company had sufficient scientific strength to undertake the management of the Atlas program. Excerpts of his report are contained in U.S., House, Subcommittee of the Committee on Government Operations, *Hearings, Organization and Management of Missile Programs*, 86th Cong., 1st Sess., February 4-March 20, 1959, pp. 29 and 64.

[42] *Aviation Week*, January 28, 1957, p. 28. The estimate for aircraft may be too low, for 41 percent of the cost of a B-58 bomber was accounted for by electronics. However, bombers may carry more electronic equipment than fighters. The fact that 80 percent of the engineers working on the B-58 were electronic engineers indicates the importance of electronic equipment even to aircraft. *Electronics*, February 7, 1958, p. 14.

[43] *Ibid.*, May 20, 1957, p. 24C; *Aviation Week*, November 25, 1957, p. 96; and *Aviation Age*, January 1958, p. 19.

[44] The percentage of the cost attributable to the G and C systems varied with each missile, ranging from 25 percent for the Thor IRBM to 75 percent for the Sparrow I and Eagle air-to-air missiles. *Aviation Week*, September 23, 1957, p. 104, October 14, 1957, p. 34, December 22, 1958, p. 19, and December 12, 1960, p. 100. *Electronics*, January 31, 1958, p. 16.

meteorological satellites. Manned space flights have been made; scientific probes of the moon and the planets have been undertaken, and preparations for manned flights to, and exploration of, the moon are being made.

This country's expenditures for space activities mounted rapidly after the National Aeronautics and Space Administration was created in 1959. Moreover, the task of performing the research and development and production of equipment for many of these activities fell to the aviation industry. With the expansion of the scope of its activities, it was renamed the Aerospace Industry. Since it was already working on the rockets and re-entry vehicles required for our missile programs, the industry was able to adapt to the space age. For example, the same rockets were usually used in both defense and space programs, and the experience with re-entry vehicles was adaptable to the manned space capsules. Thus, although a new technology was required for some aspects of space exploration, much existing knowledge could be applied to the area. The growth in importance of research and development expenditures and the increased use of electronic equipment continued in this period. However, the additional facilities required in this interval were financed primarily by the firms.

In the commercial field, the big change in the early 1960's was the conversion of the airlines' fleets to turbine-powered planes. As a result of this development, Boeing replaced Douglas as the pre-eminent firm in this respect. Boeing's 707 and 720 airliners accounted for 170 of the 302 jet-powered air transports which were in operation by U.S.-owned, scheduled, domestic, and international airlines at the end of 1961.[45]

Although our analysis will focus on the relationship between the aerospace companies and the government, one further development affecting the commercial airlines should be mentioned. At the time this study goes to press it seems that another technological evolution in airplane travel will start with the introduction of the supersonic air transport. Since the development of this airliner requires government participation, a brief discussion of the problems associated with supersonic aircraft is presented in Appendix A.

---

[45] Although additional numbers of the Boeing 707 and 720, the Douglas DC-8, and the Convair 880 have been produced and placed in operational service since the end of 1961, Boeing has still retained its position.

Summary

The rapidity of change in the industry has led one observer to conclude that change is the only factor which remains constant in the industry.[46] The industry has in fact undergone great change and has been subject to considerable fluctuation. It became an important sector of the economy during World War I, faded until civilian airplane travel began in full scale, and then became the nation's largest industry in World War II. It again experienced a decline with the end of that war, but has once more come into prominence. Now approximately 50 percent of the industry's $15.8 billion sales volume is accounted for by programs nonexistent ten years ago— missiles and space.[47] This industry which originally manufactured only aircraft has expanded into other activities including electronics. In addition, emphasis in the industry's output has shifted from production to research and development. These developments naturally have left their mark upon the structure of the industry.

---

[46] Richard Rutter, "Missile Makers again Shifting to a Vast New Field—Space," *The New York Times*, Western Edition, May 7, 1963, p. 13.

[47] U.S., Bureau of the Census, *Backlog of Orders for Aerospace Companies*, Current Industrial Report Series M37D, April 25, 1963, p. 2; Gilbert Burck, "Hitching the Economy to the Infinite," *Fortune*, June 1962, p. 124; *Aviation Week*, March 18, 1962, p. 62.

2.

DEFINITION AND IMPORTANCE OF THE AEROSPACE INDUSTRY

DEFINITION

Before we evaluate the aerospace industry it is important to define its proper bounds. According to one definition the industry engages in "the research, development and production of manned and unmanned vehicles and supporting equipment for movement above the earth's surface." [1] According to another, the "aerospace industry encompasses all companies or activities from business flying to air transport to military aircraft to space craft." [2] The former definition is too narrow, because it lacks several products that should be included. The latter definition is too broad because the transport companies logically should not be included in the industry.

Since government data must be used, it is logical to examine the government agencies' official definitions of the industry. The Census Bureau regularly reports on the aerospace industry; in addition the reports of two other agencies regularly refer to it. The title of the Census Bureau's quarterly report, "Backlog of Orders for Aerospace Companies," [3] was adopted in 1961 when the scope of the

---

[1] Merrill Lynch, Pierce, Fenner & Smith, *Aerospace in the Sixties and Beyond* (1961), p. 2. The term "aerospace" was defined by the Aerospace Industries Association to mean "an operationally indivisible medium consisting of the total expanse beyond the earth's surface."

[2] Letter from Charles C. Gerusa, Promotion and Marketing Manager of *Aviation Week and Space Technology* (McGraw-Hill), dated August 1, 1962.

[3] U.S., Bureau of the Census, *Backlog of Orders for Aerospace Companies,* Current Industrial Report Series M37D, April 25, 1963. These reports present data on the sales, new orders, and backlogs of these companies.

survey was enlarged in recognition of the expansion of the industry into missile and space projects.[4] In early 1963, the report surveyed sixty-seven companies which produce, assemble, develop or have prime system responsibility for complete aircraft (SIC Industry 3721); complete missile or space-vehicle systems (SIC Industry 1925); complete aircraft engines and complete engines or propulsion units for missiles and space vehicles (SIC Industry 3722).[5] Those companies which *only* manufacture complete propellers (SIC Industry 3723) or miscellaneous aircraft or missile parts (SIC Industry 3729) are not within the bounds of this survey. However, if the surveyed companies produce these products, then their sales of these products are included in the published figures.[6]

The Federal Trade Commission and Securities Exchange Commission issue quarterly reports on the sales and profits of those companies which manufacture aircraft and aircraft parts.[7] While the FTC-SEC data are clearly defined as referring only to companies primarily classified in SIC Industry 372,[8] the trade literature commonly refers to these data as pertaining to all aerospace companies. Firms primarily manufacturing missiles must be considered part of the industry but are excluded from the FTC-SEC surveys. To the extent that the aircraft and missile manufacturers are the same, many of the latter are included in the survey. Some, however, are excluded, but their sales and profits cannot be combined with the mentioned aircraft manufacturers, for they are classified somewhere in the Ordnance and Miscellaneous category, and the data for the missile manufacturers cannot be abstracted.[9]

The Bureau of Labor Statistics publishes employment statistics for the aircraft and aircraft-parts industry (SIC Industry 372) and for the Ordnance Industry (SIC Industry 19).[10] Many trade sources

---

[4] Previously the reports were entitled, "Backlog of Orders for Aviation Companies."

[5] Instructions for form M37D, pp. 2-3, and letter from Maxwell R. Conklin, Chief, Industry Division, Bureau of the Census, dated July 2, 1962.

[6] Letter from Mr. Conklin, *op. cit.*

[7] U.S. Federal Trade Commission-Securities Exchange Commission, *Quarterly Financial Reports for Manufacturing Corporations.*

[8] *Ibid.* This definition corresponds to the Census of Manufactures' definition for SIC Industry 372 and is also the definition used by the Census Bureau in its pre-1961 M37D series, *Backlog of Orders for Aviation Companies.*

[9] *Ibid.*, p. 6.

[10] U.S., Bureau of Labor Statistics, *Employment and Earnings for 1909-1960*, 1961, pp. 42 and 215-216.

quote only the former set when discussing the level of employment in the aerospace industry.[11] However, by making an appropriate adjustment to the ordnance data, employment in the aircraft and missile industry theoretically could be estimated.

Thus, the three government agencies do not define clearly the aerospace industry nor do their implied definitions agree. The Census includes missiles in the industry, but the other agencies make no attempt to broaden the aircraft-industry definition. If these latter data are used as statistics which supposedly describe the aerospace industry, clearly they must be recognized as underestimates.

Another government attempt to define the industry was made in 1958 and 1959 when the Labor Department and the Electronic and Aircraft Industry trade jointly defined the bounds between the two industries. This controversy was conducted within the framework of the Walsh-Healy Act.[12] This law attempts to prevent any single manufacturer from obtaining a competitive advantage. The aircraft manufacturers argued that a wage differential hurt them in competing against electronics firms for guidance systems and automatic and semiautomatic equipment, such as navigation and control systems.[13] In essence, the aircraft firms argued that they and the electronics firms were competitors and should therefore be counted as one industry.

A final definition of the aerospace industry was never issued,[14] but the Labor Department proposed that the Aircraft and Guided Missile Industry perform the functions of:

Manufacture and assembly of airplanes, lighter-than-air craft, gliders, drones, guided missiles, aircraft type engines, guided missile propulsion systems, aircraft and guided missile airframes, aircraft propellers and parts, and accessories especially designed for use with or on the above

---

11 See, for example, *Aerospace Facts and Figures, 1962,* pp. 66-67.

12 *Aviation Week,* December 1, 1958, p. 35; February 23, 1959, pp. 60 ff., and September 7, 1959, p. 25.

13 *Ibid.,* December 1, 1958, p. 35. Actually the aircraft firms which manufactured the electronics equipment would not have had to pay the same minimum wage for this type of work as for aircraft assembly, but in practice, with the same union representing workers in both fields, they did. *Ibid.,* February 23, 1959, p. 60.

14 Letter from Clarence T. Lundquist, Administrator, Wage and Hour and Public Contracts Division, U.S. Department of Labor, dated September 28, 1962.

mentioned products . . . and specialized aircraft and guided missile serv-
icing equipment.[15]

The Aerospace Industries Association (AIA) in commenting on
this proposed definition asked for the inclusion of

. . . electronic, hydraulic, electrical, pneumatic, and mechanical systems
for purposes such as flight control, guidance, airborne intelligence, telemetering and navigation; and/or major assemblies for use in such systems for such vehicles, which are especially designed for and perform
specific functions in such vehicles; and specialized ground support serv-
icing equipment which is especially designed for and performs specific
functions in such vehicles, engines and systems.[16]

The Electronics Industries Association concurred with the Labor
Department's proposed definition but wanted to exclude guided
missiles.[17] It argued that the AIA definition created an artificial dis-
tinction between defense electronics for aircraft-missile use and
similar electronic equipment for other use. On the other hand, the
AIA noted that the prime contractor in the weapon-system concept
of management established the overall specifications for avionic
equipment.[18] The only significant question in this argument is the
extent of the competition between the airframe manufacturers and
the avionics companies, for not even this proposed definition of the
aircraft and guided-missile industry was adopted.[19]

Although more will be said in Chapter 6 about the extent of this
competition between the former aircraft companies and the electronic firms, at this stage mere mention is made of some examples

---

[15] Excluded were: Electrical and electronic manufacturers, and electrical and electronic equipment and parts therefor, such as ignition and lighting systems, communications equipment, guidance systems, intelligence systems, navigation systems and
ground-support equipment. Also excluded were engine, flight and navigation instruments and photographic and de-icing equipment. Quoted in *Aviation Week*, February 23, 1959, p. 61. The definition of the aircraft manufacturing industry is contained
in Sec. 50-202.23 of the code of Federal Regulations.

[16] Quoted in *Aviation Week*, February 23, 1959, p. 61.

[17] However, missile construction is basically very similar to aircraft and airframe
construction. *Ibid.*, February 25, 1957, pp. 78-80; July 22, 1963, p. 124.

[18] Quoted in *ibid.*, February 23, 1959, p. 65. Electronic avionic equipment is designed for aviation purposes. This includes communication, navigation, identification,
weapons delivery, radar, instrumentations, display, and automatic controls systems.
See *ibid.*, March 26, 1962, p. 19.

[19] Letter from Clarence T. Lundquist (see n. 14). Neither this letter nor the
trade literature indicates why the definition of the aircraft industry was not revised.

which indicate that this competition does exist. For instance, three airframe and four electronic companies competed for one particular air-defense missile-study contract.[20] Moreover, an undersecretary of the Air Force stated that development and production contracts will go to the electronic companies for those vehicles which are primarily electronic devices with airframes designed to house the systems.[21] These contracts have in many previous instances been awarded to the airframe manufacturers.

The performance of our planes and missiles has come to depend heavily on electronic equipment. This increasing importance of electronics provides another justification for including at least some specialized electronic equipment carried in aircraft or spacecraft within the industry's bounds. Moreover, since it is possible to substitute complex ground-support equipment for complex spacecraft equipment, some former systems might also be included. For instance, this substitution has simplified the Surveyor spacecraft.[22] Since substitutes should logically be grouped together in defining an industry, there is some justification for including the ground-support equipment in the industry.[23] The scientific electronic instrumentation for the satellite payloads also must be included, because the satellite would be useless without this equipment.[24] All

20 *Aviation Week*, February 23, 1959, p. 67. Numerous other examples could be cited including the Mauler missile and a new antitank missile. The competition for the latter item was won by Hughes Aircraft, which is an electronics company, over Martin and McDonnell, two airframe manufacturers. *Missiles and Rockets*, August 13, 1962, p. 9; *Aviation Week*, October 12, 1959, p. 69. More recently there has been competition between the electronic and airframe manufacturers for the Lunar Reconnaissance Module. *Missiles and Rockets*, June 17, 1963, p. 13.

21 *Electronics*, June 13, 1958, p. 26. The Eagle missile is an example. Grumman produces the airframe and launcher but Bendix Aviation, an electronics firm, is the prime contractor. *Aviation Week*, September 19, 1960, p. 121.

22 *Missiles and Rockets*, December 3, 1962, p. 32.

23 Other examples of the need for ground-support equipment can be found in: *Aviation Week*, February 25, 1957, pp. 215 ff., July 22, 1957, p. 55, and October 24, 1960, p. 32; *Missiles and Rockets*, May 30, 1960, p. 66; and U.S., House, Subcommittee No. 4 of the Select Committee on Small Business, *Hearings on the Aircraft Industry*, 85th Cong., 2d Sess., June 27-28, 1958, p. 154.

24 The scientific payload of the OAO and Tiros satellites cost more than the launching vehicle. *Missiles and Rockets*, September 17, 1962, pp. 62 ff. In addition, one might note that some electronic equipment has been developed almost exclusively for aerospace applications. Thus, at one time, around 70 percent of the sales of both telemetering equipment and instrument-type magnetic tape recorders were used in conjunction with aircraft or missiles. See *Electronics*, June 20, 1957, p. 15, and August 10, 1957, p. 22.

these factors plus the delegation to one firm of management and technical responsibility for a given (weapon) system,[25] make it appear artificial to define the aerospace industry in such a manner as to include the aviation industry but exclude the electronics industry.

Rather the definition of the aerospace industry should be analogous to that of the automobile industry. The Census definition of the Motor Vehicles and Parts Industry (SIC 3717) includes not only "establishments engaged in manufacturing or assembling passenger automobiles," but also manufacturers of automotive engines and some other auto parts.[26] Those parts which are excluded are usually products not manufactured by the assemblers of automobiles, where the technology is significantly different, such as tires and glass.[27] The value added for SIC Industry 3717, when combined with that of the excluded industries which manufactured auto parts in 1958, accounts for more than 63 percent of the total;[28] tires, tubes, and glass for nearly half of the remaining 37 percent. These calculations point out that the 1958 definition of the motor-vehicle industry encompasses a significant portion of the manufacturing on the final product.

Since airplanes, missiles, and spacecraft are all manufactured by assembling many parts and systems, the aerospace industry should

---

[25] A weapon system is an aggregation of subsystems which are functionally and sometimes physically interdependent. *Aviation Week*, May 18, 1959, p. 59. The Defense Department has provided the following definition of a weapon system: "A system composed of equipment, skills, and techniques, the composite of which forms an instrument of combat usually . . . having an air vehicle as its major operational element. The complete weapon system includes all related equipment, materials, services, and personnel required solely for the operation of the air vehicle . . . so that the instrument of combat becomes a self-sufficient unit of striking power within its intended operational environment."

[26] U.S., Bureau of the Census, *Census of Manufactures, 1958, II*, Inventory Statistics, Part 2, 1961, p. 37A-1.

[27] The excluded SIC industries are 3011 tires and tubes; 3211 autoglass; 3429 auto hardware; 3461 autostampings; 3519 diesel engines; 3599 carburetor, piston; 3641 sealed beam and lamps; 3642 motor lighting fixtures; 3694 ignition equipment; 3691 storage batteries; and 3651 auto radios. Although ignition equipment and batteries are excluded, they are manufactured by one or more of the auto firms.

[28] The value added of all industries manufacturing or assembling autos or auto parts was $9,912 million. This included the value added of SIC Industry 3211, all glass, of which only a portion is automobile glass. The value added of SIC Industry 3717 is $6,412 billion. Since auto glass was overestimated, the 63 percent is an underestimate of the value added of the auto industry in relationship to the expanded definition.

be defined in such a manner that a significant portion of the manufacturing on the final product is included in the industry. Since electronic equipment accounts for 40 to 50 percent of the cost of a missile,[29] and since a large portion of avionics research and development is done by airframe manufacturers, electronic subsystem manufacturers must not be excluded arbitrarily from the industry definition.[30]

It is apparent that none of the cited definitions is broad enough for our purposes. We shall, therefore, present an operational definition of the industry and then list the types of products which would be included within the scope of the definition. According to our definition *the industry would develop and manufacture vehicles, subsystems and parts essential for both atmospheric and space flight, whether manned or instrumented, or necessary for effective operation in flight or space.*[31] Obviously military and commercial aircraft, aircraft and missile engines, engine parts, propellers, guided missiles, and guided-missile components and subassemblies are all included in the industry. These products are manufactured by firms classified in SIC industries 3721, 3722, 3723, 3729, and 1925.

Two essential components for the effective operation of space vehicles, missiles, and satellites, are the re-entry vehicles, and the guidance and control systems. The former are classified in Industry 3729, already included in the industry, but the latter are manufactured by firms usually classified in SIC industry 3662. However, estimates of the value added and number of employees accounted for by these electronic products can be obtained and added to the available data for the nonelectronic products included in the definition. Similar information may also be obtained for many other products which theoretically should be classified within the indus-

---

29 *Aviation Week*, January 1, 1957, p. 27.

30 For instance, see the Martin Company's advertisement in *ibid.*, August 1, 1960, p. 35. "Without electronics, it is impossible to design, build, test, launch, guide, track, or communicate with a missile. That is why 40 percent of Martin's 7500 engineers are electronic and electrical engineers."

31 Our definition was influenced by the following statement: "A space capability is compounded of all other knowledge in chemical propellants, ballistics, special materials, rocket engine design, radar, and communications, computers, servomechanisms, nuclear energy, human factors work, and much ground support equipment to mention only the most obvious." U.S., House, Committee on Science and Astronautics, *Military Astronautics*, 87th Cong., 1st Sess., May 8, 1961, p. 1.

try. These include aircraft flight, nautical and navigational instruments, automatic pilots, telemetering equipment,[32] electronic navigational aids, electronic aircraft and missile control, guidance, and check-out systems; and electronic airborne communication and computer equipment.[33] Other products which should be included theoretically are electronic airborne counter and counter-counter measures, and scientific instruments used in communication, scientific and weather satellites. To our knowledge, data for these products cannot be abstracted from the published Census data. It is doubtful that these omissions would result in a serious bias in any quantitative estimate of the importance of the industry, but in principle they should be included within the industry. Consequently all estimates are slightly understated.

As with any definition, inconsistencies arise; the jet fuel for powering aircraft and the liquid propellants designed to propel liquid missile rockets are not included in the industry, whereas the solid propellants are included since they constitute an integral part of the solid-fueled rocket. A second inconsistency is the inclusion of the payload of a satellite but not the warhead of a missile nor the occupant of a spacecraft.

Our definition recognizes that research, development, and production of electronic equipment is within the scope of the industry. Furthermore, this definition is consistent with the practice of allowing the prime systems contractors either to produce or merely to supervise the production of electronic subsystems. Moreover, this definition is operational and allows us to evaluate the importance of the industry to the economy.

IMPORTANCE

There are several dimensions in which the economic importance of this industry can be measured. These include sales volume, the number of employees, and value added. The sales of the industry

---

[32] One of the objects of space flight is to obtain scientific information which is then relayed back to earth by telemetering equipment. It was previously noted that the biggest market for this equipment is the result of this function.

[33] These systems were included for it has been noted that the important systems for Project Apollo, in addition to the Saturn rocket, are the re-entry vehicle, the environmental and attitude control systems, power supplies, communications systems, on-board propulsion, guidance and control systems, and pilot displays, *Aviation Week*, August 29, 1960, p. 27.

can be measured easily, but the other data required a considerable amount of estimating. The Census Bureau estimates the yearly sales of a number of aerospace companies.[34] This figure may be used as an estimate of the sales of the industry, for the Bureau includes all firms which have prime system responsibility for the research, development, and production of aviation, missile, and spacecraft systems.

Under the contractual form of procurement known as weapon-system management, it has been the government's practice to award a prime contract to a particular firm, known as the manager, and require it to award the subsystem contracts. Since the managing firm includes the dollar volume of its subcontracts in its own sales figures, the dollar value of these subsystems is included in the Census estimate. By including only the sales of the weapon-system managers, an unduplicated estimate of the shipments of the industry is obtained, after the value of the subcontracts awarded by one prime manufacturer to another prime is subtracted.[35] Since this particular Census report has been issued only since 1961, as previously noted, no valid comparison with earlier years can be made.

In any event, in 1961 the unduplicated sales of the aerospace industry were $14.9 billion, accounting for 2.9 percent of GNP. In 1962, industry sales rose to more than $15.9 billion and continued to account for 2.9 percent of GNP.[36] These figures indicate that the industry is growing and making a significant contribution to our economy. It is, therefore, worthy of study.

The importance of this industry may also be measured in several other dimensions, which have the advantage that a comparison over time is possible. For this purpose, the first data to be examined are for the aircraft industry, SIC No. 372; subsequently the data for the missile industry will be added to these figures. Finally, estimates for the electronic products included in the aerospace industry will be made and added to the mentioned data. Both the employment data and the value-added figures will be used for this procedure.

The number of employees, *using the 1957 SIC definition of the*

---

34 *Backlog of Orders for Aerospace Companies* (see n. 8).

35 Although a valid sales estimate for the firms in the industry is obtained, these data do not provide us with any information about the distribution of activity between the prime and the subsystem manufacturers.

36 *Ibid.*, M37D (61-5), May 9, 1962, p. 1, and M37D (62-5), June 25, 1963, p. 1.

industry is indicated by Table 21: in 1947 there were 239,000, and in both 1954 and 1958, approximately 783,000 employees in the industry. The accuracy of these figures should be checked before the employment figures for the missile industry are added. The 1958 data can be compared with the 1958 Census of Manufactures,

TABLE 21

NUMBER OF EMPLOYEES AND PRODUCTION WORKERS IN SIC INDUSTRY 372, 1947-1962a

Year	Employees (000)	Production workers (000)
1947	239.3	176.7
1948	237.7	175.2
1949	264.2	196.6
1950	283.1	209.4
1951	467.8	348.4
1952	670.6	495.4
1953	795.5	586.2
1954	782.9	560.2
1955	761.3	525.5
1956	837.3	561.0
1957	895.8	591.4
1958	783.6	499.4
1959	755.4	462.6
1960	673.8	392.5
1961	668.9	378.4
1962	707.3	389.3

SOURCE: U. S., Bureau of Labor Statistics, *Employment and Earnings for 1909-1960*, pp. 215, 216; *Employment and Earnings*, Vol. 8, No. 7 (January, 1962), pp. 12, 14 and Vol. 9, No. 8 (February, 1963), pp. 12, 14.

a Based upon the 1957 SIC definition.

because both were obtained from the same SIC classification. However, in order to compare the two estimates for 1947 and 1954, the pre-1957 SIC classification must be used.

For 1958, Census estimated that 765,000 were employed by plants classified in SIC Industry 372; the BLS estimate was 783,600.[37] This was an error of less than 3 percent. The BLS data which were issued before the revisions resulting from the adoption of the 1957 Standard Industrial Classification[38] indicate that 764,100 persons were

[37] *Census of Manufactures, 1958*, p. 37 B-4; U.S., Bureau of Labor Statistics, *Employment and Earnings for 1909-1960*, pp. 215-216. Moreover, it was determined that this discrepancy would not be the result of the differing averaging procedures used by the Census Bureau and the Labor Bureau. If the Census method of using the average of four specific months had been used by BLS, the latter's estimate would have been reduced by only 2,400.

[38] U.S., Bureau of Labor Statistics, *Employment and Earnings, Annual Supplement*, V, No. 11 (May 1959), p. 66.

employed by the aircraft and parts industry in 1954. The Census Bureau's figure for 1954 was 822,500 [39]—an error of less than 10 percent. Similarly, for 1947, the respective figures were 264,100 employees according to the BLS but only 219,700 according to the Census.[40] The discrepancy is in the neighborhood of 15 percent. While the percentage differences between the BLS and Census estimates for the earlier years are perhaps uncomfortably high, use of either set of data would correctly indicate the trend of employment in the industry.[41]

In measuring the importance of the aerospace industry in this dimension, workers engaged in the production of missiles should also be included. However, estimates of the number of these workers are not available for years before 1958. It is, therefore, important to determine the extent of the resulting bias. Missiles gained in relative importance only after 1957, but approximately 1 percent of the 1954 federal government budget was allocated to missiles. Consequently, the 1954 estimate of aerospace employment is somewhat low because employees engaged in the manufacture of missiles are excluded. This would later appear as an overestimate of the rate of growth of importance of the industry.[42]

For 1958, three estimates of employment in missiles are available. The Census estimated that 108,431 people were employed in SIC Industry 1925—complete missiles. The BLS's figure for employment in all of SIC Industry 192, of which SIC Industry 1925 was the predominant part, was only 64,400.[43] The Bureau of Employment Security's October, 1958 estimate of missile employment in

---

[39] U.S., Bureau of the Census, *1954 Census of Manufactures, II, Industry Statistics*, p. 37B-3.

[40] U.S., Bureau of Labor Statistics, *Employment and Earnings; Annual Supplement*, May 1954, p. 62; *1954 Census of Manufactures, II, Industry Statistics*, p. 37B-3.

[41] Moreover, the large errors in 1954 and 1947 are in opposite directions, that is, the Census estimate is lower in 1947 but higher in 1954. This would seem to indicate the absence of a systematic bias. The Bureau of Labor Statistics has noted that its employment statistics are not strictly comparable to the Census Bureau's estimates. For the differences see BLS's, *Employment and Earnings Statistics for the United States, 1909-1960*, p. 1-E.

[42] The underestimate of 1954 employment is probably slight, since the proposed aircraft expenditures in the 1954 budget were twelve times that of missiles. Moreover, the appropriations for fiscal year 1954 were not all spent in that period. In addition, the airframe manufacturers performed a considerable amount of the missile work, and missile employment may have been included partly in the aviation industry data.

[43] U.S., Bureau of Labor Statistics, *Employment and Earnings Statistics for the United States, 1909-1960*, p. 42.

SIC Industry 19 was approximately 80,000.[44] Although the estimates differ, they are of the same order of magnitude. The Census' employment estimate for missiles was added to its airplane and airplane-parts employment figures and the totals compared with all manufacturing employment as estimated by the Census. Using these data, it is estimated that the aerospace industry accounted for 1.4 percent of total manufacturing employment in 1947, for 5.3 percent in 1954, and for 5.7 percent in 1958.[45] It should be noted that none of the mentioned estimates include employment figures for electronics products. After the value-added data have been presented, which correspond to the mentioned employment figures, the 1958 estimates of employment and value added in a select group of electronics industries will be made and added to the aircraft and missile data.

Value-added estimates for 1947 and 1954 are available only for the aircraft and aircraft-parts industry, but the 1958 data may also be obtained for the missile industry. The exclusion of the data for the latter industry in the earlier years again overstates the growth rate. The data indicate that the aircraft-missile industry accounted for 1.2 percent of the total value added of all manufacturing industries in 1947, 5.4 percent in 1954, and 5.8 percent in 1958.[46] Despite the exclusion of some categories of electronic equipment, these preliminary estimates, nevertheless, indicate the enormous importance of the industry to the economy.

The value added and employment figures for the electronic portion of the aerospace industry can be estimated once a list has been prepared of the products included within the scope of the industry. It should be remembered that the electronics products which have been included in the industry definition are the major subsystems required for flight. Components such as transistors, tubes, and re-

---

[44] U.S., Bureau of Employment Security, *Industry Manpower Survey No. 95*, "Missiles and Aircraft Recent Manpower Development," April, 1960, p. 9. The data for October 1958 are nat presented, but the October 1959 data and the rate of change are given. However, those data do not agree with an earlier estimate presented in *Industry Manpower Survey No. 93*, "Manpower in Missile and Aircraft Production," August, 1959, p. 7. The data differ because Survey No. 95 uses the 1957 standard industrial classification, while Survey No. 93 uses the 1945 industry classification.

[45] The BLS estimates indicate a similar trend. The figures are 1.7 percent, 4.8 percent, and a little less than 5.5 percent for 1947, 1954, and 1958, respectively.

[46] The combined value added by the aircraft, aircraft parts, and (in 1958) missile industries totaled (in millions), $955, $6,287, and $8,077 for 1947, 1954, and 1958, respectively. Total value added for all manufacturing industries was (in billions), $74.3, $117, and $141.3 for 1947, 1954, and 1958, respectively.

sistors, which are used to manufacture these systems, are not included. The 1958 Census of Manufactures shows that information could be obtained for the following electronic systems which are within the scope of our definition: Aircraft flight, nautical, and navigational instruments and automatic pilots (SIC 38111—this category includes the gyroscopes necessary for the guidance systems); communications equipment (SIC 36621 airborne communications equipment is included in this industry); electronic navigational aids (SIC 36624); electronic aircraft and missile control, guidance, and check-out systems (SIC 36625); other electronic equipment (military, industrial, and commercial equipment—SIC 36626—part of this industry should be included as telemetering equipment is included herein); computing and accounting machines (SIC 35712, for airborne computers are included in this industry).

Since the value-added and employment data are available only for the four-digit industries, the following procedure was used to obtain estimates both of the number of employees engaged in this production process, and the magnitude of value added which was generated. The ratio was computed of the sales of the product to the entire sales of the four-digit industry in which the product was classified. This ratio was then applied to the number of employees of the four-digit industry which were producing this product. The value added of the primary industry associated with this product was estimated in a similar manner. None of the mentioned products were manufactured entirely within the four-digit industry to which the product was assigned. Therefore, another step was necessary to obtain the estimates of the number of employees and the value added, associated with the total sales of each product, not just with the sales of those plants which were classified in the primary industry. The data for the primary industry were merely multiplied by the reciprocal of the coverage ratio for that product.[47] The proce-

---

[47] It is obvious that this procedure may overestimate the variables through double counting, for some of the sales of these electronic products may have resulted from firms in the aircraft or missile industries, and the employees of this industry have already been counted. However, there are sales of products primary to the aircraft and missile industries which are made by firms other than those in these two industries (i.e., the coverage ratios of Industries 372 and 1925 combined is not 100 percent). To the extent that these sales are excluded, there is an underestimate of the various variables. Second, other electronic subsystems useful in space and the research and development expenditures associated with the electronic systems, which have been included within the scope of the industry, are also excluded. Our procedure assumes that, in the absence of a better estimate, these errors cancel.

TABLE 22

COMPUTATIONS FOR VARIOUS ELECTRONIC INDUSTRIES: NUMBER OF EMPLOYEES AND AMOUNT OF VALUE ADDED WHICH SHOULD BE INCLUDED IN THE AEROSPACE INDUSTRY, 1958

SIC number	Primary 4-digit industry (in thousands of dollars)		Sales ratio: Product to total industry col. 2/col. 3	Primary industry employees	Value added of primary industry (in thousands of dollars)	Attributable to product:		Coverage ratio[a] (percent)	Attributable to aerospace industry	
	Product sales	Total sales				Number of employees col. 4 x col. 5	Value added col. 4 x col. 6 (in thousands of dollars)		Number of employees, reciprocal of col. 9 x col. 7	Value added, reciprocal of col. 9 x col. 8 (in thousands of dollars)
(1)	(2)	(3)	(4)	(5)	(6)	(7)	(8)	(9)	(10)	(11)
38111	466,969	1,000,235b	46.6	67,456	606,530	31,434	282,643	72	43,658	392,560
36621c (part)	118,633	2,414,620d	4.9	129,515	1,297,583	6,346	63,582	81	7,834	78,496
36624	191,713	2,414,620d	7.9	129,515	1,297,583	10,232	102,509	94	10,885	109,052
36625e (part)	669,115	2,414,620d	27.7	129,515	1,297,583	35,876	359,430	72	49,827	499,208
36626f (part)	50,367	2,414,620d	2.0	129,515	1,297,583	2,590	25,952	80	3,238	32,440
357112g (part)	54,031	1,104,194	4.8	80,864	579,103	3,881	27,797	91	4,265	30,546

SOURCE: *Census of Manufactures, 1958*, pp. 38A-17, 38A-26, 36D-7, 36D-15, 36D-19, 36D-20, 35F-6, 35F-9, and 35F-10.

a Defined as the ratio of value of shipments of primary products made by plants classified in the industry to total shipments of primary products made by all producers. It measures the extent to which all shipments of primary products of an industry are made by plants classified in the industry.

b This includes $143,642,000 composed of repairs, miscellaneous sales, and research and development. The amount of research and development attributable to Product 38111 should be included in the product's sales. However, this figure cannot be estimated and is, therefore, excluded.

c Only the airborne communications equipment portion of this industry is included, that is, SIC No. 3622112, 3622122, and 3622152.

d This includes $317,190,000 composed of repairs, miscellaneous sales, and research and development. The amount of research and development attributable to Products 3622112, 3622122, and 3622152 should be included in the product's sales. However, this figure cannot be estimated and is, therefore, excluded.

e Sonar equipment, which is included in product 36625, was excluded from our calculations. This estimate was obtained by taking the total of the product (No. 36625) by the primary industry and reducing this figure by the ratio of total nonsonar sales of the product to total sales of the product by all industries. The value of total shipments of product 36625 by industry 3662 is $704,332,100. Total sales of the product are $917,856,000. Total nonsonar sales are $872,303,000.

f Only telemetering equipment was included.

g Only "other electronic computers" were included, for the Census stated that these were primarily for aircraft and missile use.

dure is illustrated in Table 22. The computations indicate that in 1958, 119,400 more employees should be included in the industry, and an additional $1,142 million should be attributed to the value added of the industry. Our estimate of the 1958 level of employment is 993,300, accounting for 6.2 percent of total manufacturing employment. With a value added of $9,219 million, the industry accounted for 6.5 percent of the value added generated by all manufacturing industries.

These employment data can be compared with another set of estimates of the level of employment in the aerospace industry. This other set of data is not strictly comparable with our estimates, for it includes the employees who manufacture subsystems and electronic components. Employment figures for these items were not included in our estimates. Nevertheless, the Bureau of Employment Security's three Industry Manpower Surveys of the Missile and Aircraft Industry may be used to check the accuracy of our estimates.

The manufacturers of aircraft, missiles, and artificial satellites were included in the BES's definition of the aerospace industry.[48] Missile activity consists of research and development and production of complete missiles, launching devices, ground control and testing units, propulsion units, warheads, fuel, electronic components, and other parts.[49] Our definition of the industry did not include warheads, fuel if manufactured by the chemical industry, and electronic components used in the production of electronic subsystems. The BES's estimate of employment in nonaircraft plants is derived from a Department of Defense list of plants which were engaged in missile manufacture.[50] This list included manufacturers who received subcontracts and may have included some of the third- and fourth-tier subcontractors. It may even have included manufacturers of such electronic components as transistors, diodes, and the like, which were explicitly excluded from our industry definition. Furthermore, the surveys included government-owned facilities for research, development, testing, and production, but excluded Department of Defense and NASA personnel engaged in administration, planning, and procurement.[51] Certain nonmanufac-

48 *Industry Manpower Survey No. 95*, p. 3.
49 *Ibid.*, p. 1.
50 *Ibid.*, p. 6.
51 *Ibid.*, p. 1, *Industry Manpower Survey No. 102*, p. 6.

turing industries such as SIC industries No. 73 (Miscellaneous Business Services), No. 89 (Miscellaneous Service), and No. 91 (Federal Government) were also included.

Despite the differences in the industry definitions, the BES and our estimates of total aerospace employment are of the same order of magnitude. The BES has two estimates of October, 1958, employment. Its survey of that date indicated that 948,500 were employed in the industry, but a later survey indicated that the October, 1959, figure of 978,000 [52] was virtually unchanged from the 1958 level. These figures are slightly smaller than our previous estimates of 993,000 employees for all of 1958.

According to the BES, the August, 1961, level of employment in the aerospace industry was 982,000.[53] The most spectacular gain in employment between October, 1959, and August, 1961, occurred in SIC 19, which includes primary-missile activity, and SIC 36 in which electronic equipment is classified (Table 23). This growth

TABLE 23
EMPLOYMENT IN MISSILE ACTIVITY IN INDUSTRIES OTHER THAN SIC 372,
OCTOBER, 1959, AND AUGUST, 1961

SIC industry	October, 1959		August, 1961	
	Establishments	Employees	Establishments	Employees
19	33	100,500	36	139,600
36	82	87,000	132	141,200
73	21	18,400	34	32,700
38	22	17,700	33	22,000
91	16	18,600	28	42,800
89	8	10,700	12	18,900
35	24	5,100	31	8,100
28	. . .	. . .	13	6,000

SOURCE: U. S., Department of Labor, Bureau of Employment Security, *Industry Manpower Survey No. 95*, p. 9; *Industry Manpower Survey No. 102*, p. 6.

in the importance of electronics, mentioned previously, was the reason for making our estimate of employment in this sector of the industry. It is difficult to compare the sales and employment trends of the entire aerospace industry, not only because the SIC indus-

---

[52] *Industry Manpower Survey No. 95*, pp. 4, 7.

[53] *Industry Manpower Survey No. 102*, p. 5. The BES estimate of employment in the aircraft sector of the industry is always lower than the corresponding BLS figure, thus indicating a possible bias. The BES underestimates are 34,000 in October 1958, 31,000 for October 1959, but 100,000 for August 1961.

trial classification was changed in 1959, but also because the data relating to missile employment are not available for years before 1958. However, employment in the industry has probably not grown as rapidly as sales. The BES estimates indicate that there was virtually no increase in employment in the industry between October, 1958, and August, 1961,[54] while sales increased from $11.5 billion in 1958 [55] to $14.9 billion in 1961. What has happened is that the number of technical personnel employed by the industry has increased while the number of production workers has declined. Since the former are paid more than the latter, and the sales of the industry are often of a cost-plus nature, the dollar volume of sales may rise purely for this reason. This change in the composition of the industry's work force has been the result of the shift of the product mix generated by the industry.[56]

SUMMARY AND CONCLUSIONS

In this chapter, a definition of the industry was developed. One of the features of this definition was the inclusion of a portion of the electronics industry within the scope of the aerospace industry. Moreover, when the relative economic importance of the aerospace industry was measured, the findings indicated that the electronics section accounted for a significant portion of the industry's economic activity. However, the industry makes a large contribution to the nation's economy even if this electronics output is excluded from our estimates.

---

54 However, the possibility that the BES data for 1961 have larger underestimates than do the data from earlier years was noted in footnote 53. Moreover, the BES data for August 1962 indicate that employment in the aerospace industry had risen to 1,117,000 people. The electronics industry continued to show a large increase in missile and spacecraft employment. See, Bureau of Employment Security, *Industry Manpower Survey No. 105*, "Missiles, Spacecraft and Aircraft," May 1963, pp. 4-5.

55 U.S., Bureau of the Census, *Backlog of Orders for Aircraft Companies, Summary for 1958*, Facts for Industry Series M37D-U8, March 23, 1959, p. 3. *Aviation Week*, March 9, 1959, p. 68, gave an estimate of $11.8 billion.

56 It has been estimated that technical personnel account for 20 percent of an airplane plant's work force. This ratio may be as high as 50 percent in a space facility. *Ibid.*, September 22, 1958, p. 26. *Aviation Age*, March, 1958, p. 108.

3.

THE STRUCTURE OF THE AEROSPACE INDUSTRY
IN THE EARLY 1960'S: THE PARTICIPANTS
IN THE MARKET

An analysis of the structure of the aerospace industry is presented in this and later chapters. The discussion focuses primarily on the market relationships which are the result of government demand for industry products, for this segment of the market accounts for more than 90 percent of the dollar volume of aerospace industry sales. Because of our emphasis on the role of government in this industry, the relationship between the airplane manufacturers and the airlines will not be discussed. This chapter is concerned primarily with the number of firms selling to the government and the role of the government as a buyer and the role assumed by management companies in assisting the government.

NUMBER OF SELLERS

Estimates were obtained from several sources of the number of aerospace firms which were actively engaged in selling to the various government agencies. For instance, for 1962 the Census Bureau's quarterly reports, "Backlog of Orders for Aerospace Companies," indicate that there were 64 firms which produced, assembled, developed, or had prime system responsibility for complete aircraft, complete missile or space vehicle systems; and complete aircraft engines, and complete engines or propulsion units for missiles and space vehicles.[1] A second source, the FTC-SEC *Quar-*

---

[1] Firms primarily engaged in the manufacture of airplane and missile parts are not included in the survey. In early 1963, the Census Bureau reported that 67 firms were included in the survey.

terly Financial Reports for Manufacturing Corporations, surveys only 51 aviation companies. The former source more nearly represents the type of information we desire. However, there is no way of determining accurately whether the 64 firms surveyed by the Census Bureau represented the entire population of firms with prime-system responsibilities.

Several other sources were consulted in order to verify the Census data. A count of firms which in 1962, according to *Aviation Week and Space Technology,*[2] manufactured aircraft, missiles, drones, engines, and power plants, yielded only 50 such companies. This figure is an estimate of the number of firms which have prime contracts, but firms with subcontracts must also be included in the industry. A check of the 1961 edition of the *Fortune Plant and Product Directory of the 500 Largest U.S. Industrial Corporations* indicated that 53 of the listed firms were engaged in the manufacture of planes, engines, or missiles (SIC Nos. 3721, 3722 and 1925). Moreover, the inclusion of the firms active in Industry 3729 showed that 80 of the 500 largest firms were to some degree active in the aircraft and missile industry. Since the definition of the aerospace industry also included parts of SIC industries 35, 36, and 38, any list of participants in the industry must also include contractors active in the appropriate sectors of these SIC industries. An additional 23 firms were active in the sectors thus indicating that 103 of the 500 largest firms were to some extent active in the aerospace industry.[3] All evidence seems to indicate that the Census survey of prime manufacturers is a minimum estimate of the number of firms involved, but the survey probably yields a reasonable estimate of the number of prime contractors, for no other list appeared to be as comprehensive.

Additional Census data provide another partial count of the number of firms active in the aerospace industry in 1958. There were 113 firms in Industry 3721, 186 in 3722, 17 in 3723 and 1097 in 3729. However, no data are available for Industry 1925, for the pre-1957 industry definitions were used to count the number of firms, and that particular SIC classification was not created until

---

2 *Aviation Week,* March 12, 1962, pp. 70-78, 179-180, and 194-195.

3 A very cursory examination of lists of subcontractors of major importance, published occasionally in *Aviation Week* and a partial membership list of the Aerospace Industries Association indicated that at least another 129 firms were noteworthy of being classified in the aerospace industry.

1957.[4] However, the trend in the number of firms in several of these industrial classifications can be examined (Table 24). The number of firms increased between 1947 and 1954 as the aviation industry expanded to meet the demand for military aircraft during and after the Korean War, but it is interesting that the number

TABLE 24
NUMBER OF FIRMS IN SIC INDUSTRY 3721, 3722, 3723, AND 3729,
FOR 1947, 1954, AND 1958

SIC Number	Year	Number of firms
3721 Aircraft	1958 1954 1947	113 . . . . . .
3722 Aircraft Engines	1958 1954 1947	186 202 54
3723 Aircraft Propellers	1958 1954 1947	17 16 12
3729 Aircraft Equipment, n. e. c.	1958 1954 1947	1097 1054 301

of firms did not increase between 1954 and 1958. This may be attributable to the post-1957 slowdown in the demand for aircraft, for the increase in missile activity is not as yet reflected in SIC 3729, because the pre-1957 definition of the industry, in which missile activity is not counted, was used. At some later time it will be necessary to compare the 1958 and later Census data on the number of firms included in the revised definition of Industry 3729. Then it will be possible to measure the effect that the missile and space programs have had on the number of firms active in the industry.[5]

---

4 U.S., Senate, Committee on the Judiciary, *Concentration Ratios in Manufacturing Industry, 1958*, Report Prepared by the Bureau of the Census, 1962, p. 38. Since the pre-1957 definition of each of these industries is used, missile parts would not be included in Industry 3729. A different Census publication indicated the existence of 114 companies active in Industry 3721. Of these 114 companies, 102 were primarily classified in the industry. U.S., Bureau of the Census, *Enterprise Statistics: 1958*, Part 1, General Report, Series ES 3 No. 1, 1963, p. 69.

5 However, conceivably, this expansion will not occur in Industry 3729 but in various other SIC industries, such as electronics, instruments, and so on. An examination of the 1958 concentration ratios, based on the 1957 SIC classification, of product classes 37292 (guided-missile components) and 37294 (research and development in guided-missile components) yielded figures of 55, 80 and 96-99 for 4, 8, and 20 firms

The concentration ratios by SIC industry, though unlikely to explain the competitive practices of the aerospace industry in view of the peculiar relationship between the firms and the government, are presented in Tables 25 and 26. These data, however, can provide some information about the structure of the market. In Table 25, the concentration ratios apply to each of the relevant four-digit SIC industries and are based on the pre-1957 SIC classification. On

TABLE 25

PERCENTAGE OF VALUE ADDED AND SHIPMENTS ACCOUNTED FOR BY THE 4, 8, AND 20
LARGEST FIRMS IN SPECIFIED CLASSIFICATIONS,[a] 1947, 1954, AND 1958

Industry classifications	Year	Percentage by number of largest firms		
		4	8	20
3721	1958[b]	59	83	99
3722	1958	56	77	92
	1954	62	81	93
	1947	72	88	98
3723	1958	97	99	100
	1954	91	98	100
	1947	98	99+	100
3729	1958	27	39	55
	1954	20	32	52
	1947	37	58	75

SOURCE: U. S., Senate, Committee on the Judiciary, *Concentration Ratios in Manufacturing Industry 1958*, Report Prepared by the Bureau of the Census (1962), p. 38.

a The concentration ratios for industries 3721 and 3723 are based on the percentage of the industry's value added accounted for by the 4, 8, and 20 largest firms. The other data are based on value of shipments.
b Data are not available for earlier years.

the other hand, the data in Table 26 are based on shipments by product class, regardless of the industry of origin, and these figures are based on the 1957 SIC classification.

The concentration ratios are relatively high in three of the four segments of the industry. This is true for both the SIC industry classification and the product groupings. The exception is SIC 3729, where, as previously noted, the research and development of missiles components is relatively concentrated whereas the sales of

respectively. Such ratios may be associated with a large number or an increasing number of firms. However, one should be wary of reaching such a conclusion for the shipments of aircraft parts and components, which constitute the other part of Industry 3729, were much less concentrated, with ratios of 20, 33, and 56 for 4, 8, and 20 firms respectively.

miscellaneous aircraft components are unconcentrated. These data indicate that twenty or fewer firms account for virtually all sales of most aerospace products.[6] This is not surprising since the system method of contracting, which was mentioned briefly in Chapter 2, has tended to concentrate sales within a few firms. This contractual

TABLE 26

PERCENTAGE OF SPECIFIED AEROSPACE-PRODUCT SHIPMENTS: 4, 8, AND 20 LARGEST FIRMS, 1954 AND 1958

Industry classification	Year	Percentage by number of largest firms		
		4	8	20
3721	1958	62	83	97
	1954	55	79	97
3722	1958	56	74	99
	1954	63	81	91
3723	1958	96	98	99
	1954	90	96	99
3729	1958	20	34	60

SOURCE: U. S., Senate, Committee on the Judiciary, *Concentration Ratios in Manufacturing Industry 1958,* Report Prepared by the Bureau of the Census (1962), pp. 159-60.

arrangement will be explored in more detail in the following chapter. The conclusion to be stressed is that despite the relatively large number of firms in the industry, a few firms account for most of the sales.

THE TYPES OF AEROSPACE FIRMS

At one time it was possible to distinguish clearly between firms which were in the aircraft industry and those excluded from it. The former group included the manufacturers of specialized parts for aircraft, the manufacturers of both piston and jet aircraft engines, and propellers, and, finally, the assemblers of airplanes known as the airframe manufacturers. Several operations were often embodied in one firm, such as United Aircraft.

Originally, specialized parts, including the engines, were supplied by the government to the airplane manufacturing firm which

---

[6] In addition, the performance of research and development in the aerospace industry is also concentrated in the hands of a small number of firms. The four aerospace firms with the largest research and development programs accounted for 50 percent of the industry's research and development work. The eight largest accounted for 71 percent. National Science Foundation, *Funds for Research and Development in Industry, 1958,* NSF 60-35, May 1960.

constructed the airframe and assembled the entire airplane. Part of the metal forging and machining of the airframe components was subcontracted, especially at times of peak of demand,[7] but the construction of the airframe was the most complex operation and accounted for the largest percentage of the cost of the plane.[8] Now, the electronic equipment is often the most critical item in the development of a new system and may account for the largest percentage of the cost.[9]

This change has expanded the scope of the industry and has had two main effects on the structure of the industry as will be pointed out below. First, each aircraft firm had to obtain a capability in electronics in order to be able to integrate the airframe and electronics subsystems. Second, several electronics firms have entered the industry and obtained some prime systems contracts for guided missiles.

While satisfactory classification of the aerospace firms by function is difficult, several arbitrary divisions are suggested. First, there are the prime system contractors that have the responsibility of developing and delivering a finished system to the government. In addition, under the weapon-system form of contracting, these prime contractors supervise the work of their subcontractors and integrate the subsystems into a final finished product. An alternative form of contracting has the manufacturers of the guidance systems and rocket engine working in conjunction with the prime contractor, but the latter still retains the responsibility for the overall performance of the system.[10] Two groups of companies currently qualify as prime contractors. The first includes the eleven remaining airframe manufacturers,[11] which not only have system responsibility for air-

---

[7] See the books of Harlan and Day, as cited in chap. 1, n. 20.

[8] U.S., Senate, Subcommittee of the Committee on Armed Services, *Hearings, Military Procurement*, 86th Cong., 1st Sess., July 13-31, 1959, p. 209.

[9] *Ibid.*

[10] In this case, the manufacturers of the rocket engines and guidance systems, and so on, are called associate contractors. For an illustration of this system of contracting see U.S., House, Committee on Armed Services, *Weapons System Management and Teams System Concept in Government Contracting*, 86th Cong., 1st Sess., 1959, pp. 128 ff. Hereafter cited as *Weapons System Hearings*.

[11] The companies are: Boeing, Douglas, General Dynamics, Grumman, Ling-Temco-Vought, Lockheed, Martin, McDonnell, North American Aviation, Northrop, and Republic. Several of these companies also manufacture large civilian transport planes. Peck and Scherer count only 10 because Martin is no longer considered to be an airplane manufacturer, *op. cit.*, p. 195. Also see *Aviation Week*, November 9, 1959, p. 29; and *Missiles and Rockets*, June 19, 1961, pp. 40 ff.

planes but also for the larger ballistic missiles. The second group includes those firms originally classified in the electronics industry which have the prime contracts for the smaller, guided, surface-to-air, air-to-air, air-to-surface, or surface-to-underwater missiles. A representative list of firms which in 1962 had such contracts would include Raytheon, Western Electric, Bendix Aviation, Hughes Aircraft, Emerson Electric, Sperry-Rand, and Minneapolis-Honeywell.[12] The electronics companies were not the only firms which had prime system responsibility for the smaller guided missiles, for several of these missiles were developed by the airframe manufacturers. It was noted previously that the armed services, in awarding prime contracts, chose between the electronics and airframe manufacturers primarily on the basis of which was the more difficult chore to perform, the construction of the airframe or the development of the electronics components going into the airframe.[13]

Another group of firms, often called associate prime contractors, are the manufacturers of propulsion units for rockets and power plants for aircraft. The major producers of aircraft engines are General Electric, General Motors (Allison Division), United Aircraft, and Westinghouse. Aerojet, North American Aviation (Rocketdyne Division) and Thiokol were the primary rocket-engine manufacturers until the early 1960's when Bell Aerospace, United Aircraft, Lockheed, and Hercules Powder among others entered this segment of the industry.[14] An interesting question, discussed in Chapter 7, is why the manufacturers of aircraft engines did not become the major rocket-engine producers, for this is in marked contrast to the experience of the airframe manufacturers which became the manufacturers of all the larger and many of the smaller missiles.[15]

The manufacturers of specialized aerospace systems and parts

---

[12] Chrysler, which is neither an electronics company nor an airframe manufacturer, also has had prime contracts.

[13] *Aviation Week*, May 23, 1960, p. 67.

[14] Several airframe manufacturers, namely North American and Lockheed, are also active in this segment of the industry.

[15] The experience was not uniform, for companies like Grumman, McDonnell, and Republic had had no missile contracts by 1960. See Peck and Scherer, *op. cit.*, p. 195. One explanation for the aircraft companies obtaining missile contracts is that the military did not appreciate the lesser importance of "metal bending skills" and the greater emphasis on electronics. *Aviation Week*, May 23, 1960, p. 67.

form another group of companies.[16] They are usually classified by the prime or associate prime contractor, responsible for choosing other firms to develop the subsystems and to integrate the various systems, as subcontractors which manufacture communication, guidance, and control systems, life-support systems, instruments, rocket-motor cases, valves, ground-supply or other aerospace equipment. These firms generally are listed as the first-tier subcontractors of the prime contractors, even though in many cases they themselves have prime contracts for another missile or may be associate prime contractors on still another project. The competitive relationship between the prime contractors and these subcontractors is examined in greater detail in Capter 7. In addition, the relationship between these first-tier electronic subcontractors and their subcontractors, the manufacturers of electronic components, is discussed in Appendix C.[17]

Finally, one should note that there are other sellers in this industry. It was decided arbitrarily not to discuss their behavior, for they either accounted for only a small percentage of the industry's sales or sufficient data could not be obtained. These companies include the manufacturers of light civilian planes, drones, and helicopters.

The Government as a Buyer

Since the government's 1962 purchases accounted for 94 percent of the industry's total sales,[18] a complete understanding of the structure of the industry requires that the government's role as a buyer be examined. The government cannot be considered a monopsonist, for each of the military services and NASA conduct their own procurement. Even within each of these autonomous units separate units compete for the funds allocated to that branch. Thus the Army purchases short-range, ground-to-ground missiles and some types of short-range support aircraft. The Navy may purchase planes, missiles fired from ships, or missiles fired from planes. The Air Force purchases ballistic missiles, bombers, fighters, and air-

---

16 These firms have also been called the subsystem manufacturers because the missile or airplane itself is called the system.

17 Electronic components are used in the manufacture of electronic systems and include such products as tubes, transistors, relays, resistors, capacitors, and filters.

18 *Ibid.*, March 12, 1962, p. 62. The 1961 ratio was lower but this was a result of large commercial orders because of the introduction of turbine planes.

to-air missiles. Both NASA and the military services buy rocket engines. The list could be extended further, but the basic point is that the government cannot be considered as a single buyer.

Several developments since 1961 have served to introduce more uniformity into the purchasing decisions of the armed forces. First, the programming concept developed by Secretary of Defense McNamara and Assistant Secretary of Defense Hitch has provided the major impetus in this direction. In this concept, a program package consisting of an interrelated group of planned military systems is developed, costed, and analyzed. This package would consist of systems which both support each other and are substitutes for each other. The programming is based upon the major missions of the armed forces, and the selection of systems to be purchased within each mission category is determined by the cost of each system and its effectiveness in performing the assigned task.[19]

In addition, NASA and the Air Force have coordinated their development policies for programs such as the large-scale rockets. One agency has the responsibility for each program, but the knowledge is shared between the agencies. This is another factor which has seemed to increase the government's appearance as a single buying unit.

However, there still is considerable rivalry among the Armed Services and lately between the Armed Forces and NASA in vying for jurisdiction over a particular mission or assignment. As an example, our nuclear deterrence can be implemented either by the Navy with the missiles aboard its Polaris submarines, or by the Air Force with its bombers and ICBM's. This tends to lead to competition between the services for this mission. The ultimate selection of the service to perform the task within the programming concept depends upon the operational effectiveness and cost of each weapon. In the past there have been numerous such jurisdictional disputes (e.g., among the most important were the controversy between Air Force and Navy over the B-36 versus carriers, and the

---

19 *Misiles and Rockets*, May 8, 1961, pp. 17-18 and March 25, 1963, pp. 77-78. The nine major programs are the Strategic Retaliatory Forces, Airlift and Sealift Force, Reserve Forces, Ground Forces, General Purpose Forces, General Support, Research and Development, Civil Defense, and Military Assistance.

Moreover, the Armed Services Procurement Regulations apply to all the services thus providing another push towards uniformity in procurement practices.

dispute between NASA and Air Force about each agency's jurisdiction in space).[20]

This interservice rivalry, depending on the effectiveness of specified weapons, probably has had a beneficial effect on the industry's
performance.[21] Once a contract for a specified system has been
awarded to a particular firm, there is little likelihood that this contract will be removed from its jurisdiction and awarded to some
other firm. There are few instances in which this has been done.
One exception occurred during the development of the BOMARC
missile. General Electric originally had the Thumper antiaircraft
missile and Michigan Aeronautical had the Wizard program. The
two were merged and the renamed program was awarded to Boeing.[22] However, if a contract was rarely taken from one firm and
awarded to another, there have been instances in which second
sources have been developed in follow-on procurements or when
a variant of the system was introduced. This technique was used
when the Nike X was introduced. A firm different from the one
which held the Nike Zeus contract was chosen as the prime contractor. Since a research and development or production contract
for a specified system is usually awarded only to one firm, there is
no competition between firms for a particular system once the contract has been awarded.

However, even after contracts have been awarded, the force of
competition is felt indirectly through interservice rivalry because
pressure is placed on the firms holding contracts with the agency
whose mission is in jeopardy. This interservice rivalry thus has
encouraged interproduct competition, especially in the prespace

---

20 *The New York Times*, October 9, 1949, Section 4, p. E1 and October 25, 1959,
Section 4, pp. E2, E5. The Air Force is still attempting to compete with NASA in the
manned space flights.

21 R. Schlaifer, *Development of Aircraft Engines* (Cambridge, Mass.: School of
Business Administration, Harvard University, 1950), p. 11, indicates that the development of the jet engine was stimulated by interservice competition.

22 U.S., Senate, Permanent Subcommittee on Investigations of the Committee on
Government Operations, *Pyramiding of Profits and Costs in the Missile Procurement
Program*, Part 4, *The BOMARC Program*, 87th Cong., 2d Sess., May 22-25, 1962, p.
782.

Similarly, the OSO satellite was developed for NASA by Ball Brothers, but when
the advanced OSO satellite was to be procured, feasibility studies were awarded to
Ball Brothers, Republic Aviation, and STL. Republic was awarded the production
contract for the satellite.

age era when the aviation firms often worked exclusively for one agency.[23] Moreover, this interproduct or interservice competition often comes from sources outside the aerospace industry. For instance, there is some indication that the time slippage of the MIDAS satellite, which was designed to warn of impending missile attacks, may have caused a curtailment of the satellite project and an expansion of our Ballistic Missile Early Warning System.[24]

A more important consideration is that the government, as a buyer, needs the industry as much as the industry needs the government. The government does not have the facilities or skilled manpower to produce aerospace items and often finds it difficult even to supervise the day-to-day operations of its prime contractors.[25] In fact, these government agencies have often assigned the task of direction and coordination to private companies, known as management companies.

---

[23] Peck and Scherer, *op. cit.*, p. 342. Boeing and Republic have in the past specialized in Air Force work whereas Grumman and Chance-Vought worked for the Navy. Since 1930 Grumman has produced more than 25,000 planes, of which 23,500 were carrier-based. *Aviation Week*, May 20, 1963, p. 104. If an agency loses a mission, the size of the market of firms specializing in work for this agency has been permanently reduced. Since NASA was established, many aerospace firms have attempted to reduce their reliance on a given service and obtained contracts from the space agency. The diversification has somewhat reduced the firms' vulnerability to possible cancellations of a service's mission.

[24] The Ballistic Missile Early Warning System is a land-based radar system. *Aviation Week*, August 6, 1962, p. 26 and February 18, 1963, p. 40. *Missiles and Rockets*, February 17, 1964, p. 9. As other recent examples of such interproduct competition, the following should be noted: The Polaris and Minuteman missiles were considered substitutes, and there was a dispute over the number of each to be installed. *Ibid.*, May 2, 1960, p. 14. The phasing out of our bomber fleet was noted by the headline, "More Minutemen Sought to Replace B-52's." *Aviation Week*, November 26, 1962, p. 27. Ford was endeavoring to reduce the weight of its Shillelagh missile in order to meet the competition from other lighter antitank systems. *Missiles and Rockets*, March 11, 1963, p. 9. The nuclear plane was considered to be in competition with missiles. *Aviation Week*, April 1, 1963, p. 81. Our manned spacecraft are considered to be substitutes. The Saint Inspector Satellite was canceled when it was discovered that Gemini would be operational first. DynaSoar (X-20) and Gemini are considered in the same manner, though there is a slight technological difference between the two. *Ibid.*, February 25, 1963, p. 26 and March 18, 1963, p. 31. Similarly, in the past, interceptor-fighter planes were considered substitutes for antiplane missiles such as the BOMARC. U.S., House, Subcommittee of the Committee on Government Operations, *Hearings, Organization and Management of Missile Programs*, 86th Cong., 2d Sess., 1960, pp. 47-48.

[25] The armed services have had more difficulty on this score than has NASA, which has a large in-house technical staff. But even NASA, as it has grown, has found it difficult to evaluate alternative approaches effectively and has turned to private industry for this type of assistance.

Management companies perform the government's function of supervision and coordination[26] and often suggest to the contractors, through the appropriate government agency, an alternative approach to a technical problem. This function is known as system management and has at various times been in the hands of Ramo-Wooldridge, the Space Technology Laboratories of Thompson-Ramo-Wooldridge, the Aerospace Corporation, Bellcomm, Inc. (a division of American Telephone and Telegraph), and General Electric. All these companies except Aerospace are profit-seeking firms. The role of the nonprofit organization in evaluating federally sponsored research contracts has been questioned,[27] but the only important point to be considered in this study is why these corporations came into existence and why they are still required.

The Air Force was the first to use these management companies. NASA, which was established only in 1959, did not use them initially, but as its tasks expanded, it, too, required their services. The manner in which NASA uses these companies will be discussed after the relationship between the Air Force and the management companies has been presented.

In 1954, the Air Force assigned Ramo-Wooldridge the task of supervising the development of our missile programs. This responsibility rested with the company until 1960, despite several organizational changes that occurred in the private firm. The Space Technology Laboratories Division of Ramo-Wooldridge was established in 1956 and became a wholly-owned subsidiary of Thompson-Ramo-Wooldridge when Thompson Products merged with Ramo-Wooldridge. Because Thompson-Ramo-Wooldridge was not allowed to bid on projects which Space Technology Laboratories was managing,[28] the parent company sought to yield this management role.[29] This was accomplished in 1960 when this func-

---

26 U.S., House, Staff Study Prepared for the Committee on Science and Astronautics, *Independent Nonprofit Federal Research Contractors*, 87th Cong., 2d Sess., October 10, 1962, p. 1. For further information about the role played by management companies in assisting the government, see *Organization and Management of Missile Programs*, 1959.

27 The pros and cons of using nonprofit firms, as compared to profit-making organizations, as systems managers have been examined in *Independent Nonprofit Federal Research Contractors*, pp. 7-8.

28 *Aviation Week*, January 26, 1959, p. 35.

29 *Ibid.*, February 16, 1959, p. 31. As early as 1957, there had been some discussion that technical staff management was not an appropriate function for a company

tion was transferred to the Aerospace Corporation. The functions of this nonprofit firm include: directing and managing of systems; judging the technical aspects of industrial proposals; and originating scientific and technical ideas.[30]

NASA required the assistance of management companies when the Apollo project threatened to dilute its scientific strength. NASA argues that it and the Air Force have different approaches to the problem, but the difference between the two management approaches is one only of degree. Thompson-Ramo-Wooldridge had both the technical direction and the systems management responsibilities in performing its job for the Air Force, but the Aerospace Corporation, Bellcomm, and General Electric performed only advisory functions for NASA.[31] However, the tasks which Bellcomm and General Electric agreed to execute are similar to those assigned to the Aerospace Corporation. Bellcomm is to prepare overall systems specifications, study check-out and launch, and develop mission assurance.[32] General Electric is to look at total reliability factors with respect to engines and to every other factor up to the completed Apollo boosters and spacecraft.[33] In other words, it is to perform the overall check-out, and coordinate the work of two of NASA's prime contractors, North American Aviation and Boe-

---

like Ramo-Wooldridge. The argument was that the company's talent yielded low returns on these types of contracts as compared with production contracts. *Ibid.*, June 24, 1957, p. 29. The argument is erroneous because Space Technology Labs in managing the Atlas, Titan, and Minuteman missile programs earned a fee averaging between 9.2 and 9.3 percent of its costs. This fee was larger than those earned by any of the companies it supervised. *Ibid.*, April 30, 1962, p. 26. The company was hurt, since it could not compete for any type of missile contract because of the conflict of interest provisos. This excluded Thompson-Ramo-Wooldridge from the market and reduced its potential sales. If Thompson-Ramo-Wooldridge had been able to obtain a substantial share of the market, and even if it had earned a lower percentage fee, total profits would have risen. Also see *Missiles and Rockets*, March 19, 1962, pp. 30 ff. For an additional discussion of the conflict of interest provisions which apply to the technical advisory firms, see *The New York Times*, September 18, 1962, pp. 1 and 19.

[30] *Independent Nonprofit Federal Research Contractors*, p. 5

[31] U.S., House, Subcommittee on Manned Space Flight of the Committee on Science and Astronautics, *Hearings, 1963 NASA Authorization*, Pt. 2, 87th Cong., 2d Sess., March 6-April 10, 1962, p. 873. Also *Aviation Week*, April 2, 1962, p. 38.

[32] *Ibid.*, September 17, 1962, p. 87. U.S., House, Subcommittee of the Committee on Government Operations, *Hearings, Systems Development and Management*, Pt. 5, 87th Cong., 2d Sess., 1962, pp. 1695-1718.

[33] *1963 NASA Authorization*, Pt. 1, February 27-May 3, 1962, p. 16. For other information about General Electric's role see *Aviation Week*, July 22, 1963, pp. 290 ff.

ing Aircraft.[34] Bellcomm will decide what must be done and General Electric will see that it is done properly.[35]

From this discussion it is possible to conclude that neither the Defense Department nor NASA has a sufficient number of skilled personnel to perform technical management. In some cases, the agencies delegate responsibility for technical decisions to the management companies. For these reasons one might infer that the various agencies do not have the technical expertise to be the well-informed buyers that one commonly associates with oligopsony. It follows that these agencies then turn to some of the sellers of the industry's products to assist them in performing a part of the buying function.[36] As a consequence, one observer characterized this market as one in which a single buyer, with large and inelastic demand, faces a few sellers who are aware of the urgency of the buyer's needs.[37] Moreover, at one time good military strategy dictated that the armed services try to maintain a broad industrial base and assure the survival of the industry upon which the security of the country depended.[38] Work was spread among contractors in order to prevent bankruptcies. In addition the government built many of the manufacturing facilities of the aircraft industry and provided the industry's working capital in the form of progress payments. These actions thus protected the industry against many financial risks.

---

[34] *Aviation Week*, April 2, 1962, pp. 45-47. *1963 NASA Authorization*, Pt. 2, p. 382. North American already has the responsibility of integrating the guidance and control systems with the spacecraft. Boeing, which is building the first stage of the Saturn V booster, also is responsible for integrating the total booster with other stages built by North American and Douglas.

[35] *Aviation Week*, April 2, 1962, p. 45. General Electric's role has been expanded. It now also performs the support functions at the Mississippi Test Facility. *Ibid.*, April 22, 1963, p. 28.

[36] In the weapon-system approach, the prime contractor also carries out functions that might well be performed by the government. These will be discussed below, including integration of the subsystem and overall supervision.

[37] J. P. Miller, "Military Procurement Policies: World War II and Today," *American Economic Review, Papers and Proceedings*, XLII, No. 2 (May 1952), p. 455. This was written at a time when weapon systems were simple compared with those being developed at this time.

[38] For instance, see the testimony of Northrop's President in *1963 NASA Authorization*, Pt. 2, pp. 395-397. U.S., Senate, Preparedness Subcommittee of the Committee on Armed Services, *Investigation of the Preparedness Program*, 82d Cong., 1st Sess., 1952, p. 20. One general testified that "Boeing needs the BOMARC casework because they had just lost a wing subcontract on North American's canceled F-108." *Pyramiding of Profits and Costs . . .* Pt. 4, p. 769.

A more detailed discussion of some aspects of the government's role in protecting the industry against financial risk is presented in Chapter 5. In addition, Chapter 4 includes an analysis of the institutional arrangements used by the contracting agencies to protect the government's interest. At this time, however, it suffices to mention that the government has attempted to establish multiple sources of supply in order to insure that no single contractor becomes dominant in any major area of importance.[39] An increased number of competitors can be obtained easily by broadening the base of supply and spreading contracts among several firms. The Air Force pursued this policy in the ICBM program when the Titan was started,[40] and NASA, in turn, has followed suit in its awards both for the rocket boosters and propulsion units.[41] This is one of many institutional arrangements which became necessary as a result of the structure of the market.

SUMMARY AND CONCLUSIONS

In this chapter we have discussed one aspect of the structure of the industry, namely the number of sellers and buyers. We concluded that there are a substantial number of sellers operating within the industry, but all available evidence indicates that the sales of most aerospace products are concentrated in the hands of a small number of firms. It was noted further that classification of aerospace firms by the type of activity in which they are engaged is difficult. However, several arbitrary divisions were suggested. These categories included prime contractors, associate prime contractors, subcontractors which manufacture systems, and subsystem manufacturers. A partial description of the type of firm which operates in each area was also presented.

In examining the buying side of the market, we decided arbitrarily to focus our attention on the government's position as a buyer. It was noted that the government's procurement was per-

---

39 *Aviation Week*, May 2, 1960, p. 25, November 13, 1961, p. 32, December 4, 1961, p. 26, and February 18, 1963, p. 32.

40 *Organization and Management of Missile Programs*, pp. 66-67.

41 *Aviation Week*, November 13, 1961, p. 32, and April 18, 1962, p. 28. *1963 NASA Authorization*, Pt. 2, pp. 825-826. However, the S-IV and S-IVB Saturn stages were both awarded to Douglas, because both relied on the same technology! *Missiles and Rockets*, November 26, 1962, p. 92.

formed by several agencies with the result that the government could not be considered as a single buyer. It was also concluded that the interservice rivalry for the authority to perform particular missions may have had a beneficial competitive effect. Finally, we observed that the government hired firms active in the industry to assist it in buying.

4.

STRUCTURE OF THE INDUSTRY: THE NATURE AND DEVELOPMENT OF COMPETITIVE PRACTICES

CURRENT COMPETITIVE PRACTICES

Since the main emphasis of this chapter is on the competitive practices prevailing in the industry, the analysis of the historical evolution of these practices has been relegated to the final section of the chapter.

Currently, the competitive practices of the industry are dissimilar from those of most others. It is not the absence of price competition that sets this industry apart, for there are many industries in which the prevailing structure precludes price competition; but in those industries, there is usually some form of nonprice competition, for the pressure to compete for the sales of a specified product must find some outlet.

The difference between this industry and most others is that at the time of the competition for sales not even a prototype of the product is usually available. The Armed Services and NASA want an airplane, rocket, or space vehicle which has some operating characteristics. Only time will tell whether these specifications actually can be translated into an operational system. Requests for proposals for reducing these specifications into an operational system are submitted to the aerospace firms which then suggest alternative techniques of performing this task. Each firm prices its own technical proposal, but the quoted price is usually not the variable

58

which determines the recipient of the contract award.[1] The proposals are evaluated by various boards within each agency, and the contract is awarded to the firm which presents the most promising approach.[2] The form of contract and the price at which this work is done is then subject to negotiation between the government and the successful bidder. This, then, is the extent of the competition between the sellers for the right to develop a specified aerospace system. In essence, firms are selling ideas, and the concern with the best proposal or design is awarded a contract. Thus, one cannot characterize the competitive process by any of the standard terms generally used in analyses of this type. Moreover, once a firm is chosen to develop a system, the firm becomes a monopolist of that particular product, for, generally, duplicate research and development contracts are not awarded.[3]

Some characteristics of this competitive process should be noted. At the time of the competition the feasibility of developing the proposed system is uncertain. The competition for the government's business thus revolves around each company's ability to demonstrate its technical competence to develop the product, for the firms are competing for the right to develop the proposed system for a particular governmental agency at the latter's expense. Only if a product closely approximating the original specifications can be developed will it be ordered into production.

If a successful bidder were to agree to undertake this research

---

[1] U.S., House, Subcommittee of the Committee on Government Operations, Hearings, *Systems Development and Management*, Pt. 3, 87th Cong., 2d Sess., 1962, p. 894. Heavy weights are given to past performance, personnel, and the quality of the technical proposal. It has been suggested that price is now a more important consideration in selecting a contractor than it was before the 1960's. However, the government may decide that the least cost is not necessarily obtained by accepting the lowest bidder. This was especially true when firms placed "unnecessarily low" bids in the hope of obtaining cost-plus contracts. This point will be examined in greater detail below.

[2] We shall not discuss the internal organization of the governmental agencies through which these proposals are routed. The proposed designs and final configurations often are quite different, but the design proposals have a value in predicting the outcome of a specified program. See Merton J. Peck and F. M. Scherer, *The Weapons Acquisition Process: An Economic Analysis* (Cambridge: Harvard University Press, Division of Research, 1962), pp. 364-365.

[3] The interproduct rivalry discussed in Chapter 3 is ignored at this stage. In addition, any political pressures which work behind the scenes to influence the choice of contractor are also excluded from discussion.

and development for a fixed price, it would have to receive a substantial risk premium to accept these uncertainties. Firms are often unwilling to undertake risky ventures even when substantial profits are available. Research and development contracts are often of the cost-reimbursement type both because of this risk aversion on the part of the bidder and the government's desire to prevent high profits which might accrue to successful firms. Moreover, in the past, the government was also believed to attempt to protect the financial position of concerns whose efforts might be unsuccessful. With this type of contract, the government pays only for the firm's actual expense of performing the work, plus a profit fee. Whether the government actually pays less than it would have if a fixed-price contract, even with a substantial risk premium included, had been awarded is a subject for conjecture.[4] The argument is that with the financial burden shifted to the government, the firms have little incentive to minimize costs. Actually, as we shall see below, cost overruns are an inherent feature of these contracts.[5]

-----

[4] Firms presumably would only bid for contracts in areas in which they had expertise, thus reducing the size of the premium necessary to induce a firm to accept the uncertainties. However, in several segments of the market, eventually there would be only one or at most two firms competent to produce specified systems. It was previously observed that the government, in order to assure the success of its mission, wants to maintain multiple sources.

[5] Despite the faults of the cost-reimbursement contract, several legal questions about the government and the firms are avoided when these contracts are used. If a system only approximating the original specifications is developed under a fixed-price contract, the question arises whether the contract has been fulfilled and the government's requirements met. The firm may insist that it had completed its assignment. However, with a reimbursement-type contract, the government may insist that alternative approaches be tested in order to bring the product closer to the original specifications. With no financial risk, firms are more likely to agree. (For the problem in the use of fixed-price contracts when technological changes are involved, see *The Wall Street Journal*, August 20, 1963, p. 6. This discusses the TVA-Westinghouse Electric Co. dispute over turbine-generators, but is not *directly* relevant to the aerospace industry.)

Second, suppose there has been an award of a fixed-price contract concerning research and development of a system, which actually could not be developed. Such a situation is most likely to occur when the system requires a technological revolution. Due to the uncertainties, most firms would not have bid for such fixed-price contracts, but one firm might have underestimated the magnitude of the task, bid for and been awarded the contract, and was now in difficulty. The firm could legally be forced to continue working on the contract until bankrupt, but this would not aid the government, for it would not have obtained its new system and would have forced a supplier into bankruptcy or reorganization. Moreover, this method of procurement would lead most firms to bid only on "safe" contracts and might inhibit technological progress in aerospace systems.

Whereas the development of these new large-scale systems, which involve scientific breakthrough, almost always is performed under reimbursement-type contracts, there are other forms of procurement contracts. Government purchases of standardized products are usually made through competitive bidding for fixed-price contracts. This type of action needs no further explanation, but the negotiated fixed-price contract should be examined.

The negotiation of fixed-price contracts may take two forms. In the first, the government and a firm which is the sole producer of a system, negotiate the price at which the item will be supplied. This form of "sole source" procurement usually follows the successful development of a system with the production order going to the concern which originally developed the item. Since there is only one source of supply and price, the price must consequently be negotiated.[6] At this stage of the procurement process, the organization which has developed the system is the sole producer of that particular item, but it may face the competition of other systems which may perform a similar if not identical task. Thus the inter-product competition provided by alternative systems may tend to limit the freedom of action of any one firm.[7]

In the second type of negotiated procurement, known as "two-step negotiation,"[8] a form of price competition exists. This procurement means is used when the item is not standardized and may be developed in different ways. Since the procuring agency is interested in developing a system with a specified set of technical characteristics, it issues a set of specifications and requests technical proposals. From these proposals a source list of companies whose items meet the specifications is obtained. Each of these approved companies is then asked to price its own technical proposal, and the lowest bidder is awarded the contract.[9] Thus, systems whose

---

6 Not all these negotiated procurements with sole-source suppliers result in fixed-price contracts, for the first production contract may still contain cost uncertainties. Under such situations, incentive-type cost reimbursement contracts are often used.

7 In addition, if the system is to be produced in large quantities, the procuring agencies may establish a second source of supply. In either case, the market power of the seller has been curtailed.

8 U.S., Senate, Subcommittee of the Select Committee on Small Business, *Hearings, Government Procurement, 1960,* 86th Cong., 2d Sess., April 5-8, 1960, pp. 113-115.

9 Often, if the bid is considered unreasonably low, the company is requested to confirm its bid. However, it is not told the direction of the suspected error. *Ibid.,* pp. 52-53.

development is comparatively simple are procured by price competition.

On the other hand, the major weapon and space systems, which account for the bulk of the industry's output, are not procured competitively. Thus, two basic problems must be examined. First, the reasons for not awarding such research and development contracts on the basis of price competition have been examined, but the rationale for not awarding production contracts on this basis needs further elaboration. Second, the absence of price competition necessitates the protection of the buyer's interests by the introduction of some institutional arrangements. It is probably erroneous to assume that these arrangements have always been successful.

THE EXTENT OF COMPETITION AND INSTITUTIONAL ARRANGEMENTS OF THE BUYER

After a system has been developed, it might be appropriate to award the production contract on the pasis of price competition. However, there are several factors which reduce the likelihood that this happens. Sealed-bid procurement requires the preparation of blueprints upon which the bids are based,[10] and this takes time. A sufficiently long interval must elapse for competitors to prepare and submit their bids. Since a system is often required at a specific instant, time is often the variable which is the scarce resource. In such a situation, the buyer will search for methods which minimize the length of the development-and-production process. Little time is lost if the production contract is awarded to the successful developer. Furthermore, development and production often can overlap in time without either being delayed by an intervening competitive process. These are probably sufficient reasons to curtail the use of competitive bids.

In addition, the tooling expenses incurred in preparing the experimental models need not be duplicated if the firm which de-velops the system also manufactures it. For competition to be beneficial, the reduction in cost per unit resulting from the entry of another firm would have to be large relative to the additional tooling costs which would be incurred by the second firm. This is

---

10 U.S., House, Committee on Armed Services, *Weapons System Management and Teams System Concept in Government Contracting*, 86th Cong., 1st Sess., 1959, p. 49.

not likely to be the case, for the typical modern weapon and space system is manufactured in small quantities. Second, even if manufactured in large quantities, the reduction in costs resulting from increased production through the learning curve would lower the original firm's costs relative to that of potential entrants.[11] Thus there are reasons for justifying the award even of a production contract on a noncompetitive basis.[12]

In many industries, buyers have the opportunity to purchase an undifferentiated product from several sellers. Even if products are differentiated, they may be close substitutes for each other. The market power of any seller is thus limited by the availability of other firms' products which the buyers consider substitutes. This competitive environment does not always prevail in the aerospace industry.

Since both the research-and-development and production contracts are awarded only to one firm, the procuring agencies' only source for the desired system is that firm. In some instances, another firm's system may be adapted to meet the buyer's needs should the desired system prove inadequate or too costly. This may be an additional restraint on the behavior of firms. However, it may be equally expensive to modify an existing system, and the second system's performance may not be equal to that planned and desired. Another source of possible competition is the interproduct interservice rivalry mentioned in the previous chapter. This competitive influence would protect the country by providing alternative serv-

---

11 U.S., House, Special Investigation of the Committee on Armed Services, *Hearings, Aircraft Production Costs and Profits*, 84th Cong., 2d Sess., February 16-March 22, 1956, p. 1762. Peck and Scherer, *op. cit.*, p. 206.

12 There are very few examples of systems which have been awarded to two or more firms. The guidance system of the Navy's Sidewinder, air-to-air missile, which was produced in relatively large quantities, was manufactured by two firms. Similarly, the guidance system for the Polaris, which was not produced in such large quantities, was manufactured by two firms. *Aviation Week*, May 2, 1960, p. 37. Hughes Aircraft and Minneapolis-Honeywell were chosen as the second source for the Polaris guidance system. Hughes, which was to build the computer and maintain system responsibility, and Minneapolis-Honeywell, which was to build the gyro-stabilized platforms, were to compete with General Electric.

The Air Force had three firms build the B-47, but this again was an example of a system where large quantities were produced. On the other hand, production contracts for nuclear submarines, which are as complex as planes and are manufactured in small quantities, are awarded by sealed bidding. *Government Procurement, 1960*, p. 263.

ices which could accomplish the assigned task, but it does not necessarily protect a particular procuring agency.

If there are reasonable "back-up" sources for each system, and if the interproduct interservice rivalry exists, then a competitive environment is created. Reasonable substitutes do not exist for many aerospace systems, especially those requiring large research and development costs. Thus, one can conclude that once the research and development contract has been awarded, competitive forces do not always prevail in this industry.

One additional restraining force may apply even in this noncompetitive environment. The action of the aerospace firms may be limited by the realization that they must deal with the same buyers in the future. Their ability to obtain future contracts is based on their previous performance. However, in this case desirable economic results may be obtained only if the buyers devise institutional arrangements and standards which produce the same outcomes as emanate from the competitive process.

Without price competition, one possible institutional device is the use whenever opportunity exists of other forms of competition, such as the management competitions, which provide procuring agencies with alternative technical approaches to any problem. Since interfirm rivalry for a particular project occurs only at the outset of the development stage, one would expect that some form of the competitive process would occur at this juncture. Surprisingly, many projects are not even subject to competition at this stage. If the sample is representative of the population, the analysis of 99 Armed Forces' weapon systems and 21 NASA projects would indicate the extent to which competition occurs at any point in the procurement process.[13] Of the 99 weapon programs, only 36 were subject to competition at any stage of the procurement process.[14] At least 18, and perhaps 20, of NASA's first 21 major projects involved some form of competition at the onset of the procurement process.[15] The explanation for this difference between the procurement practices of the two agencies is that NASA's projects were all new, with no company having an advantage because of previous

---

13 Peck and Scherer, *op. cit.*, pp. 329-332. It should be noted that not all military projects concerned the aerospace industry.

14 *Ibid.*, p. 329.

15 *Ibid.*, p. 331.

contracts. On the other hand, 39 of the Defense Department's 99 projects had evolved from other projects.[16] The firm which held the original contract had an advantage if the Department of Defense believed that some of its efforts would have to be duplicated if the follow-on contract were awarded to another firm. It is impossible to prove that this was the Defense Department's attitude, but the fact remains that in only 5 of the 39 systems which evolved from earlier projects was there any competition.[17] As the scope of NASA's activities broadened, its newer projects also were awarded noncompetitively to firms which had gained experience on earlier contracts. The Gemini project is the prime example of this approach, for it was awarded to McDonnell on the grounds that the firm had considerable experience with the Mercury capsule.[18] However, the Gemini is so advanced that it has been considered a new model and not a modified Mercury.[19]

This does not explain why there was no competition in twenty-nine of the sixty remaining Defense Department projects which were unrelated to previous systems. Various reasons advanced by Peck and Scherer include: there was only one firm with the know-how or capability; there was a lack of interest in a small study contract which was awarded noncompetitively (this firm then gained an inside track for the larger awards which followed once the feasibility of the project was established); and a proprietary interest in the idea or system required that the contract be awarded to a specified firm.[20] The second reason sounds unrealistic, but may in fact provide an excellent explanation. For example, in the late forties, firms showed little interest in competing for missile study contracts, for it was doubtful that missiles would ever prove useful. However,

---

16 *Ibid.*, p. 332.

17 *Ibid.*

18 U.S., House, Subcommittee on Manned Space Flight of the Committee on Science and Astronautics, *Hearings, 1963 NASA Authorization*, Pt. 2, 87th Cong., 2d Sess., March 6-April 10, 1962, p. 382. Similarly, the second-generation Syncom was to be built by Hughes Aircraft, which was building the first Syncom. However, the second contract was awarded before the first satellite was even launched. *Aviation Week*, June 25, 1962, p. 31, and August 20, 1962, p. 81.

19 *Ibid.*, May 13, 1963, p. 54. However, the Gemini system has turned out to be more sophisticated than originally planned. Similarly, there have been six basic models of the Atlas missile. The first and last missiles have been similar only in name and concept, yet there has been only one prime contractor. *Ibid.*, February 25, 1963, pp. 54 ff.

20 Peck and Scherer, *op. cit.*, pp. 336-337.

Convair accepted such a contract. Although the project originally was very small and was stretched out, it eventually evolved into the Atlas ICBM, a major missile for which there never had been any competition. Similarly, the Air Force may have felt that Convair had a proprietary interest in the Centaur project, for the company was the first to suggest a hydrogen-oxygen upper stage for the Atlas.[21]

Even when the design competitions were used it is unlikely that the government obtained their full benefit. The bidders were not always required to demonstrate their competence by suggesting technical trade-offs which could reduce development time or costs without affecting the overall performance of the system.[22] This possibility of substitution was almost completely ignored until 1962, when the Defense Department suggested that firms when bidding should package their proposals by discussing alternative solutions.[23]

Since a competitive environment is unlikely to be created once the original contract has been let, the government has sought substitutes for the cost-plus fixed-fee contracts which have usually been awarded to the organizations undertaking the research and development. With such contracts, firms assume no financial risk, and may, therefore, be less efficient than if they bore part of the cost overruns. Since the cost overruns on these cost-plus fixed-fee contracts have often been sizeable,[24] Defense Department and NASA have tried to increase the use of incentive-type contracts. Under the

---

[21] U.S., House, Subcommittee on Space Sciences of the Committee on Science and Astronautics, *Hearings, Centaur Program*, 87th Cong., 2d Sess., May 15-18, 1962, p. 4. Previous research had been performed by several other companies to demonstrate the feasibility of using a liquid-hydrogen engine. None of these companies were airplane manufacturers, *ibid.*, p. 111; *1963 NASA Authorization*, Pt. 3, p. 1290.

[22] *Aviation Week*, March 12, 1962, pp. 211 and 227. The governmental agencies have been responsible for the deficiencies, for they have often invited proposals before usable and realistic specifications have been worked out. *Systems Development and Management*, p. 228.

[23] Similarly, researchers at the RAND Corporation have applied economic analysis to military problems in order to obtain efficient decisions. Some of the economic techniques suitable for this purpose are discussed in Charles J. Hitch and Roland N. McKean, *The Economics of Defense in the Nuclear Age* (Cambridge: Harvard University Press, 1961), pp. 105-158. These techniques have also now been accepted in the Defense Department. See Alain C. Enthoven, "Economic Analysis in the Department of Defense," *American Economic Review, Papers and Proceedings*, LIII, No. 2 (May 1963), pp. 413-423.

[24] For dissatisfaction with the size of overruns on CPFF contracts, see *Aviation Week*, November 7, 1960, p. 33; June 21, 1961, p. 36; June 4, 1962, pp. 35-36; and June 25, 1962, pp. 28-29. Also *Missiles and Rockets*, March 25, 1963, p. 33.

terms of these contracts, contractors and the government share both in overruns and underruns in some specified proportion, say 20 to 80 percent. Since the firms do not have to meet a market performance standard, an artificial arrangement must be devised which will penalize inefficient and reward efficient firms.[25] The use of these contracts theoretically encourages the well-managed programs and efficiency which a competitive environment could have provided automatically.

Another type of incentive contract is based upon meeting or exceeding technical specifications or deadlines, with a superior performance rewarded with greater profits. This is known as the incentive-fee contract, a type used increasingly since 1962.[26]

The government must convince its contractors to accept these incentive contracts.[27] The firms will do so only if the risks and un-

---

[25] Expression of the government's desire to use more incentive-type contracts can be found in *Aviation Week*, April 30, 1962, pp. 26-27 and *Missiles and Rockets*, November 26, 1962, p. 49. A partial measure of the success of these contracts can be found from an examination of Titan III's costs. Virtually the entire program has been procured through incentive-type contracts. Costs had only risen by one-third of 1 percent in the first ten months of the booster's development. *Ibid.*, January 27, 1964, p. 9.

[26] Thus, Bendix Aviation was awarded a NASA contract to operate five Mercury tracking and communications stations. The agreement provided for reimbursement of costs plus a fixed fee of 3 percent. The company was also eligible for an extra fee of as much as 7 percent if its performance was superior. *Aviation Week*, June 25, 1962, pp. 28-29. However, incentive-type contracts, based on performance, are not new to the industry for they were used as early as 1959 for the Thor nosecone. *Aviation Week*, September 14, 1959, pp. 35-37. Another example was the contract for a carrier-based all-weather attack aircraft. U.S., House, Subcommittee of the Committee on Appropriations, *Hearings, Department of Defense Appropriations, 1963*, Pt. 4, *Procurement*, 87th Cong., 2d Sess., p. 497. *1963 NASA Authorization*, Pt. 2, p. 387.

Recently, Space Technology Laboratories built the Vela Hotel Satellite for ARPA under such an incentive-type contract. A basic fee of 7.75 percent was contemplated, but this could have reached 14.5 percent or been reduced to 0.5 percent depending upon the performance of the satellite. *Aviation Week*, October 28, 1963, p. 28. The first satellite launched was so successful that the number of subsequent launchings could be reduced, thus saving money.

NASA's first large incentive-fee contract was for the Orbiter system. The contract included bonuses and penalties for cost overruns and reductions, for time delays, and the technical performance of the system. The object was to discourage performance exaggerations and deliberate underbidding. A definitive contract was submitted to the bidders thus eliminating the letter contracts and post-selection negotiations. Any disagreement with the specifications had to be stated at the time of the bidding. *Ibid.*, October 7, 1963, p. 32.

[27] Firms have been afraid of accepting incentive-type contracts, for the Tax Court, in January 1962, had rendered an unfavorable decision to Boeing in its appeal of one of the Renegotiation Board's rulings. Boeing in 1952 had earned 88.8 percent of its profits from incentive-type contracts. Firms feared that all incentive-type con-

certainties inherent in research and development contracts are reduced. This can be accomplished if the program and the tasks assigned to the contractor are clearly defined and specified. Thus, an additional advantage inherent in the cost-plus incentive-fee contracts is the requirement that the buyer clearly define the desired system before selecting the contractor to develop the system. Since 1962, both NASA and the Defense Department have moved in this direction. NASA has had conceptual design competitions before selecting the hardware developer,[28] and the Defense Department has introduced a program definition phase in its procurement actions.[29] After bids based on technical proposals have been received, the buying agency narrows the choice to the most promising approaches and awards study contracts to the two or three firms which submitted these proposals. These companies determine the alternative system characteristics and study the technical difficulties associated with each. On the basis of these studies the program is defined, and the firm whose approach is most feasible is chosen to be the contractor. The object is not to proceed to the development stage until technical criteria have been well established.[30]

---

tracts would be treated similarly in the future. *Ibid.*, April 30, 1962, pp. 26-27. It should be noted that the particular type of contract chosen in the Boeing case is no longer used, for in essence it was a cost plus percentage-of-cost contract. It is, therefore, unlikely that the new incentive contracts will be treated similarly by the court. Recently, Douglas expressed the hope that more of its business would use incentive contracts because the profit margins were higher. *The Wall Street Journal*, February 4, 1964.

In another vein, industry spokesmen have commented on the administrative burdens which result from the imposition of governmental arrangements which are designed to provide incentives to the aerospace firms. *Aviation Week*, July 1, 1963, pp. 98-99.

28 *Ibid.*, July 2, 1962, p. 352.

29 *Ibid.*, April 2, 1962, p. 22 and August 27, 1962, p. 27; *Missiles and Rockets*, June 11, 1962, p. 15, and March 9, 1964, pp. 14-15. *The Wall Street Journal*, March 5, 1964, p. 7. This "projected definition phase" establishes specifications, defines interfaces, and so on. Other techniques have also been developed for predicting electronic equipment reliability. *Aviation Week*, January 6, 1964, p. 76.

30 Hitch and McKean, *op. cit.*, p. 251, have argued that design competitions are useful only if the buyer is informed enough to make rational decisions solely from the brochure. If not (we have already noted that the government often lacks skilled technical personnel), exaggeration is encouraged. They, therefore, have suggested that competition in research and development be encouraged and that prototypes be built.

However, if the development of prototypes is expensive or time-consuming, this approach may not be feasible. Nevertheless, competitive study contracts introduce an element of competition and are likely to reward the buyer with useful information

As another method of promoting efficiency, the government has recently begun to evaluate the performance of its contractors. Those performing well will be awarded other contracts in the future. Contracts presumably will be withheld from those firms which have frequently failed to meet deadlines or experienced substantial cost overruns. Among the factors to be considered is a comparison between the promises contained in the proposals and the actual results.[31] This evaluation will force bidders to be more realistic in both their cost and technical estimates, for their performance will be downgraded if they fail to meet these targets.[32] Consequently, the source upon which the government depends for much of its technical information must provide more reasonable estimates. This will, in turn, aid the government in selecting a more meaningful mix of projects to support.

Finally, the procuring agencies have attempted to reduce the costs of systems by several other institutional arrangements. These have tended to reduce the importance of the systems method of procurement. First, the Defense Department decided to support actively the development of components and subsystems. These would then be available when required for the development of advanced systems. These subsystems consequently would not have to be developed on a "crash" basis with a concomitant increase in costs.[33]

Government agencies have always negotiated with the prime manufacturer on the items which could be produced "in house,"

---

which will improve the probability that an appropriate choice will be made. Without such competition, the government has less information on which to base its decision. The firms will want to perform well on these study contracts, for they may be rewarded with research-and-development and production contracts.

[31] *Aviation Week*, February 4, 1963, p. 95, and April 15, 1963, p. 32.

[32] In the past, no penalties were levied for such inaccuracies. The firm had everything to gain and nothing to lose if it were exceedingly optimistic. If it asserted that it could deliver a system which promised a real "break-through" at a nominal cost, the military would most likely be willing to award the firm a CPFF contract. The firm would have no risk; all its out-of-pocket costs would be recouped; and at most only some opportunity costs would be incurred if its resources were tied up on this project. This would occur if the fee remained fixed while the project continued. A more likely occurrence would be for the firm to receive another contract to perform additional work. Profits would also rise. Eventually, the conclusion would be reached that both the cost and technical aspects of the proposal had been overoptimistic. This puffing did not hurt the firm under the old system, but with the adoption of the new system, the contractor would receive "demerits."

[33] *Ibid.*, August 27, 1962, p. 27, and October 1, 1962, p. 89. NASA is now moving in the same direction. See *ibid.*, October 28, 1963, p. 29.

with the remaining items being subcontracted.[34] Despite the general acceptance of these "make or buy" provisions, one example should suffice to indicate how the government might reduce costs by further focusing its attention on this subject. The prime contractor of the Pershing missile stated its intention to perform one particular task itself, claiming that no other firm was qualified to handle the job. The Army, however, found five firms capable of undertaking the project, and saved money in the process.[35]

Although fully developed large-scale systems are not likely to be procured through competitive bidding, it is possible for the government to insist that it will furnish the prime-systems manufacturer with many major subsystems. The government can obtain these subsystems through sealed bids under a method of procurement known as "break-out."[36] After a system has been developed, certain items used in large quantities are no longer procured from the developer and manufacturer of the system. Instead, the item is broken out from the rest of the system and the blueprints obtained from the development process are used to obtain sealed bids. The government then provides the subsystem to the prime contractor as government-furnished equipment. The reduction in costs stems from two sources. First, even if the subsystem had been procured at the same price as before, the prime cannot charge a fee on government-furnished equipment, whereas it can if procured from one of its subcontractors. However, the more substantial saving can be expected to result from the use of the competitive mechanism.[37]

The essence of our discussion has been the necessity to introduce institutional arrangements which promote efficiency in the absence of an effectively operating market mechanism. However, it should also be emphasized that governmental introduction of many of these devices is relatively new. The recent increase in the use of incentive contracts and evaluations of contractors was not instituted

---

34 *Ibid.*, November 17, 1958, p. 58. Peck and Scherer, *op. cit.*, p. 388. U.S., House Report 1121, Committee on Government Operations, *Organization and Management of Missile Programs*, 86th Cong., 2d Sess., September 2, 1959, p. 43.

35 *Government Procurement, 1960*, p. 136.

36 *Aviation Week*, July 27, 1959, and June 4, 1962, p. 356.

37 In the chapter on performance, the extent of the reduction in costs which results from competitive bidding will be noted.

until the early 1960's. Any inefficiencies which may have arisen may be attributable partly to the government's failure to seek actively those institutional arrangements which promoted efficiency and protected its interests.

THE EVOLUTION OF COMPETITIVE PRACTICES

It would be appropriate to consider the evolution of the described competitive practices, for competition was not always of this type. Initially, new airplanes involved noncompetitive negotiation between individual firms and the government. Later contests were based on drawings and were known as "paper" competitions. Although the 1926 Aircraft Production Act[38] authorized such design competitions, most interwar competitions were based on prototypes.[39] Prototypes of the aircraft desired by the Army Air Corps and Navy were built. The government could thus compare the performance of each airplane with the others and order that firm's plane which most closely approximated its needs.

However, the competing concerns bore the financial risk inherent in this type of procurement. The Air Corps *usually* bought prototypes at cost, but this was not a legal requirement.[40] The cost of prototypes rose from $10,000 in the 1920's to $600,000 by 1939.[41] Many firms were reluctant to engage in such competitions, for the risks were too great for most firms whose financial condition, just before World War II, was already precarious.[42]

The military services were concerned lest the productive base of the industry be destroyed, but under the laws existing in the late 1930's, contracts could not be awarded unless won through competitive action. A new law, enacted in 1939, was designed to reduce the financial risks of the airplane manufacturers and encourage

---

[38] 44 Stat. 784, 787.

[39] Peck and Scherer, *op. cit.*, pp. 344-345. This was required because improved features were often included in the designs, and the state of aeronautical engineering knowledge prevented a proper evaluation from drawings.

[40] *Ibid.*

[41] U.S., Senate, Committee on Military Affairs, *Hearings on An Act to Provide More Effectively for the National Defense by Carrying Out the Recommendations of the President in his Message of January 12, 1939 to the Congress*, 76th Cong., 1st Sess., 1939, p. 33; also U.S., House, Committee on Military Affairs, *Hearings on a More Effective National Defense*, 76th Cong., 1st Sess., 1939, p. 18.

[42] *Ibid.*, p. 10.

them to build prototypes (which, in turn, might enable them to win an award).[43] Under its terms those prototypes built for, but not winning, the competition could be purchased for a percentage of the development and manufacturing cost. The runners-up were purchasable for 75 percent of the costs, but this ratio declined to 60 and 50 percent, respectively, for models ranked third and fourth.

Since this new law, developed to encourage prototype competition, was not enacted until 1939, the services in the mid-thirties had reverted to the design competitions,[44] which were authorized again by the 1947 Armed Services Procurement Act.[45] As has been noted, because of the complexities of modern weapon and space systems, this approach became the customary method of competition in the industry. Since it may cost close to a million dollars even to bid on a complex, important weapon system,[46] the cost of competition at a later stage of the development cycle would certainly be prohibitive.

Although design competitions are being used again, the desire to introduce institutional arrangements which will reduce the impact of cost reimbursement contracts has led to the contracting of feasibility studies.[47] In working on these contracts, firms study the technical problems which are likely to be encountered both in the development and operation of the system. The theoretical solutions to these problems assist the purchasing agency in deciding on the final specifications of the system. This procedure is extremely

---

[43] 53 Stat. 560.

[44] Peck and Scherer, *op. cit.*, p. 346. Moreover, the development of aeronautical engineering enabled the services to reach better decisions about the designs of the planes. The B-17 award resulted from a self-financed project at Boeing. *Ibid.*, p. 339. The B-25 contract was awarded in a design competition which occurred in 1937. *Weapons System Hearings*, p. 18.

[45] 10 U.S.C. 2304.

[46] Peck and Scherer, *op. cit.*, p. 35. This cost, however, is borne by the government if the bidders have a substantial amount of government business, for this is an allowable expense allocated to overhead and prorated to government work. Another source indicates that the expense of proposal competition may not be quite that high. A figure of $250,000 is presented in *Aviation Week*, October 9, 1961, p. 28; and a third source indicates a figure of $500,000. *Systems Development and Management*, Pt. 3, p. 894. The TFX competition cost Boeing $10 million, but much of this was reimbursed. *Fortune*, March 1963, p. 96.

[47] Peck and Scherer, *op. cit.*, p. 346. An interesting use of this type of contract was made by NASA in awarding the Apollo feasibility studies to the Convair division of General Dynamics, General Electric; and Martin. North American Aviation, however, was awarded the development and production contract. *Aviation Week*, October 31, 1960, p. 31, and December 11, 1961, p. 37.

useful in situations where a large technological advance is required because a number of uncertainties are reduced before the design competition. Moreover, all firms interested in developing the system must undertake some research in this area, if the research and development contract is not to go by default to the firms which have the feasibility-study contracts.

At the other extreme, some planners have suggested that the government again use the prototype method of competition.[48] This suggestion was stimulated by the TFX controversy where the decision to award the contract to General Dynamics rather than to Boeing was based on a design competition. Similarly, a recent RAND report has indicated that the money spent for the procurement of prototypes yields desirable results including improved aircraft performance and options.[49] The successful development of the McDonnell F4H Phantom fighter has produced a similar request.[50]

It is true that the McDonnell plane was procured after competitive flight testing against the Chance-Vought F8U-3, but the development contract which had been awarded to McDonnell was not based on a prototype competition. Actually, the two planes were competitors only because both could perform the same mission, that is, both were carrier-based all-weather fighters. The McDonnell aircraft was a twin engine two-seater, whereas the Chance-Vought plane was a one engine single-seater. The development of the McDonnell plane began in September, 1953, when the company received a contract for a plane to be designated the AH-1. Changes were incorporated in the specifications, a new design suggested, and the plane redesignated the F4H-1.[51] The Chance-Vought plane was an improved version of their earlier carrier-based fighter, the F8U-1.[52] The McDonnell plane was judged su-

---

[48] *Aviation Week*, April 22, 1963, p. 31. The selection of the LEM descent engine will in fact be made on the basis of prototypes built by Rocketdyne and STL. *Ibid.*, March 2, 1964, p. 33.

[49] This report by B. H. Klein, T. K. Glenman, Jr., and C. H. Shubert, *The Role of Prototypes in Development*, RAND Report RN 3467-PR (Santa Monica, Calif.: The RAND Corp., 1963) was included in U.S., Senate, Permanent Subcommittee on Investigations of the Committee on Government Operations, *Hearings, TFX Contract Investigation*, 88th Cong., 1st Sess., 1963, pp. 1105-1115.

[50] *The New York Times*, Western Edition, February 26, 1963, p. 8.

[51] *Aviation Week*, October 13, 1958, p. 66.

[52] *Ibid.*, July 14, 1958, pp. 54 ff.

perior after the competitive flight testing.[53] Two facts must be emphasized. Mass production of the planes did not begin until the
flight tests of the prototype were completed. However, the development contracts for these prototypes were not awarded simultaneously, with the production contract to be awarded to the winner of
the prototype competition. The original contracts were let either
through design competitions or as follow-on contracts.[54] However,
at the time that the Navy was forced to choose an all-weather
fighter, two models were available.

Prototype competitions such as those between the F4H-1 and
F8U-3 differ from their counterparts of the twenties and thirties
mentioned above. In the newer competitions several contracts may
be awarded on the basis of paper designs, the subsequent prototypes then compared, and the superior craft ordered into production. In earlier competitions the armed services issued specifications and, without any contracts, the airplane manufacturers simultaneously built prototypes which were tested against each other.
The advocates of prototype development do not suggest a return
to this form of procurement, but stress that multiple and parallel
systems must be developed and tested quickly.[55] This provides
flexibility and insures that the procuring agency will have the relevant information when it must choose a new system.

However, with the absolute cost of development rising, and with
this figure increasing relative to the cost of the total system, it may
be impossible to underwrite the expense of these parallel development programs.[56] While competitive prototype development might
have been appropriate at an earlier time, such a course of action

---

53 *Ibid.*, December 22, 1958, p. 22. Other references to this competition include
ibid., June 9, 1958, p. 43; U.S., House, Subcommittee of the Committee on Appropriations, *Hearings, Department of Defense Appropriations, 1960*, Pt. 5, *Procurement*,
86th Cong., 1st Sess., 1959, pp. 371-375; *Hearings, Department of Defense Appropriations, 1958*, Pt. 1, 85th Cong., 1st Sess., 1957, p. 1213; U.S., Senate, Committee on
Armed Services, *Hearings, Military Procurement Authorization, Fiscal Year 1962*,
87th Cong., 1st Sess., April 4-19, 1961, pp. 578-579.

54 For example, the F8U-3 was a follow-on version of the F8U-1 and F8U-2. The
original competition for the F8U-1 was a design competition won by Chance-Vought,
Aviation Week, July 14, 1958, p. 57.

55 RAND Report 3467-PR in *TFX Contract Investigation*, p. 1106; R. R. Nelson,
"Uncertainty, Learning and the Economics of Parallel Research and Development
Efforts," *The Review of Economics and Statistics*, XLIII, No. 4 (November 1961), p.
353.

56 This is one reason why Secretary of Defense McNamara reviewed and canceled
the DynaSoar program, for it duplicated many aspects of the Gemini program.

must probably be ruled out in the sixties. The Navy spent $136.5 million on the unsuccessful development of the F8U-3 [57] and the low bid for development of the TFX was $580 million[58]—and the original cost estimates are usually low! The rapid rise in development cost has eliminated the likelihood of many future prototype competitions.[59]

In addition to changing the competitive practices of the industry, the growth in complexity of modern weapon and aerospace systems also has led to changes in the method of procurement, culminating in the weapon-system form of contracting. With this form of procurement the government chooses the prime contractor to manage and coordinate a particular project. Since this form of procurement is relatively new, it is necessary to discuss its evolution.

In the design competitions before World War II, as exemplified by the development of the B-25 bomber, the contractor did not propose to develop each piece of equipment *de novo*. North American, in its B-25 bid, appended a list of 210 pieces of basic equipment or off-the-shelf items which would be used. The company chose existing equipment best suited to the design submitted by North American.[60] In 1945, when North American bid for the XP-86 jet fighter (later known as the F-86 Sabre) it again suggested that 210 items would be government-furnished equipment, but this represented only 50 percent of the plane's equipment. Moreover, some of these items required considerable development to be adapted to the specific needs of the airplane.[61]

Before the war, the government directly procured the essential

---

[57] *Department of Defense Appropriations, 1960,* 86th Cong., 1st Sess., 1959, pp. 38 and 813

[58] *TFX Contract Investigation,* p. 208. On the other hand, if only a prototype were being developed, the cost of development might be somewhat less. However, the data necessary to substantiate this hypothesis are not readily available.

[59] At the other extreme, there have been arguments that the amount of bidding be reduced and that contractual awards be made primarily to firms which are most qualified. *1963 NASA Authorization,* Pt. 2, p. 407. *Aviation Week,* October 15, 1962, p. 25, October 22, 1962, p. 29, and November 5, 1962, p. 23. In the Hardsite ICBM defense program based on a solid propellant antimissile missile Douglas, Lockheed, Martin, and North American Aviation were chosen on the basis of their skill to undertake such studies. Lockheed, however, dropped out, because it did not want to share the costs of the study program.

[60] *Weapons System Hearings,* p. 19. In fact, 80 percent of the B-25 items were furnished by the government to the contractor.

[61] *Ibid.*

subsystems and delivered them to the airframe manufacturer for installation in the plane. However, at the end of the war, there began "a trend toward procurement of systems and equipment through the airplane prime contractor, a trend that resulted from the increasing need for adaptation and integration with other equipment with the airplane."[62] While firms manufacturing sophisticated subsystems remained in the industry, the growing complexity of the systems[63] required that more components be designed for a particular system. Thus it was natural for the Air Force to advocate the idea that a single prime contractor be responsible for developing, coordinating, and integrating the entire program.[64] According to its advocates, the advantage of this form of procurement approach is that with control and responsibility concentrated in one firm, the development time of a particular system is likely to be minimized.[65] Though the choice of subcontractors and the amount of in-house effort are subject to review by the government, there are areas in which the prime contractor may take advantage of its position.[66] The analysis of this topic is postponed until Chapter 7.

SUMMARY AND CONCLUSIONS

In the first portion of this chapter we examined the competitive practices currently prevailing in the industry and concluded that

---

[62] *Ibid.*, p. 20. Testimony of J. L. Atwood, President of North American Aviation, Inc.

[63] The complexity of even an airplane has increased so substantially that the number of engineering man hours expended in the research and development effort (up to the production of the 200th plane) increased by a factor of 73 between 1940-1942 and 1959. *Ibid.*, p. 16.

[64] *Ibid.*, p. 21. The Air Force itself should have been responsible for this function, but except for a few top-priority projects, it delegated this task. A possible explanation was a shortage of qualified technical personnel. *Ibid.*, pp. 311, 456.

[65] Furthermore, the various subsystems are interdependent so that integration is definitely required, for a change in the performance of one of the components may be offset by a change in one of the other systems. For instance, radar range can be increased in various ways. However, each method would affect the speed and range or configuration of the airplane to some extent. *Ibid.*, p. 15. As an example, the F-86 had several systems whose functions overlapped. The integration of these systems would have saved weight. *Ibid.*, p. 105.

[66] The government had argued that it would not allow a weapon-system manufacturer to intrude on other firms' business. See U.S., Senate, Subcommittee of the Select Committee on Small Business, *Hearings, Military Procurement, 1955*, 84th Cong., 1st Sess., April 20-May 5, 1955, p. 163. Also *Aviation Week*, February 25, 1957, pp. 248 ff.; *Ibid.*, October 12, 1959, p. 75, and March 13, 1961, p. 227; and Air Force Procurement Instruction 53-101.

competition, if it existed at all, occurred mainly at the initial stages of the procurement process. Once the research and development contract was awarded, competitive forces did not always prevail in this industry. The several situations in which this conclusion did not hold were noted also.

It was then mentioned that in the absence of competition it was up to the buyer to introduce institutional arrangements and standards to protect his interest. These arrangements could be devised so that outcomes similar to those emanating from the competitive process would result. Several such institutional devices were examined and their effects noted. A major conclusion from the discussion was that the introduction of these arrangements occurred only recently. Thus, in the past, the buyer has not always protected his interest, but since the early 1960's there has been renewed interest on the government's part to seek arrangements which promote efficiency.

The last portion of this chapter examined the evolution of the industry's competitive practices so that the current structure could be put in its proper perspective. The complexity and cost of modern weapon and space systems has been partly responsible for the absence of rivalry after the initial design competition. Moreover, the procurement practices of the government have also changed in response to this increase in complexity and cost.

5.

STRUCTURE OF THE INDUSTRY: CONTRACTS AND THEIR USES; THE OVERALL FINANCIAL RISKS OF AEROSPACE FIRMS

CONTRACTS AND THEIR USES

It is necessary to investigate the types of contracts in order to determine the risks which have been imposed on the aerospace firms. So much has been written about the various types of contracts and uses for which they are specifically designed that little else can be added here.[1] However, in order to obtain a complete understanding of the structure of the industry, a review of these contracts must be undertaken.

Basically the contracts may be classified into four categories: fixed price, cost reimbursement, special incentive, and special purpose. These categories may be further subdivided, as will be illustrated below.[2] The Armed Services Procurement Regulations (ASPR) direct that, in negotiated contracts, the firm fixed-price contract is to be used unless circumstances indicate that another type of con-

---

[1] See Frederick T. Moore, *Military Procurement and Contracting: An Economic Analysis*, RAND Memorandum RM 2948-PR (Santa Monica, California: The RAND Corporation, June 1962), pp. 2-12. U.S., House, Committee on Armed Services, Special Subcommittee on Procurement Practices of the Department of Defense, *Hearings Pursuant to Section 4, Public Law 86-89*, 86th Cong., 2d Sess., April 25-June 9, 1960, pp. 59-63 and 157-166. (These hearings will hereafter be cited as *Procurement Practices Hearings.*)

[2] The types of contracts which may be used have been listed in the Armed Services Procurement Regulations, Section III, Pt. 4. 10 U.S.C., Chapter 137, Section 2306. The one type of contract forbidden is the cost plus percentage-of-cost. With this type of contract a firm's profits increase proportionately with its costs. It was decided that this contractual form might be subject to abuse.

tract is more appropriate. Although used for contracts amounting to only 41.5 percent of fiscal 1963's procurement dollar,[3] it is considered the basic type of Armed Service procurement contract. Although still accounting for less than 50 percent of the total procurement dollar, the percentage of Department of Defense funds committed through fixed-price contracts has been increasing since fiscal 1961 (Table 27).

TABLE 27

PERCENTAGE OF THE VALUE OF MILITARY-PROCUREMENT ACTIONS ACCOUNTED FOR BY SPECIFIED TYPES OF CONTRACT, 1951-1961

Fiscal year	Firm fixed price	Fixed price redeterminable and escalation	Incentive	Cost reimbursement	
				Fixed fee	Other
1951	43.9	34.3	9.1	8.6	4.1
1952	29.8	40.3	12.0	13.3	4.6
1953	31.8	24.0	24.0	16.3	3.9
1954	38.0	7.3	25.2	23.8	5.7
1955	39.7	13.3	22.0	19.7	4.4
1956	36.4	14.1	19.2	24.1	6.2
1957	35.3	13.5	17.8	29.9	3.5
1958	27.8	13.4	19.2	33.2	6.4
1959	32.8	11.0	15.3	34.3	6.6
1960	31.4	12.4	13.6	36.8	5.8
1961	31.5	15.2	11.2	36.6	5.5
1962	38.0	10.8	12.0	32.5	6.7
1963	41.5	7.6	15.8	20.7	14.4

SOURCE: U. S., Defense Department, Installations and Logistics Division, *Military Prime Contract Awards and Subcontract Payments*, July-December, 1963, p. 45; U. S., House, Committee on Armed Services, Special Subcommittee on Procurement Practices of the Department of Defense, *Hearings Pursuant to Section 4, Public Law 86-89*, Pt. 4, *Procurement*, 87th Cong., 2d Sess., 1962, p. 545.

It should be noted that the firm fixed price need not require competitive bidding, but can be obtained through negotiation: it implies merely that the contractor is obligated to furnish a specified quantity of a paritcular product at a price not subject to *any* adjustments. Whereas 41.5 percent of fiscal 1963's military procurement dollar was spent through firm fixed-price contracts, only about 13 percent of that year's expenditures were contracted through competitive bidding.[4]

The remainder of the "fixed-price contracts," accounting for 23.4

---

[3] Office of the Assistant Secretary of Defense, Installations and Logistics, *Military Prime Contract Awards and Subcontract Payments*, July-December 1963, p. 45.

[4] *Ibid.*, p. 35. This figure has remained relatively constant since 1956. In 1959 only 12.9 percent of the procurement dollar was awarded through formal competitions. *Procurement Practices Hearings*, p. 136. In fiscal year 1961, 11.9 percent of the mili-

percent of fiscal 1963's military procurement dollar, are in reality not fixed-price contracts at all. The fixed-price escalation contracts provide that the contract will be revised upward or downward upon the actual occurrence of certain specified contingencies. The Armed Services recognize (and the ASPR concur) that the government should assume the risk of these contingencies rather than force the contractor to include a risk premium in his firm fixed price. The fixed-price contract with redetermination specifies that when the level of production costs is uncertain, an initial price be negotiated with the stipulation that it be redetermined at intervals, when the level of costs can be determined more accurately. At the time of redetermination the initially negotiated price will be readjusted, with the new price based upon the actual cost data available at that time. The surprising element is that the redetermined price may be applied to items already produced as well as to future production.[5] It is possible that this type of contract may induce inefficiencies, for the contract is, in essence, a form of the prohibited cost plus a percentage of cost contract. The firm could negotiate an initial price, produce a few items, and then discover that its costs were higher than the originally negotiated price. Both the price and fee would be redetermined upward, not only for all future production, but also for the items already produced. The only requirement upon the firm is that it submit and substantiate the relevant cost data.[6] Thus, a contract which has been called fixed price can in fact be a cost-plus contract.

The last of the fixed-price contracts is called fixed-price incentive. Initially, a target cost, a target profit, a ceiling price, and a profit-sharing formula are negotiated. If the final cost is less than the target cost, the contractor's profit increases according to some

tary procurement dollar involved formal competition, U.S., House, Subcommittee of the Committee on Appropriations, *Hearings, Department of Defense Appropriations, 1963*, Pt. 4, *Procurement*, 87th Cong., 2d Sess., pp. 492-494, and 575.

The procurement actions of NASA have shown a similar pattern, with 17 percent of the expenditures of the first half of fiscal 1961 spent through fixed-price contracts, and only 9 percent through formal competition. U.S., House, Subcommittee on Manned Space Flight of the Committee on Science and Astronautics, *Hearings, 1963 NASA Authorization*, Pt. 2, 87th Cong., 2d Sess., March 6-April 10, 1962, p. 381; *Aviation Week*, June 25, 1962, pp. 28-29, and July 16, 1962, p. 33.

[5] *Procurement Practices Hearings*, p. 159.

[6] The military services have discontinued this type of contract, but an anlysis of its features was still required in order that the trend of government contractual practices could be understood.

profit-sharing formula, say 80-20, with the larger share going to the government; that is, 80 percent of the reduction in costs accrues to the government and the remainder goes to the firm. If actual costs exceed target costs, the contractor shares the increased costs with the government until some profit floor is reached. Theoretically, this form of contract should provide the contractor with an incentive to improve his performance and reduce the costs of production. However, it is possible that these contracts invite firms to negotiate on the basis of unrealistically high target estimates in order to be able to obtain extra profits through the incentive features of the contract, when the actual costs of production are reduced.[7] Were this the case, the use of this type of contract would be self-defeating. Regardless of the merits and demerits of these contracts they, too, should not be considered fixed-price contracts.[8] As seen from Table 27 the use of this contract was increased beginning in fiscal year 1962.

In fiscal year 1963, 35.1 percent of the Defense Department's procurement dollars were obligated through cost-reimbursement type contracts.[9] These contracts include the cost contract (no fee), usually given to nonprofit institutions; the cost-sharing contract, in which a firm and the government share the cost of a specified project in some agreed proportion; and the cost-plus-a-fixed-fee contract (CPFF). In this last type of contract, the government and firm estimate the total cost of a project and establish the fixed fees which will be paid to the firm. The procurement law[10] limits the allowable fees, but in practice the fees have been considerably less than this maximum. If the cost of completing the project exceeds

---

[7] The need for greater cost analysis in the setting of target prices has been noted in *Department of Defense Appropriations, 1957*. 84th Cong., 2d Sess., 1956, pp. 22-35; U.S., Senate, Permanent Subcommittee on Investigations of the Committee on Government Operations, *Pyramiding of Profits and Costs in the Missile Procurement Program*, Pt. 4, 87th Cong., 2d Sess., May 22-25, 1962, pp. 684, 712, and 810 ff.

[8] The Defense Department had stopped classifying incentive-type contracts as fixed-price type contracts. This can be observed in comparing the data for fiscal year 1951 in *Procurement Practices Hearings*, p. 133, with similar data in *Department of Defense Appropriations, 1963*, p. 495. The former shows fixed-price contracts accounting for 87.3 percent of the procurement dollar; in the latter source, fixed-price contracts are claimed to account for 78 percent of the total, with incentive-type contracts accounting for an additional 9 percent. However, *Military Prime Contract Awards and Subcontract Payments* still classifies the incentive contracts under the fixed-price category.

[9] *Military Prime Contract Awards and Subcontract Payments*, p. 45.

[10] 10 U.S.C. 2306(d).

the original estimate, the government assumes the costs, but the supplier theoretically receives no extra compensation.[11] The major incentive for a company to operate efficiently stems from the knowledge that its workforce and facilities cannot be employed on other projects, thereby foregoing the opportunity to earn additional profits.[12] Since the CPFF contracts provide firms with a minimum of incentive, the government has tried recently to curtail their use, and to substitute incentive-type contracts.[13] As can be seen from Table 27, the percentage of the procurement dollar committed through CPFF contracts dropped from almost 37 percent in fiscal years 1960 and 1961, to 20.7 percent in fiscal year 1963. There has been a concomitant increase in incentive-fee reimbursement contracts.

There are also special incentive contracts designed to encourage contractor efficiency. In the performance-type incentive contract, the fees paid to the contractor are based on his ability to surpass certain criteria such as the minimum level of performance of the system. The value-engineering contracts are designed to encourage firms to maintain value-engineering staffs which study means of reducing costs.[14] The costs of the group are paid by the government, the savings are split with the firm.[15]

---

[11] There is evidence which seems to contradict this statement. Moore made a study of 2,501 CPFF prime contracts in which costs were revised upwards. The data show that there were at least 93 contracts in which the fee rose proportionately more than costs. In another 1,715 cases, fees rose in about the same proportion as costs. Some of the increase in costs may be attributable to an expansion of the scope of work, for which an increase in fees is justified, but this incidence seems to suggest that firms receive extra compensation even with overruns on CPFF contracts. Moore, *op. cit.*, pp. 40-43.

[12] Actually, the only scarce resources whose use the firm must forego on other projects are its facilities and its management. If skilled aerospace workers, technicians, or engineers are scarce resources, they too represent an opportunity cost, but if the firm could easily hire additional workers, this is not so. However, new engineers may not be substitutes for the experienced personnel already working for an aerospace firm.

[13] Used very sparingly has been the cost-reimbursement contract with incentive fee, which has characteristics similar to the aforementioned incentive-type contracts.

For a statement of the desire to reduce the number of CPFF contracts which have been awarded, see *Aviation Week,* May 6. 1963, p. 99.

[14] "A value engineering study is an intensive appraisal of all the elements of the design, manufacture or construction, inspection, installation, and maintenance of an item and its components, including the applicable specifications and operational requirements, in order to achieve necessary performance, maintainability, and reliability at minimum cost." *Procurement Practices Hearings,* p. 165.

[15] The special-purpose contracts have no particular significance for this study.

The trend in the composition of the mix of contracts awarded by the government is of interest, for it indicates the extent of the risk borne by the firms. As shown in Table 27, the percentage of the Defense Department's procurement dollar spent through cost-reimbursement contracts had risen steadily between fiscal 1951 and fiscal 1961, but has declined since then. The CPFF contracts accounted for 37 percent of the Defense Department's procurement dollar in fiscal 1961,[16] but for only 21 percent in 1963. It has been claimed that 82 percent of NASA's money was spent through the CPFF contract.[17] This estimate is probably high, since NASA did award some incentive-type contracts, and 9 percent of NASA's funds were distributed through fixed-price contracts.[18] In 1951 the CPFF contract accounted for only 13 percent of the Defense Department's procurement dollar. It must be remembered further that many of the "fixed-price contracts" do not require fixed prices. Incentive contracts have been included in this category.

This enormous increase in the incidence of cost-reimbursement type contracts was not peculiar to the aerospace industry, but was common to all defense and space-oriented firms. It stemmed from the increased emphasis on research-and-development-type work and the coincident decline in the importance of actual production. This increasing importance of research and development was of particular significance to the aerospace industry, for its ratio between research and development and sales averaged more than five times that of the comparable ratio for all manufacturing industries.[19] Moreover, this ratio has increased even for the aerospace industry, from a level of 18.7 to 18.9 percent in 1957-1958, to 24.2 percent in

---

16 *Department of Defense Appropriations, 1963*, p. 545.

17 *Aviation Week*, June 25, 1962, pp. 28-29; and July 16, 1962, p. 33. The literature often does not distinguish between CPFF and other cost-reimbursement type contracts. Thus these data often also refer to the incentive-type contracts.

18 In addition to the increase in cost-plus type contracts there has been a concomitant decline in the percentage of the military-procurement dollar committed through formally advertised contracts, and an increase in sole-source procurement. *Department of Defense Appropriations, 1963*, p. 575; U.S., Senate, Subcommittee on Defense Procurement of the Joint Economic Committee, *Progress Made by the Department of Defense in Reducing the Impact of Military Procurement on the Economy*, 87th Cong., 1st Sess., June 12, 1961, p. 19; and U.S., House, Procurement Subcommittee of the Committee on Armed Services, *Procurement Study*, Pt. 2, 86th Cong., 2d Sess., May 23-31, 1960, p. 147.

19 National Science Foundation, *Research and Development in the Aircraft and Missile Industry (1956-1961)*, Reviews of Data on Research and Development No. 39, NSF 63-19, May 1963, p. 8.

1961. The figure has probably increased even further because of the growing importance of the Apollo project.

Since cost-reimbursement contracts are usually awarded for research and development work, this increase in the incidence of CPFF contracts is not unexpected. The type of contract awarded to a firm does, however, affect both the risk borne by the contractor and the firm's expectable profits for performing its tasks.

The Financial Risks

RISKS ASSOCIATED WITH CONTRACTS

Although it is impossible to make a quantitative estimate of the risk involved in accepting the various mentioned contracts, general observations about the degree of risk can be made. Very little risk is involved in the CPFF contracts, for the companies are assured of recovering *all* out-of-pocket costs and are even assured of a modest fee in the event of a substantial cost overrun. A large overrun does impose an opportunity cost on the firm, since its resources cannot be used on other contracts. This is only a diminution of its profit potential and not an actual accounting loss.[20]

With incentive contracts, a financial loss is possible if there is no guarantee of a minimum profit fee, but usually there is a profit floor which eliminates this possibility. Under the terms of these contracts, the government and contractor share all overruns and underruns of costs in a fixed proportion, usually 80-20, with the larger share accruing to the government. As compared to the CPFF contract, the firm assumes a larger risk with incentive-type contracts, for every dollar's worth of overrun reduces the firm's profit fee by twenty cents. Without a profit guarantee, if an overrun is large enough the firm can sustain a loss on the contract. However, for assuming this risk the fee on incentive contracts is usually larger than on CPFF contracts. Moreover, the firm also may increase its earnings by sharing in any underruns with the government.[21]

---

[20] If the government were to rate contractors by their ability to minimize cost overruns, firms with frequent substantial overruns might not obtain contracts in the future. Financial losses and even failures might be a consequence.

[21] Overruns or underruns may be shared in the same or in different proportions. In fact, asymmetrical sharing formulas are often used. These asymmetrical formulas are even used for cost overruns or underruns alone. For example, if the government were anxious to minimize the possibility of extreme overruns, it might share them with a

Further, errors in the estimated target costs are likely to be biased in the firm's favor by being on the high rather than the low side, thus providing a margin of safety. In addition, firms are often guaranteed a minimum fee regardless of the size of the overrun. Both factors thus virtually eliminate the risk of loss.

Finally, one can determine the size of the overrun necessary for the firm to sustain a loss if, in fact, a small fee was not guaranteed. If the negotiated profit fee was 8 percent of the originally estimated cost, and the sharing formula was 80-20, an overrun of 40 percent would be required for a loss to be sustained. If the firm wanted to avoid a risk it could attempt to negotiate a 90-10 or even 95-5 ratio, which would naturally reduce the profit potential. Based on these ratios, losses would not be incurred until the overruns exceeded 80 and 160 percent respectively. In the past, incentive contracts have been negotiated when the estimated variation in the negotiated price was approximately 10 percent,[22] with the result that the risks associated with the incentive contracts were probably not extremely high. This is corroborated by Moore's analysis of eighty incentive contracts accepted by North American Aviation.[23] Moore's study indicated that the firm sustained a loss on only two contracts. With the government now pushing the use of incentive contracts at the early stages of the procurement process, the risks borne by firms in accepting this type of contract will naturally increase. However, not enough data have been accumulated as yet to provide an estimate of the extent of the risk.

When a firm accepts a fixed-price contract, it is committed to produce an article at that price. Even under these conditions the risk imposed is not likely to be very high, for the terms of a majority of the fixed-price contracts are determined through negotiation. The risk which the firm bears depends on the "tightness" of the cost estimates which are negotiated. Companies can estimate their costs more accurately than the government negotiators, which means that a firm would hardly be forced to accept a price which is low relative to its cost. Furthermore, evidence presented below indi-

---

95-5 formula for costs up to 110 or even 120 percent of those originally estimated. However, if costs exceeded this figure, all further overruns might be shared 80-20. Moore, *op. cit.*, p. 74.

22 *Ibid.*, p. 66.

23 *Ibid.*, pp. 47-49.

cates that these negotiated prices are not very low, for when items previously procured through sole-source negotiation are obtained through competitive bidding, prices drop. Second, a study made by the Renegotiation Board [24] indicated that in the 1950's the highest rate of return on sales was made on fixed-price contracts. Although part of this high rate of return may in fact have been a risk premium, the combined evidence seems to indicate that bidders do not bear a large risk in accepting negotiated fixed-price contracts.

When a firm enters a fixed bid in a competitive situation, it naturally accepts a much larger risk. However, it is not necessary for us to evaluate the extent of this risk, for we have been merely trying to determine the relationship between the degree of risk which a firm accepts and the size of the profit margin provided to the firm. In a competitive environment, profit margin size is automatically determined by the operation of the price system. In a noncompetitive situation, this is not the case, and the profit fee is a subject of negotiation.

GOVERNMENT-FURNISHED FACILITIES, WORKING CAPITAL, AND OPPORTUNITY COSTS OF AEROSPACE FIRMS

Since the contractual arrangements established between the government and the aerospace firms do not increase the size of the overall risks that the contractors already bear, it is only necessary to evaluate the overall financial risks faced by the aerospace firms. This can be done if one asks: What would the firms lose if they received no more contracts? It was noted before that an indefinite "large number" of the facilities used in this industry are owned by the government. An exact figure is important, for it would show the extent of the reduction of the financial impact on firms faced with possible contract cancellations. In 1959, the Air Force owned twenty-nine plants which were operated by contractors and were separate from any contractor-owned complex of buildings.[25] There were thirty-eight additional Air Force-owned, contractor-operated plants

---

24 Merton J. Peck and F. M. Scherer, *The Weapons Acquisition Process: An Economic Analysis* (Cambridge: Harvard University Press, Division of Research, 1962), p. 208.

25 U.S., Senate, Subcommittee of the Committee on Armed Services, *Hearings, Military Procurement*, 86th Cong., 1st Sess., July 13-31, 1959, p. 670.

located within a complex of contractor-owned plants.[26] If the firm should become bankrupt, the owners would experience a smaller loss than they would have sustained had they owned all their operated facilities.

These plants were built during World War II and the Korean War when the industry was unwilling to build to meet the demands of a situation considered temporary. Since the Korean War, very few government-financed facilities have been built, with the exception of some limited-purpose items such as rocket test stands.[27] Despite its intention not to finance the construction of new facilities in the early 1960's the government paid for two plants which were designed for the fabrication of Minuteman ICBM stages.[28]

By the late 1950's a broad mobilization base was no longer required, and high-volume production ceased. The government, therefore, directed that, wherever possible, procurement awards be made to privately financed plants.[29] Moreover, in selecting contractors the government placed greater emphasis on the availability of contractor facilities both for production and testing.[30] This trend

---

[26] *Ibid.*, p. 671. For an indication of the way company-government-owned complexes were financed, see U.S., House, Subcommittee No. 4 of the Select Committee on Small Business, *Hearings, The Aircraft Industry*, 85th Cong., 2d Sess., June 27-28, 1958, pp. 164-165.

[27] *Aviation Week*, October 6, 1958, p. 26; U.S., Senate, Subcommittee of the Select Committee on Small Business, *Hearings, The Role of Small Business in Government Procurement, 1961*, 87th Cong., 1st Sess., April 25-26, 1961, pp. 86-87. Specialized test facilities are still being financed by NASA and the Defense Department; see *Aviation Week*, February 25, 1963, p. 39; and *Department of Defense Appropriations, 1963*, p. 578. Harlan states that in the Korean War no new facilities contracts were awarded to the airframe manufacturers, but only to subcontractors. Neil E. Harlan, *Management Control in Airplane Subcontracting* (Boston: Division of Research, Graduate School of Business Administration, Harvard University, 1956, p. 19.

[28] *Aviation Week*, July 30, 1962, p. 26. *Department of Defense Appropriations, 1963*, p. 578 indicates that the Air Force built facilities in fiscal years 1960 and 1961 valued at $17.1 million and $33.1 million respectively. These expenditures were expected to fall to $6.8 million by fiscal year 1963. These facilities were considered distinct from production equipment, which the Air Force was financing at the rate of $37.4, $69, $77.8, and $84.4 million in fiscal years 1960-1963, respectively.

[29] See Department of Defense directives 400.13-.14 and *Procurement Practices Hearings*, pp. 357-358.

[30] In evaluating proposals, NASA has stated that it considers in-house test capabilities almost as important as production facilities. *Missiles and Rockets*, May 20, 1963, p. 67. Moreover, it was decided that all large-scale solid-fuel rocket research and development would be done in company-owned plants. Thus the companies had to develop their own facilities at considerable risk, since they were not certain of obtaining the contracts. *Ibid.*, April 22, 1963, p. 15.

actually began in the 1950's with the expansion of the missile programs.[31] It is thus not surprising that the capital expenditure of the aerospace firms increased, with the fixed assets of the twelve major airframe manufacturers rising in value from $154 million in 1952 to $431 million in 1956.[32] At the end of 1961 the net book value of the fixed assets of the eight airframe companies for which comparable data could be obtained was $422 million, compared with $231 million in 1956.[33] The evidence seems to indicate that the firms have bigger stakes in the industry, and as a result, the risk associated with potential failure has increased.[34]

Nevertheless, the contractual relations in the industry have not changed significantly since the end of World War II. Fees are still set at approximately the same percentage of estimated cost as they were when the government owned a larger percentage of the facilities. Since firms are accepting these rates and are, in fact, expanding their plants and eagerly bidding for government contracts, one interpretation is that profit rates were too high in the past.[35]

On the other hand, this industry does not face another problem

---

[31] Contractors' expenditures had accounted for 37 percent of the funds which had been invested in missile facilities, machinery, and equipment by 1958. The contractors' investment was mainly in land and buildings, with the firms spending 76 percent of the funds committed for this purpose. The Air Force expenditures on machinery and equipment accounted for 56 percent of this total. *Aircraft Industry Hearings,* p. 164.

[32] *Aviation Week,* July 7, 1958, p. 54. Part of this increase might have been the result of mergers.

[33] The companies for which the data are fairly comparable are Boeing, Douglas, Lockheed, Grumman, McDonnell, North American, Northrop and Republic. Both Martin and General Dynamics were excluded because they were engaged in mergers which distorted the figures. The data were obtained from the annual reports and are net of depreciation or reserves.

[34] Another risk faced by all firms, including those in this industry, is the loss of contracts with consequent loss of skilled manpower. A firm may be viewed as possessing a set of skills which would disintegrate were the company forced to curtail production and reduce its workforce with the possibility of not being able to rehire at a later date. How this should be evaluated and measured is a difficult question. Virtually everyone, including the U. S. Tax Court, has recognized that one of the primary assets of the industry is its manpower. Were this manpower to disappear, the firm would have to go out of existence just as surely as if its physical assets were destroyed. However, the major contractors might reduce the magnitude of their subcontracts and maintain their staffs by increasing the scope of their "in-house" activity. See *Aviation Week,* November 18, 1957, p. 101.

[35] For an opposite view, see Walter Guzzardi, Jr., "G.E. Astride Two Worlds," *Fortune,* June 1962. On the other hand, it is also possible that other risks may have diminished since the end of World War II. The increased risk resulting from more company-owned facilities might have been offset by a diminution of other risks. Consequently, the fees required by firms might have remained unchanged.

common to most others. Once a project is undertaken, the aerospace firm is confident of recouping not only its cost but also of earning some profit.[36] Thus, when the Skybolt contract was canceled, Douglas did not lose any money, as Ford did when its Edsel was dropped. One reason for this difference is that the aerospace companies are, in effect, contractors working with government specifications and under government contracts, and are thus not subject to the vicissitudes of market acceptance. On the other hand, these firms may be subject to very sudden program cancellations. This is a risk most other firms do not face.

There is an additional difference between this and other industries. Usually a firm provides its own working capital. This may be obtained by using company funds or, more commonly, by borrowing from financial institutions. A cost is incurred in either case, be it an opportunity cost as in the first example or an accounting cost as in the second. In this industry, a firm's need for working capital, and consequently the level of its costs, is reduced, since the government provides the working capital through progress payments. These payments are reimbursements made to firms by the government for a specified percentage of the costs incurred by the contractors. Payments are made periodically, usually monthly, as the work moves toward completion.[37] Firms prepare estimates of the expenditures incurred in the latest period in the production development of a specified item, and submit these data to the government, which then makes reimbursement for a specified percentage of these costs. Were it not for additional restrictions, working capital would be required only for the month for which the firm was carrying this burden, plus the time elapsed from cost-estimate preparation to reimbursement receipt. If it is assumed that two months are required for this process,[38] then the firm's opportunity cost of financing work in progress would be the cost of this

---

[36] This statement applies in principle only to the cost reimbursement type of contract, but the aerospace firms seldom incur a loss on government fixed-price contracts. The situation is different in the commercial segment of the industry, where Douglas and General Dynamics experienced losses in developing their jet airliners.

[37] For a discussion of progress payments, see *Pyramiding of Profits and Costs . . .*, Pt. 1, pp. 164-167.

Progress payments are common in certain other sections of the economy where long lead times are required in constructing capital equipment.

[38] According to one industry spokesman, two months would be a reasonable estimate of the time required for this process.

working capital for three months. If the relevant interest rate was 6 percent, then the opportunity cost would be 1.5 percent of the total value of the contract.

Moreover, in the past when the government decreased the size of these progress payments, it increased the fee paid to the contractor to help meet the cost of borrowing money to finance work in progress. This was so in 1957, when progress payments were reduced from 100 percent to only 70 percent of the material and direct labor costs.[39] Higher profit margins were subsequently allowed to all contractors affected by this action.[40] Although the opportunity cost of the firms was increased when progress payments were reduced, they received additional compensation.[41]

Some additional restrictions increase the firm's opportunity costs. No progress payments can be made until a definitive contract has been drawn up, although the firm may start committing funds as soon as it receives a letter of intent from the government.[42] This letter (more precisely, it is a statement of intent to make a formal award later) is an interim contract which obligates the government to reimburse the firm for expenses undertaken on behalf of the government, but it does not establish a final price, fee, or other terms. While the firm is operating under the authority of a letter of intent, it must be self-financing.

There is some recent evidence, probably representative, indicating the length of time that firms operate under the terms of interim contracts. An examination of these data would yield an estimate of the additional costs attributable to this factor. United Technology, a subsidiary of United Aircraft, was selected as the prime contractor for the Titan III-C first stage in May, 1962. This contract, covering work extending into the summer of 1966, was formally awarded to the company late in March, 1963.[43] The contract encompasses

---

39 *Aviation Week*, August 19, 1957, p. 31.

40 *Procurement Practices Hearings*, p. 217. *Aviation Week*, November 4, 1957, p. 26.

41 In January, 1961, the government increased the size of the progress payments. Peck and Scherer, *op. cit.,* p. 169.

42 U.S., Senate, Subcommittee of the Select Committee on Small Business, *Hearings, Small Business Participation in Defense Subcontracting*, 86th Cong., 1st Sess., April 23-24, 1959, p. 202.

43 *The Wall Street Journal*, March 25, 1963, p. 9. The elapsed time between the letter of intent and the definitive contract for most missiles was at least ten months. U.S., House, Subcommittee of the Committee on Government Operations, *Hearings, Organization and Management of Missile Programs*, 86th Cong., 1st Sess., February 4-March 20, 1959, pp. 43-44.

almost fifty months' worth of work, including the nine to ten months covered only by the interim contract. If it is assumed that the money is spent evenly over the lifetime of the contract, then the cost of the working capital employed during the life of the *interim* contract can be calculated and prorated over the total value of the contract. Our best estimate of the cost of the working capital employed by United Technology is 2.5 percent of the committed funds and .5 percent of the total value of the contract.[44] This probably is an overestimate, since funds are not spent evenly over time, and since it takes time to get a project started and to hire new employees. Consequently, less than the average monthly expenditures will be spent in the early months of the contract.

This estimate is supported by the data on the negotiations between NASA and Boeing for the Saturn I-C booster.[45] NASA awarded the Saturn first-stage contract to Boeing on December 15, 1961, and the company worked for fourteen months under the terms of this interim contract. However, the interim contract was for $50 million, whereas the final contract set a figure of more than $418 million.[46] If it is assumed that the entire $50 million was spent, with expenditures spread evenly, then the opportunity cost of the working capital employed during the life of the interim contract can again be calculated. Our best estimate is that the cost was .5 percent of the total value of the contract.[47]

There is a second restriction which limits the use of progress pay-

---

[44] The figures were obtained in the following manner: Funds were committed for ten months while the interim contract was in effect. The funds were spent equally, and the interest cost of the total working capital thus committeed would average 6 percent for five months, or 2.5 percent of the committed funds. But the life of the contract is fifty months, and thus only 20 percent of the total funds would have been committed in the first ten months, provided the money is spent equally in every month. Thus a charge of .5 percent of the total value of the contract is attributable to the absence of progress payments during the period in which the firm operates with a letter contract.

[45] *Missiles and Rockets*, March 4, 1963, p. 15; and *Aviation Week*, March 4, 1963, p. 30.

[46] The Gemini Spacecraft, Intruder A-6 plane and F-1 (Saturn) engines are examples of other recent systems in which the value of the definitive contract has been a large multiple of the value of the interim contract. *Missiles and Rockets*, April 8, 1963, p. 10; *Aviation Week*, June 17, 1963, p. 39; *The Wall Street Journal*, March 31, 1964, p. 14.

[47] If the money were spent evenly over fourteen months, then the interest cost of the average dollar would be 6 percent for seven months or 3.5 percent. However, the $50 million were only 12 percent of the total value of the contract, and the cost attributable to the entire contract cannot be in excess of .5 percent.

ments. If the contract is small (less than a half-million dollars) or the contract's duration is for fewer than six months, then firms must use their own funds for working capital.[48] Since these contracts are a negligible portion of the total contracts of large firms, the overall opportunity cost attributable to a firm's use of its capital will not be increased appreciably. For small firms this may have quite an impact,[49] but there is evidence that the smaller contracts are awarded higher fees to compensate for this increased cost.[50]

Finally, there are additional opportunity costs for which an aerospace firm expects compensation. Even in the era when the aerospace firms had to contribute only a small percentage of the plant and equipment necessary for production, they still contributed something. The firm's relevant opportunity cost is the return obtainable on the capital invested in the productive process. To obtain an estimate of this cost, the ratio of sales to net fixed assets was estimated for a number of aerospace firms for 1955, one of the last years in which firms contributed only a small percentage of the required capital. With an average ratio in the neighborhood of 25 or 30 to 1, firms should have received a fee of approximately .2 percent of their sales in order to obtain a 6 percent return on their capital.[51] If, because of the risk, 6 percent was considered too low and a 10 percent return on capital was regarded as more appropriate, then a fee of approximately one-fourth to one-third of 1 percent should have been allowed.

As noted previously, since 1956 firms have been expanding their own productive facilities. Consequently, by 1962 the ratio of sales to net fixed assets had fallen to 14 to 1. There has been a concomitant increase to .5 percent in the fee required to compensate the firms for this opportunity cost.

---

48 *Procurement Practices Hearings*, p. 203.

49 Other considerations must be taken into account in deciding whether to accept a contract of this type. If it is a study contract, a firm might accept it because it could gain access to new knowledge which would increase the firm's potential future profits.

50 Moore, *op. cit.*, p. 32.

51 This assumes that all company sales were to the government and that all company productive facilities were used for this purpose. The ratio of sales to fixed assets was much lower for firms which also had commercial business; consequently the mean ratio of sales to fixed assets is somewhat underestimated, and the opportunity cost of the capital employed in producing government systems is slightly overestimated.

Our estimate of the total opportunity costs of the aerospace firms would be the sum of: the cost of working capital during the period in which progress payments are made, the cost of working capital before obtaining progress payments, and the cost of the facilities employed in the productive process. The estimates of these respective opportunity costs were 1.5 percent, .5 percent, and before 1955, at most .333 percent. In 1962, an estimate of approximately .5 percent would be attributable to the last cost. Thus, up to 1955, a fee of 2.5 percent of sales would have covered the opportunity costs. In 1962, a fee of, at most, 3 percent would have been sufficient to cover the opportunity costs of the firms.[52]

THE ROLE OF PROFITS

Four theoretical reasons have been advanced to explain the function and role of accounting profits.[53] Included in the accounting profits of a firm are its opportunity costs—profits may also be considered a reward for innovation. Third, profits might be obtained for bearing risk and uncertainty, and, finally, they may be viewed as a monopoly return.

From the government's point of view, which of the mentioned reasons could be used to justify the level of the profit fees which have been awarded to the aerospace firms? Certainly the government would not want to argue that it was paying monopoly returns especially since it had some monopsony power. In addition, it would have difficulty proving that, in the past, the firms took great risks. It is true that in earlier years shifts in the demand for military weapons systems showed greater variability than corresponding shifts in even the most volatile nonmilitary items.[54] Moreover, technological changes, which can imperil the position of firms very rapidly, probably have occurred faster in this industry than in most other sectors of the economy. To counteract these risks, until 1956 the government had financed a large percentage of the industry's

---

52 However, the government disallows some of the firms' costs in calculating "costs" for reimbursement contracts. These costs such as advertising may, in some cases, be considered part of the normal cost of staying in business. If this were so, an additional small percentage of sales would be required to cover these costs.

53 Paul A. Samuelson, *Economics,* 5th ed. (New York: McGraw-Hill, 1961), pp. 663-667.

54 Moore, *op. cit.,* p. 97.

required facilities. In addition, the Defense Department had maintained the position of most firms.[55] Thus to a large extent the risks of the firms have been shifted to the government. Where risks have been imposed on firms, for example with incentive contracts, the negotiated fee has been several percentage points higher than when a CPFF contract is negotiated. Thus, the basic fee on a CPFF contract cannot be considered a risk premium.

In addition, our estimate of the opportunity costs of the firms was 2.5 to 3.0 percent of the volume of sales. Accordingly, this level of opportunity costs can explain only a portion of the 6 percent fee customarily paid on CPFF contracts.[56] A portion of a typical aerospace firm's accounting profits must therefore be attributed to the fourth factor and considered a reward for successful innovation or superior performance. In either case, for the government to be able to justify the level of the fees allowed on cost-plus contracts, the fee should be determined at the conclusion of the contract and not at its outset; performance cannot be judged until the results are obtained. Determining a fixed fee at the inception of the work, therefore, rewards the achievements of all firms equally, regardless of good or bad performance.

Both the Defense Department and NASA have become disturbed by the fact that the fees on CPFF contracts do not reward the performance of contractors effectively. For this reason the two agencies have started to use cost-plus incentive-fee contracts more extensively. On research and development contracts where the final price is uncertain, the incentives are based on "meeting or exceeding time schedules and standards of reliability and performance."[57] Since a superior performance earns a higher profit than an inferior job, the profits earned on these contracts could, then, be justified as a return to superior performance.

---

[55] For an overt expression of this desire to protect existing firms, see *Department of Defense Appropriations, 1957*, 84th Cong., 2d Sess. 1956, p. 29. The discussion there revolved around the need to maintain Curtiss-Wright's engineering and design potential in existence.

[56] If there are substantial overruns, the actual fee expressed as a percentage of actual costs will be less than 6 percent. Whether it would approach 3 percent would depend on the size of the overrun and the manner in which the procuring agency handles it. If a contract with an additional fee is awarded, the actual fee is not likely to approach 3 percent.

[57] *The Wall Street Journal*, March 25, 1963, p. 9.

SUMMARY AND CONCLUSIONS

In this chapter we have examined the types of contracts used in the government's procurement from the aerospace industry. Over time there has been a continual movement toward a greater use of cost-reimbursement contracts. This was the result of increased emphasis on research and development. Since 1961 there has been an attempt to decrease the use of CPFF contracts and to substitute the incentive-type contracts for them. Since the type of contract awarded can affect the risks of the aerospace firms, the risk associated with each contractual form was also investigated. We concluded that cost-reimbursement contracts imposed virtually no risk upon the firms. Incentive-type contracts did increase the risks of the aerospace firms, but it was seen that the degree of risk was not high.

Until 1956 the government also bore much of the risk and cost associated with the ownership of the industry's facilities since they had been financed by the government. The industry's risk in this area has increased considerably since the government has ceased this financing. However, the government still continues to bear the cost of the industry's working capital through the medium of progress payments.

Finally, the industry's opportunity costs were compared with the level of the fees provided in government contracts. It was concluded that the fees were larger than the opportunity costs and that the difference could be justified as a reward for superior performance. If this is true, the fees should be determined at the conclusion of the contract and not at its inception.

6.

ENTRY INTO AND EXIT FROM THE INDUSTRY

Two significant trends affecting the industry's structure are the increase in importance of research and development vis-à-vis production and the increasing emphasis placed on electronic systems. These forces have influenced entry into and exit from the industry. Aircraft firms developed electronic capabilities, and several electronics firms which did not have them competed for contracts by entering bids jointly with firms that did.

An immediate effect of the increasing importance of research and development expenditures was a reduction in the number of projects undertaken. As the absolute level of costs increased with each succeeding generation of projects, it was financially impossible for the government to undertake many such projects.[1] With the production runs of each system also becoming smaller, it is natural to expect this to affect the structure of the industry. The composition of the industry's workforce changed,[2] and fiercer competition

---

[1] There has been discussion about the correct path to follow in undertaking each succeeding project. Some have argued that the failure to contract for prototypes has unnecessarily reduced the number of projects undertaken and also increased development costs. For this view, which is particularly applicable to aircraft production, see B. H. Klein, T. K. Glenman, Jr., and C. H. Shubert, *The Role of Prototypes in Development*, RAND Report RN 3467-PR (Santa Monica, Calif.: The RAND Corp., 1963). See also R. R. Nelson, "Uncertainty, Learning and the Economics of Parallel Research and Development Efforts," *The Review of Economics and Statistics*, XLIII, No. 4 (November 1961), pp. 351-364. On the other hand, the increasing complexity of modern weapon and space systems may even make the development of prototypes expensive. Second, it is not clear whether advocates of multiple prototypes would also propose this type of development for space vehicles.

[2] In 1947, production workers constituted 74 percent of the workforce; this ratio fell to 71.7 percent by 1954 and 64.1 percent in 1958. These data were calculated from the *Census of Manufactures* for 1947, 1954 and 1958. Also, U.S., House, Subcommittee of the Committee on Government Operations, *Hearings, Systems Development and Management,* 87th Cong., 2d Sess., 1962, p. 204. A study conducted for the Aero-

for contracts ensued;[3] this may also have increased the political pressures on each company's behalf. With a smaller number of production contracts being awarded, the unsuccessful airframe manufacturers became subcontractors or merged with firms in other industries.

This increase in subcontracting to firms which have been the prime airframe manufacturers was especially noticeable in the B-70 and F-108 airplane programs. Though both were ultimately either canceled or curtailed in scope, the original intention was to provide the losing airplane firms with a part of the contract.[4] This trend, however, has not been observed with missile and space contracts.

A second effect of the industry's dependence upon research and development contracts is closely associated with the growing emphasis upon electronic equipment. Firms had to demonstrate their research capabilities in the areas in which they were competing for contracts. Since a large percentage of the work now involved electronics, almost all airframe manufacturers integrated by developing in-house electronic capabilities. At the same time, the electronics firms expanded the scope of their activities and became prime missile contractors.

AIRCRAFT FIRMS DEVELOP ELECTRONIC CAPABILITIES

Two factors required the prime airframe manufacturers to add electronic divisions to their other facilities. First, the development of the weapon-systems form of procurement required that the

---

space Industries Association indicated that hourly employees constituted only 54.4 percent of the industry's workforce in 1961. See Stanford Research Institute, *The Industry-Government Aerospace Relationship*, II, 248. These data are not strictly comparable with the Census data, but may be used as a measure of the trend.

[3] RCA claims that between 1960 and 1962 it was forced to increase the number of proposals which it submitted by 160 percent merely to maintain its proportion of business. *Aviation Week*, February 4, 1963, p. 99. However, it is difficult to determine what is meant by "its proportion." Does this mean the same level of sales, or its proportion of the value of government business? If it is the latter, this is not surprising, because aerospace expenditures were rising in this period. The competition for research and development contracts increased because it became obvious that the potential value of these contracts was increasing. Since most firms now sought more contracts, each firm might have obtained a smaller percentage of the number of contracts upon which it bid. This might also make it appear that a smaller number of contracts was being awarded.

[4] *Ibid.*, November 4, 1957, p. 33; January 12, 1959, p. 34; and March 9, 1959, pp. 68-69. Also, U.S., House, Committee on Armed Services, *Weapons System Management and Teams System Concept in Government Contracting*, 86th Cong., 1st Sess., 1959, p. 62.

prime contractor exercise overall systems integration. With the growing importance of electronic systems, this forced the airframe manufacturers to increase their in-house electronic capability. It was also considered likely that prime contracts would be awarded only to firms which had the requisite electronic capability to perform this coordination function.[5] Second, the greater emphasis on the electronic components of each system forced the prime to manufacture some electronics subsystems merely to keep the same percentage of a contract as it had previously.[6]

These factors became obvious at an early stage in the transition to the weapon-systems approach to procurement, and by 1959, most major airframe contractors had some electronic capabilities. Two paths were available for obtaining these skills. First, the firm could set up separate electronic departments within their existing organizations, or they could acquire electronic firms through mergers. Most firms used the first route, but there is some evidence that they also sought to acquire existing concerns.[7] In addition, the manufacturers of rocket engines were also moving into electronics because this equipment was needed for testing and checkout.[8] With

---

[5] *Aviation Week*, May 27, 1957, p. 37; June 24, 1957, p. 23; July 8, 1957, p. 29.

[6] However, the dollar volume of the firm's activities might increase while its percentage of the contract dollar declined.

[7] Among others, North American Aviation, Martin, Northrop, Lockheed, and the Convair Division of General Dynamics established divisions within the company. Lockheed and Northrop both purchased small electronics companies. The former bought Stavid Engineering; the latter, Page Communications. General Dynamics also acquired an electronics company, Stromberg-Carlson. See *Aviation Week*, September 23, 1957, p. 75; March 9, 1958, p. 322; May 25, 1959, p. 28; October 12, 1959, p. 70; November 16, 1959, p. 116 and December 14, 1959, p. 35; also *Electronics*, August 20, 1957. Several other merger attempts between the airframe manufacturers and electronics companies failed. Included were the proposed mergers between Martin and General Precision, Northrop and American Bosch Arma, Marquardt Corp. and Packard Bell, and Douglas and Midwestern Electronics, a small electronics company. Douglas, itself, expanded its avionics at a relatively late date, 1961. See *Aviation Week*, July 28, 1958, p. 21; May 25, 1959, p. 28; March 20, 1961, p. 87; April 2, 1962, p. 25; and October 15, 1962, p. 32. Also, *The Wall Street Journal*, October 17, 1962 and November 27, 1962. The Northrop-American Bosch Arma merger talks were held at the approximate time when Northrop was in the process of establishing its own electronics divisions.

[8] Both Thiokol and Aerojet acquired electronics firms. *Aviation Week*, July 6, 1959, p. 87; *Electronics*, March 1, 1957, p. 47. Electronics was only one of the areas into which the rocket manufacturers moved. These firms, along with some of the airframe firms, were also active in metallurgical research. The new propellants were generating too much heat for the existing rocket nozzles, which consequently had to be manufactured from new materials. *Aviation Week*, December 9, 1957, p. 33; January 13, 1958, p. 23; October 5, 1959, p. 77; May 9, 1960, p. 71; and May 21, 1962, p. 69.

the Air Force's transition from aircraft to missiles, and with the growing importance of electronics, the standard 1957 prediction was that the electronic manufacturers would expand at the expense of both the airframe and metal-working firms.[9] The implication was that the absolute share of the aerospace industry's market accruing to the airframe firms would decline.[10] Although electronic equipment has taken an increasingly larger percentage of the aerospace industry's dollar,[11] most airframe firms have not experienced financial difficulties. This can be attributed partly to a larger government budget for aerospace products, but, more fundamentally, to the aircraft manufacturers' ability to make the transition to missile and space activities by acquiring electronic capabilities. In addition to performing their usual roles of assembling the frame, the development of this electronic capability enabled the companies to expand into testing and integrating the entire system. Moreover, the overall responsibility for ground-support equipment also was assigned often to these companies.

A comparison of the 1959 electronic capabilities of the airframe firms with similar data for 1954 is indicative of this trend. A 1959 survey of the major airframe manufacturers indicated that the number of engineers employed by the airframe firms increased

9 *Electronics*, July 10, 1957, pp. 13-14.

10 On the other hand, there were fears that the weapon-system form of procurement would enhance the position of the prime contracting firm, which is usually an airframe manufacturer.

11 Because the data are classified, it is difficult to obtain a precise estimate of the avionics content of the aerospace dollar. However, a figure yielding an order of importance of the proportion of the aerospace dollar which is retained within the former airframe firms is available. Before the introduction of missiles, 90 percent of the aerospace dollar was retained within the aircraft companies, *Weapons System Hearings*, p. 48. A 1961 estimate indicated that only 30 percent of the missile dollar was spent within the aircraft companies. *Commercial and Financial Chronicle*, January 19, 1961, p. 20.

Murray L. Weidenbaum has prepared an estimate of the percentage of the missile dollar which was committed to the aircraft companies. His analysis of 35 missiles indicated that in the fiscal years 1958 and 1959 approximately 50 percent of the missile dollar was committed to the aircraft firms. Murray L. Weidenbaum, "The Impact of Military Procurement on American Industry," in J. A. Stockfish, ed., *Planning and Forecasting in the Defense Industries* (Belmont, California: Wadsworth Publishing Co., 1962), pp. 166-173. The 50-percent figure indicates the percentage of the funds committed to the aviation firms and not the amount retained in-house. Weidenbaum also indicates that 33 percent of the dollar spent for production goes to electronics (*ibid.*, p. 150). This figure, however, understates the importance of electronics, for parts both of the research and development and the assembly and testing expenditures are spent on electronics.

between 1954 and 1959. Moreover, there was also an increase in the proportion of these persons who were electronic engineers. The ratio changed from 16 percent in 1954 to 25 percent in 1959.[12]

To emphasize further the increased electronic capabilities of the airframe manufacturers, one should note that the percentage of electronic engineers employed for "in-house" research and development or manufacturing purposes doubled between 1954 and 1959.[13] Formerly, only a third of these persons were used for in-house research and development, with the remainder supervising or performing systems integration with subcontractors. By 1959, the proportions had been reversed, with two-thirds employed in-house. The ratio of electronic engineers to all engineers employed by the companies responding to the survey is shown in Table 28.

TABLE 28

PERCENTAGE OF ELECTRONIC ENGINEERS AMONG ALL ENGINEERS EMPLOYED BY A SAMPLE OF AIRFRAME MANUFACTURERS, 1954 AND 1959

Company	Percentage	
	1959	1954
Bell	38	41
Boeing	16	14
Cessna	15	3
Chance-Vought	27	26
Convair (General Dynamics)	23	29
Grumman	14	11
Lockheed	23	12
Martin	25	14
McDonnell	22	7
North American Aviation	27	9
Northrop	27	34
Republic	18	9
Ryan	19	21
Temco	37	22

SOURCE: *Aviation Week and Space Technology*, October 5, 1959, p. 101.

The airframe manufacturers' capabilities in electronics could be divided into three broad categories. The first group comprised firms which used their electronics divisions primarily for systems integration. The task of these electronics staffs was primarily to evaluate alternative approaches suggested by electronic subcon-

---

[12] Although it was predicted that this ratio would increase even further by the middle 1960's, no additional information is available to corroborate this assertion. "Avionics Grows in Aircraft Companies," *Aviation Week,* October 5, 1959, pp. 97 ff.
[13] *Ibid.,* p. 97.

tractors and to integrate the systems which were purchased from the avionics companies. Firms in this category in 1959 included Douglas,[14] Grumman, McDonnell, Republic, and the aircraft divisions of Convair, Lockheed, and North American Aviation.[15] These firms consequently had a lower-than-average proportion of electronics personnel.

A second group of companies actually competed with the avionics firms in hardware production. This group included Bell, Lockheed, the Orlando Division of Martin, North American Aviation (Autonetics division), Northrop, and Ryan. North American and Lockheed were included in both groups, causing an overlap of companies. These firms generally had a higher-than-average proportion of electronics engineers on their scientific staffs. The remaining concerns used their electronic capabilities primarily for systems integration, and usually purchased their electronic hardware. They did, however, produce some specialized products in competition with the avionics firms.

A final point about the role of electronics in the aerospace companies must be made in reference to Chrysler. Chrysler is included in the industry because it has, in the past, manufactured the Redstone and Jupiter missiles and is currently developing and producing one stage of the Saturn booster. However, it has never expanded into electronics, and is thus limited in the number of contracts on which it can bid.[16] Chrysler can afford to act in this manner, for it is basically an automobile manufacturer and only secondarily an aerospace firm. However, through coalitions, Chrysler is able to bid on contracts which require the in-house electronics capabilities not possessed by Chrysler. These coalitions are alternatives to vertical integration, and will be discussed in more detail below. Despite Chrysler's failure to develop an electronics capability, the

---

14 In the fifties, Douglas decided not to expand into electronics. C. J. V. Murphy, "The Plane Maker Under Stress," *Fortune*, LXI, No. 6 (June 1960), 299. However, this hurt the company's ability to obtain missile and space contracts. Part of these problems were attributed to the company's late—1961—entry into electronics. *The Wall Street Journal*, February 7, 1963, p. 22.

15 *Aviation Week*, October 12, 1959, p. 70. It should also be remembered that some other companies in this category obtained their first missile and space contracts at a relatively late date. See Merton J. Peck and F. M. Scherer, *The Weapons Acquisition Process: An Economic Analysis* (Cambridge: Harvard University Press, Division of Research, 1962), pp. 520-521.

16 *Aviation Week*, January 29, 1962, p. 54.

major finding of this section is that the airframe firms found it imperative to develop their electronics know-how in order to compete for missile and space contracts.

ELECTRONICS FIRMS ENTER AS MISSILE CONTRACTORS

As noted previously, it has become difficult to demarcate clearly the bounds between the airframe and electronics firms.[17] The competition between these two groups was mentioned also, but the documentation of the extent of the role played by these electronics companies has not, as yet, been presented in our analysis. In 1952, *Aviation Week's* "Annual Inventory of Airpower" listed fourteen missiles as operational or under development.[18] The electronics companies held the prime contracts for four of these missiles.[19] In 1956, twenty-six missile projects were underway, with seven of the prime contracts held exclusively by electronics firms.[20] By 1962, this list had expanded to forty-one missiles, with at least fourteen under prime contract to the avionics firms.[21] In addition the Bullpup was under contract to Martin, but a second source contract for the guidance system was awarded to Maxson Electronics. Douglas and Emerson Electric shared the Honest John contract, and the electronics division of North American Aviation had the Hounddog contract. The former airframe manufacturers had contracts for only fifteen missiles.[22] Thus, the expansion of the missile pro-

---

[17] See *Business Week,* June 14, 1958, pp. 90 ff.

[18] *Aviation Week,* February 25, 1952, p. 54.

[19] Sperry Gyroscope had the Sparrow, Western Electric the Nike, General Electric the Hermes, and Bendix the Loki. In addition, Firestone and Aerojet both held missile contracts; the former had the Corporal, the latter the Aerobee. These firms were neither electronics nor airframe manufacturers

[20] *Aviation Week,* March 12, 1956, p. 217. In addition, Douglas, Raytheon, and Sperry shared the contracts for the three versions of the Sparrow missile. Companies such as Firestone and Eastman Kodak, which held missile contracts, were not counted among the electronics firms. In 1958, there were forty-four missile programs, and the electronics companies held the prime contracts for fourteen. The electronics companies were associate primes on two more. *Aviation Age,* January 1958, p. 20. This list may include several versions of a single missile such as Sparrow I, II, III, and includes as electronics manufacturers such firms as Firestone and Eastman Kodak, which held the contracts for the Corporal and Dove missiles, respectively.

[21] This list does not include the follow-on versions of several missiles such as the Nike-Ajax, Nike-Hercules, and Nike-Zeus. However, if the manufacturers of the two systems, such as the Typhon, were different, both were counted. *Aerospace Facts and Figures, 1962* (New York: McGraw-Hill, 1962), pp. 30-31.

[22] The contractors for the remaining systems were the military services, 4; Chrysler, 2; Ford's Aeronutronics Division, 1; Goodyear, 1; and Nord, a French company, 1. Ford's division may also be classified in the electronics category.

gram saw the electronics firms enter as prime missile contractors.

To enter the industry, firms originally not considered prime system contractors were required to reorganize their internal structures. For some this reorganization came early and has benefited the company; other companies have made a belated response.

General Electric, always a staunch believer in decentralized management, announced as early as 1957 that it was attempting to fit into the weapon-system concept by putting together in one package all airborne-accessory power components which it had previously sold separately from diverse divisions.[23] It was now ready to bid on complete airborne-accessory power systems. By so doing, it was readily adjusting to the weapon-system concept of procurement. However, this process of reorganization apparently did not move as rapidly as expected or desired, for after General Electric lost the BMEWS contract to RCA, another reorganization was discussed.[24] It was again emphasized that decentralization made it difficult for General Electric to obtain large prime contracts, but since that time the company has been very successful in this field,[25] thus dispelling the early fear that electronics firms would be at a disadvantage relative to the airframe manufacturers in obtaining prime system contracts.[26]

However, other firms were not so willing to change their corporate structure, and they adjusted only in response to adverse economic developments instead of anticipating them. For instance, General Precision Instruments waited until 1962 before reorganizing and did so then only in response to a changing technological environment which threatened its economic existence. The technological changes which have affected the manufacturers of electronic components adversely are analyzed in Appendix C. General

---

23 *Aviation Week*, April 15, 1957, p. 85. Daystrom also reorganized in 1957, but it was not successful in obtaining contracts. *Ibid.*, August 12, 1957, p. 88. Its 1962 financial difficulties evidence its inability to advance rapidly in the industry.

24 *Ibid.*, October 6, 1958, p. 34.

25 Among other projects, General Electric has held contracts for the recovery portion of the Discoverer satellite, Advent, Nimbus, OAO's horizon sensors, the guidance systems for Polaris and Atlas, and the fire-control system for Polaris. The company has also performed studies for the Apollo, Voyager, and bio-satellite programs. It is also assisting NASA in a management role for the Apollo project. U.S., House, Subcommittee on Manned Space Flight of the Committee on Science and Astronautics, *Hearings, 1963 NASA Authorization*, 87th Cong., 2d Sess., 1962, p. 441; *Missiles and Rockets*, April 22, 1963, p. 10.

26 *Aviation Week*, October 12, 1959, pp. 70 and 72.

Precision Instruments, until 1962 a component-oriented firm, found that the major systems manufacturers were acquiring component lines of their own. To meet this threat, the company reorganized its divisions to emphasize its ability to manufacture complete guidance-and-control systems, and to demonstrate its management capabilities.[27]

Complete documentation of the procedures used by the electronics firms in becoming missile contractors is impossible, for the missile was a highly classified weapon in the period in which these companies entered the industry.[28] It probably was a natural development for these firms to become the prime contractors, for they were already ensconced in the electronics-system market, which accounted for the highest portion of a small missile's cost.[29] The firms already were manufacturing the most complex systems such as guidance and control. With the weapon-systems approach requiring a prime contractor, these firms were natural choices.[30]

EXITS

Peck and Scherer point out that although many firms have entered the industry, some have left it. Their data refer primarily to firms with prime system responsibility in the aircraft and missile sectors of the industry, and are presented in Table 29. The net effect of these entries and exits has been an increase of the number

---

27 *Missiles and Rockets,* May 7, 1962, pp. 37 ff. These examples show how a firm's internal decision-making procedures may be affected by changes in the industry's structure.

28 For the pattern of missile contracting, see *Business Week,* June 14, 1958, p. 96. The air-to-air missiles were manufactured primarily by the electronics companies; the large missiles went to the airframe companies, and the ground-to-air missiles were evenly divided between the electronics and airframe companies.

29 *Aviation Age,* January 1957, p. 22.

30 It is still instructive to analyze the procedures by which these companies attained their electronic capabilities. For example, Hughes decided to enter the inertial guidance field and bid for engineers. There is no evidence that the company had any contracts in this field at this time. Moreover, the classified nature of the data precludes a definite answer. *Aviation Week,* July 13, 1959, p. 101. A year later there are statements to the effect that the company was expanding its efforts and was hiring more people in the gyro and accelerometer areas. But the company was the second source for the Polaris guidance system by this time. *Ibid.,* October 24, 1960, p. 88. Minneapolis-Honeywell bid for an active role in the vehicles-control market only after having performed several USAF- and company-financed studies in which significant advances were made. *Ibid.,* November 5, 1962, pp. 56 ff. Similarly, Martin's strategy in entering the missile, space, and electronics area was to expand its self-sponsored research. *Missiles and Rockets,* June 19, 1961, pp. 40 ff.

of firms from nineteen in 1950 to twenty-six in 1960. The main increase occurred between 1950 and 1955 when missiles were first
introduced. Peck and Scherer's data for 1960 were compared with
similar information that could be obtained from *Aviation Week
and Space Technology* and *Aerospace Facts and Figures, 1961*. The
purpose of this comparison was to determine whether the latter

TABLE 29

AIRCRAFT AND MISSILE SECTORS OF AEROSPACE INDUSTRY: FIRMS WITH PRIME-SYSTEM
RESPONSIBILITY, ENTRIES AND EXITS, 1940, 1945, 1950, 1955, AND 1960

	1940	1945	1950	1955	1960
Aircraft firms	18	16	11	11	10
Entries	3	0	0	0	
Exits	5	5	0	1	
Missile firms	0	7	15	21	23
Entries	7	8	7	6	
Exits	0	0	1	4	
Aircraft and					
missiles firms combined	18	20	19	25	26
Entries	6	3	7	5	
Exits	4	4	1	4	

SOURCE: Peck and Scherer, *op. cit.*, p. 195.

data were significantly different from the former. If they were not,
it would be possible to use these trade sources for a 1963 estimate
of the number of firms active in these sectors of the industry, and to
trace the trend in the number of firms involved.

The estimates derived from the mentioned trade sources indicate that in 1960 thirteen firms were manufacturing or developing
military planes.[31] This is slightly more than Peck and Scherer's ten.
The discrepancy obviously must be due to the inclusion of firms
such as Beech, Cessna, and Goodyear, which were manufacturing
military aircraft but which probably did not have system responsibility for large weapon systems. A similar count of missile manufacturers yielded twenty-four firms, which differs from Peck and
Scherer's data by one.[32] Since the discrepancies were not large, it

---

[31] *Aviation Week*, March 13, 1961, pp. 183-197; *Aerospace Facts and Figures, 1961*,
pp. 48-51, 96, 112-113, and 116.

[32] The overall difference is 3, with our estimate of 29 against Peck and Scherer's
26. The trade sources yielded data on systems which were both operational and
under development. The discrepancy might be due to manufacturer's exit from the
industry once its one and only missile became operational, for Peck and Scherer's
data refer only to active firms.

was decided to use the same trade sources for an estimate of the number of firms active in the industry at the end of 1963. The data indicate that in 1960 one less firm was manufacturing aircraft and one more company had a prime missile contract. However, the expansion of the industry into the development and manufacture of satellites and spacecraft served to increase further the number of firms with prime systems contracts. There were seventeen firms which had spacecraft and satellite contracts. The unduplicated estimate for 1963 of the number of firms with prime contracts for either planes, missiles, or spacecraft and satellites was thirty-one.

The exits recorded by Peck and Scherer included Curtiss-Wright, Fairchild, and Bell—which left both sectors of the industry. Martin ceased being an airframe manufacturer, but remained in the missile sector, while General Electric, Firestone, and RCA left the missile section. General Electric left after its Hermes and Thumper contracts, Firestone after the Corporal missile, and RCA after Talos.[33]

After 1960, a series of mergers resulting in the formation of Ling-Temco-Vought reduced the number of aircraft manufacturers to nine. Temco Aircraft Corporation was considered one of the major airframe manufacturers, but most of its income originated from contracts obtained from other airframe manufacturers. As early as 1957, the company realized that the adoption of the weapon-system method of procurement might curtail its subcontracting business.[34] Second, since a smaller number of planes was ordered with each contract, the facilities of each of the primes appeared to be sufficient to handle the business.[35] Consequently, subcontracting was expected to diminish in volume. For these reasons, Temco wished to become a prime missile manufacturer.[36] The company purchased an electronics firm in order to acquire some in-house electronics

---

[33] RCA was the prime contractor for the land-based version of Talos, which was specifically being designed to defend land targets. *Aviation Week*, January 16, 1956, p. 37. Since the land-based Talos was considered to be a duplicate of the Nike project, Congress stated that the Army could proceed with the project if funds were withdrawn from its Nike project. The Army thereupon canceled the project. U.S., House, Subcommittee of the Committee on Government Operations, *Hearings, Organization and Management of Missile Programs*, 86th Cong., 1st Sess., 1959, pp. 120-121.

[34] *Aviation Week*, September 9, 1957, p. 75. Moreover, as early as 1956 the company had foreseen a decline in airplane production. See its *1959 Annual Report*, p. 17.

[35] *Aviation Week*, February 19, 1962, p. 27.

[36] *Ibid.*, September 9, 1957, p. 75.

and missile-component capability.[37] Nevertheless, Temco still experienced difficulties,[38] and in 1960 merged with Ling-Altec Electronics.[39] The resulting company—Ling-Temco—was oriented more toward electronics than airframe production.[40] Soon after the merger the new company was hit by the loss of the Corvus missile contract, which had accounted for 20 percent of Temco's backlog.[41] The company had no other missile-system contracts, but did have some subcontracts for missile work.

Chance-Vought, formerly a division of United Aircraft, was another airframe manufacturer highly dependent upon Navy airplane business. The Navy's aircraft procurement hit a peak in fiscal 1958 and the cutbacks were not expected to be reversed.[42] As a result, the position of companies dependent upon Navy aircraft procurement was threatened. Even before Chance-Vought sustained a decline in sales, it attempted to diversify into electronics,[43] but it too experienced financial difficulties.[44] Meanwhile, Ling-Temco merged by buying Chance-Vought's stock in the open market. Chance-Vought resisted a change in its corporate identity, but finally became a somewhat reluctant partner in Ling-Temco-Vought.[45]

There were several other significant mergers of aerospace companies, but none resulted in the disappearance of a major airframe or missile firm. Included among the other mergers were those of Martin and American Marietta, and Boeing and Vertol. The former merger enabled Martin to diversify, for American Marietta was a manufacturer of building and household supplies. Boeing's acquisition of Vertol enabled it to enter the short takeoff and landing

---

37 The firm was Fenske, Fedrick and Miller, Inc., a manufacturer of air and sea traffic control systems, automatic missile testing equipment, telemetering calibration instruments, and missile guidance components, *ibid.*, May 12, 1958, p. 105. *Electronics*, February 21, 1958, p. 8. By the end of 1959, the production of electronics and missiles accounted for 27 percent of the company's business. *1959 Annual Report*, p. 17.

38 Its sales decreased by about 15 percent between 1958 and 1959, but profits fell by more than 50 percent.

39 *Aviation Week*, May 2, 1960, p. 37.

40 Eighty percent of its business was in electronics, communications, missiles, and aerospace systems. *Missiles and Rockets*, April 10, 1961, p. 39

41 *Ibid.*, July 25, 1960, p. 14.

42 *Ibid.*, November 14, 1960, p. 35; *Space Aeronautics*, July 1961, p. 35.

43 *Aviation Week*, June 23, 1958, p. 47, and April 6, 1959, p. 125. It also bought an electronics firm. *Ibid.*, October 26, 1959, p. 125.

44 From 1958 to 1960 its sales fell from $333 to $214 million.

45 *Ibid.*, April 3, 1961, p. 29.

(STOL) and vertical takeoff and landing (VTOL) portions of the aircraft industry.[46]

We can conclude that the aerospace industry's transition from aircraft to missile and space projects tended to weaken the difference between the electronics and airframe companies. Each expanded into the other's bailiwick. Although there were some exits from the industry, the number of firms holding prime aircraft, missile, and spacecraft contracts increased between 1950 and 1963. This was the result of two offsetting movements, with aircraft firms declining and missile and space-system producers increasing. In some cases, the firm exiting from aircraft merely was classified in a different sector of the industry.

SYSTEM PROCUREMENT, COALITIONS, AND SUBCONTRACTING

The emergence of the weapon-system approach to procurement has had, as noted, a considerable impact upon the structure of the industry. One further consequence is that the aerospace firms which do not have electronics facilities have encountered difficulties in obtaining system contracts by themselves.

One solution has been the formation of coalitions. Firms such as Chrysler often team up with firms that have the required qualifications. It is, therefore, no coincidence that certain combinations of teams often bid together.[47]

General Electric has been a frequent member of teams and may be an appropriate example for analysis. General Electric is active in many areas of the aerospace industry, and manufactures re-entry

---

[46] There were numerous mergers between various electronics companies, but it is virtually impossible to examine the entire list. Since these mergers have only a minor effect on the structure of the aerospace industry, it was decided to exclude such acquisitions from our discussion.

[47] These combinations are binding only for purposes of bidding, since Defense Department and NASA may reject any member of a team. This was done on the Skybolt contract. There are several other examples.

While they were not members of a team, the Air Force did reject several of North American's suggested subcontractors for the B-70 and F-108 programs. In one case it was suspected that the firm was rejected because it had not previously been an Air Force contractor; in a second instance that the firm was a newcomer to the field. Thus, even though the prime had the responsibility for checking the firms' capabilities, the Air Force intervened because it felt that newcomers could not make substantial contributions. Thus it would appear that the USAF sought to preclude the entry of new firms and was trying to protect its established sources. See *ibid.*, December 1, 1958, p. 30; December 8, 1958, p. 34; December 29, 1958, p. 15; and May 18, 1959, p. 23.

vehicles, electronic systems, and aircraft engines, but has no airframe capabilities. In bidding for contracts in which an air or space frame is included, it must team with some other aerospace firm which has this airframe capability but is light in the other areas, such as electronics. Douglas and Chrysler have been frequent partners of General Electric.[48]

Chrysler's lack of propulsion and avionics capabilities also limits its ability to compete for a large number of prime manufacturer contracts. However, if it is a member of a team, it can bid on such projects. It joined with General Electric to bid for the lunar roving vehicle.[49] The two companies have also bid together on the Army Ballistic Missile Defense Systems Study,[50] and the Army Air Defense System for 1970.[51]

General Electric has also been a partner of North American Aviation and Douglas. Based on its experience with re-entry bodies, General Electric joined North American in bidding for the Mercury man-in-space capsule.[52] Finally, Douglas has been a frequent partner with General Electric. The two companies bid together for the Airborne Early Warning and Control Aircraft,[53] which in itself was an interesting competition, for two avionic companies submitted bids in competition with the airframe manufacturers, as the avionics content of this AEW program was extremely heavy.[54] In addition to the Douglas-General Electric team, Boeing and Ramo-Wooldridge submitted a team proposal.

General Electric also joined with Douglas in bidding for the

---

[48] It was previously noted that both Douglas and Chrysler lacked substantial electronic capabilities.

[49] *Ibid.*, January 29, 1962, p. 54.

[50] *Ibid.*, October 17, 1960, p. 27.

[51] *Ibid.*, April 22, 1963, p. 23.

[52] *Ibid.*, December 1, 1958, p. 32. By the time the Apollo competition was held, North American had obtained, through its X-15, a considerable amount of re-entry experience and bid by itself.

[53] *Ibid.*, November 24, 1958, p. 35.

[54] *Ibid.*, December 15, 1958, p. 23. Another interesting facet was that in the RCA bid, Douglas was listed as the airframe manufacturer. Thus, Douglas was submitting a bid as subcontractor in competition with itself as prime contractor. Moreover, Lockheed's bid included General Electric's radar, but Lockheed remained as the avionics subsystem developer. *Ibid.*, December 29, 1958, p. 15.

In the Apollo competition, something similar occurred. Bendix joined with Lockheed, with the former having responsibility for the guidance and control systems. At the same time, it was quoting prices on components for the Martin-Marietta bid. *Ibid.*, March 29, 1962, p. 83.

Apollo contract, but here General Electric was to have overall responsibility for reliable operations of the vehicle.[55] General Electric was bidding on this contract because it had experience with re-entry vehicles, namely the nose cones of the ballistic missiles. In fact, with the exception of the winner, all other proposals in this competition were submitted by teams.[56] Whether this was taken into account in awarding the contract to North American cannot be determined. Being not a member of a team may have been the crucial factor, for it is probably more efficient to manage a program with only one firm instead of two responsible for direction. On the other hand, the TFX (F-111) fighter contract was awarded to a team composed of General Dynamics and Grumman rather than to Boeing.[57]

Another instance in which Douglas and General Electric bid together was on the ill-fated air-launched ballistic missile, Skybolt.[58] The team won the contract, but the Air Force decided that a team does not bid as an entity but as a prime with proposed subcontractors.[59] Since the Armed Forces always have reserved the right to reject a prime's suggested subcontractors, they invoked this right for this award. The prebid alliance was then broken up, and the prime, Douglas, had to hold an open avionics competition.[60] However, this method is not standard practice even for the Air Force, since the prevailing alliance on the global communications program, which was awarded at the same time, was not divided.

The problems posed by team bidding and the selection of sub-

[55] Walter Guzzardi, Jr., "G.E., Astride Two Worlds," *Fortune*, June 1962, p. 128.

[56] Herbert Solow, "North American, A Corporation Deeply Committed," *Fortune*, June 1962, p. 170. The teams other than General Electric-Douglas were: (1) General Dynamics and Avco; (2) Lockheed, Grumman, Space Technology Labs, and McDonnell; and (3) Hughes and Ling-Temco-Vought.

[57] There has been speculation that the Navy insisted that the contractor selected for the Navy version of the TFX must have had experience with carrier-based aircraft, that is, Grumman. *Aviation Week*, December 3, 1962, pp. 21 and 26.

[58] *Ibid.*, February 9, 1959, p. 23.

[59] *Ibid.*, July 6, 1959, pp. 26-27.

[60] *Ibid.*, July 6, 1959, p. 26. In the aftermath of this award, Douglas again recommended General Electric for the subcontract, but again the Air Force rejected General Electric. Finally, Douglas selected Northrop, with General Electric acting as second-tier subcontractor to Northrop. See *ibid.*, September 14, 1959, p. 23; November 16, 1959, p. 27; and April 25, 1960, p. 23. One might mention that Skybolt's fifth failure was blamed on the guidance system (*ibid.*, December 3, 1962, p. 29) and question if an alternative approach such as General Electric's might not have been superior.

The same development occurred in the Minuteman alliance, where Boeing had to hold an open competition for the intra-site communications subcontract.

contractors stem directly from the use of the weapon-system form of procurement. It is possible that an inappropriate choice of sub-contractors, from the government's standpoint, may result either from a prime's selection of subcontractors or from the team method of bidding.[61]

In submitting a proposal in a management competition, a prospective prime contractor may automatically associate itself with another team member which would have jurisdiction over the fields in which the prime is weak. In this case, the prime contractor is also relieved of the ultimate responsibility for the performance of the subsystems under the control of the associate contractor.[62] Alternatively, it may hold symposia to brief interested firms which are specialists in specified areas. After weighing the alternative solutions to the problems of these specialized areas, the prospective prime contractor selects and works with one firm in each of these categories. In consideration for furnishing this engineering assistance to the prospective prime, these specialized firms are listed as prospective subcontractors, should the award be made to the prime firm.[63] Since the final selection of subcontractors is subject to governmental approval, these firms are not assured of becoming subcontractors, despite the fact that it may have been their efforts that enabled the prime to get its contract.[64] In fact, after the award of a contract, the prime is often expected to hold open competitions for these subsystems.[65] At this time *all firms* capable of developing

---

[61] RCA was the prospective avionics subcontractor in the proposal that Grumman submitted for the Lunar Excursion Module (LEM). It was argued that RCA's ideas were not binding because the actual requirements of the system were not known at that time. *Ibid.*, May 6, 1963, p. 23. Perhaps a more important feature was that Sperry Rand had developed some new ideas after the management competition. *Missiles and Rockets*, January 21, 1963, p. 22. RCA was, however, chosen as the subcontractor. *Ibid.*, July 8, 1963, p. 18.

[62] For example, Hughes as an associate of Convair had the ultimate responsibility for the fire-control system of the F-106 fighter-interceptor. *Organization and Management of the Missile Program*, p. 53.

[63] *Weapons System Hearings*, pp. 204-205 and 252. Before submitting its proposed list of subcontractors for the TFX, General Dynamics held an open competition for every subsystem. *Aviation Week*, December 3, 1962, p. 26.

[64] *Weapons System Hearings*, p. 620. This condition is also applicable to the situation in which a team effort was presented.

[65] *Ibid.*, p. 207. At the same time, the weapon or system acquisition process may have had another effect on the competitive structure of the industry. With the prime contractor selecting the subcontractors, there is an inherent danger that even the limited amount of competition which now exists in the industry may be destroyed. That possibility exists if each prime contractor were continuously to select the same

the systems are invited to compete, rather than just the few originally invited by the prime contractor at the initiation of the bidding.

This approach insures that no firm will be excluded automatically from competing for any subsystem. Thus a firm which submitted a very imaginary subsystem proposal with the bid of another airplane firm would have an opportunity to obtain the contract on this proposal. This would benefit the country, for the "best" approach to the problem would be used. On the other hand, the subsystem firms might react adversely.

When an avionics firm joins a team to bid for a prime contract, it often divulges proprietary information. If a further bid is based on this information, the original firm may find that it has divulged this information needlessly and thereby provided data which permitted its competitors to obtain the contract on the second round. Thus it is possible that these firms might be less willing to cooperate with the primes in bidding for contracts and save their efforts for the second round.[66] This might, of course, result in the procuring agency selecting an approach which was not the most feasible because inadequate information was provided. On the other hand, if the procuring agency blindly accepted the team or the prime's choice of subcontractors, an approach suggested by some other firm could not be implemented necessarily, for the procuring agency could not divulge the other firm's proprietary approach.

---

subcontractor to develop subsystems in a particular area without consulting any of the other subcontractors which make similar products. Even if each prime contractor had a subcontractor with whom it always did business, no harm would be done to the subcontractors if the prime contractors were divided approximately evenly among the airframe firms. However, in such working arrangements, competition between the subcontractors may diminish with a resultant decline in technological progress. The data available to test such a hypothesis are, however, not available.

[66] Another possibility is that prime contractors unable to secure the cooperation of an avionics firm would expand their own electronics capabilities. If the electronics firms refused to cooperate, they might find their market permanently reduced. It is quite likely that they would thus continue to cooperate in formulating bids. This conclusion is reinforced by another consideration. Suppose subcontractors were forced to compete after the award of the prime contract. The prospective subcontractor will probably have conditioned the prime contractor to his approach, and unless a markedly superior approach is suggested, the subcontractor is likely to have the inner track in later competitions. Moreover, the fact that his system is part of the specifications is likely to aid this subcontractor, for he has more knowledge than any other. However, the publication of this proprietary information may destroy this competitive advantage and allow other companies to overtake it.

NASA has originated a modified form of this procurement practice which overcomes most of these difficulties. It allows team bidding but reserves the right to split coalitions and to select the team of its choice. The cooperation between the primes and the subcontractors is assured, but competition between the subcontractors is not precluded, because each subsystem is judged on its own merits.[67] This is especially true when a very strong subcontract proposal is joined with a weak prime proposal. The rejection of the prime's proposal does not handicap the subcontractor, nor does a successful subcontract proposal face double jeopardy. Thus, each firm competes at each stage of the procurement process; the procuring agencies have all the relevant information; and the proprietary interests of each firm are protected.[68]

Despite all these difficulties, teams are a part of the structure of the industry and probably will continue to retain this status. In every recent major competition there have been team proposals.[69] Moreover, in evaluating the competitive effect of these teams it should also be noted that coalitions have several times provided the medium-size avionics companies with opportunities to bid for prime contracts. Firms which are too small to obtain prime contracts because they do not have capabilities in many areas have bid together, and have been successful at least on two occasions. A team headed by Hoffman Electronics, a leading force in this movement,[70] won the competition for an electronic counter-measure reconnaissance system,[71] and one headed by Stavid won the Phase I contract for defining an antimissile system.[72] Although these coali-

---

[67] The cooperation between the prime contractor and its subcontractor is also beneficial to the subcontractors, for they learn of the total system requirements. They consequently can tailor their products to the system.

[68] *Aviation Week,* October 22, 1962. In the competition for the Apollo space suit, NASA selected a team which contained a member from each of two other teams.

[69] These include the Mercury capsule, DynaSoar, the Army Ballistic Missile Defense system, the Apollo project, Bambi, and the TFX fighter. See *ibid.,* December 22, 1958, p. 23; March 9, 1959, pp. 68-69; October 17, 1960, p. 27; October 31, 1960, p. 31; April 10, 1961, p. 34; March 29, 1962, p. 83.

[70] *Ibid.,* May 6, 1957, p. 69.

[71] *Ibid.,* February 3, 1958, p. 78. The team members other than Hoffman were Cornell Aeronautical Lab, Filtron Co., Lockheed Aircraft Services, Olympic Radio and Television, Radiation, Inc., Sanders Associates, and Stanford Research Institute.

[72] *Ibid.,* February 14, 1958, p. 12. The members were Olin-Mathieson, Bausch and Lomb, and United Shoe Machinery.

tions often placed a medium-size company in the position of competing with its customers, the smaller firms are still submitting joint proposals.[73]

What have been the competitive effects of these coalitions? Clearly, a small-firms coalition is enabled to compete with the larger prime firms for the large systems contracts. However, these coalitions have not as yet obtained a prime contract for a large system such as a missile or spacecraft. Thus, the competitive effect, if any, of these coalitions must stem from the teams of large prime contractors.

These teams are found when two firms' strengths and weaknesses complement each other. The resulting coalition enables the team to enter a strong competitive bid. Thus the successful coalition of two firms unable to obtain prime contracts separately increases the effective number of entrants in management competition. This result could have been achieved through two other means whose effects must be weighed against those of the team approach. First, the partners could have merged. Teams would be preferred to mergers if the partners were competitors in any one area, for the government would have one less source of supply in the area of competition, and no new sources in any other. A possible exception would occur if a merger produced a firm with sufficient financial strength to enter a sector of the industry avoided by the individual firms because of the risk. However, teams are formed because the firms are strong in particular areas, and have the skills and presumably the facilities associated with those sectors of the industry. A merger of two such companies is not likely to result in the expansion of many facilities. Thus coalitions must be preferred to mergers.

A second alternative to coalitions would be for each of the team members to integrate vertically by expanding capabilities in areas

---

[73] One proposal was made by eleven small firms bidding for USAF Planning Study, 7990-21 (Aerospace Surveillance). *Ibid.*, April 2, 1962, p. 67.

An interesting aspect of these coalitions at their inception was that a division of one of the larger companies would often combine with the medium-size companies. This would occur even when other divisions of the larger company were competitors of the medium-size companies. Thus, American Bosch and General Electric's Light Military Electronics Division defeated General Electric's Aircraft Production Department for one contract. See *ibid.*, May 6, 1957, pp. 76-81.

of current weakness. An airframe firm might expand into electronic activities, while the electronic firms would develop an airframe capacity. Although there might be some barriers impeding the airframe manufacturer's attempt to expand within the electronics industry, they are not insurmountable, as witnessed by the aircraft industry's successful entry into electronics. However, the excess capacity[74] of the airframe industry would probably impose restraints on the electronics firms considering entering the industry. The net result would be that the airframe firms would have expanded at the expense of the electronics firms without increasing the number of competitors for the large systems contracts for which teams are usually formed. A secondary effect might be that the electronics firms would also cease competing against the airframe firms for the smaller missile contracts. This would not produce any beneficial results. If, in addition, coalitions are viewed as a short-run phenomenon, resulting from technological change, and necessary only while firms are developing their skills, it is difficult to find economic criteria on which to base a criticism of this approach. Moreover, the NASA approach of splitting team members whenever necessary virtually guarantees that no harm can be inflicted upon the buyer by this procedure.

The weapon-system form of procurement is the primary force creating problems that have been discussed in this section. If contracts were not awarded to a prime firm which is then responsible for selecting subcontractors, none of the problems involving the relationship between the prime and its subs would exist. The governmental agencies also would not be involved, for they would award subcontracts directly without dealing through an intervening prime contractor. In addition, coalitions have developed as a consequence of the economic advantages which this system of procurement has conferred upon the prime contractor.[75]

Most large aerospace firms are anxious to become prime contractors. It is therefore appropriate to measure the benefits accruing to primes that are not available to subcontractors. Prime contrac-

---

[74] *Missiles and Rockets*, June 27, 1960, p. 14. The Defense Department noted that the plant area required in the industry dropped 50 percent between 1957 and 1960.

[75] However, the problems which the weapon-system form of procurement eliminated, such as the mating of systems, would again appear.

tors, on the average, do not obtain higher overall profit rates on their contracts than subcontractors.[76] They may, however, obtain a somewhat higher fee for the work they perform in-house than do the subcontractors for similar work. The overall fee received by a contractor is a weighted average of the fees obtained for a variety of activities.[77] The prime contractor obtains, as a management fee, a percentage of the value of the subcontracts it awards. The ratio of these fees to the value of the subcontracts is lower than the composite percentage fee obtained. Since subcontractors and primes obtain the same overall fee, it is therefore likely that prime contractors receive higher rates for in-house work than do subcontractors.

Second, prime contractors have the opportunity to pursue a course of action not open to them were they subcontractors.[78] As subcontractors they would develop and produce only the limited number of systems for which they were selected, but as prime contractors they would have the option of retaining a larger share of the contract.[79]

Third, even if prime contractors did not obtain higher fees than subcontractors for their work, and if they did not retain a larger percentage of the contracts for themselves than they would otherwise have obtained, there is still a benefit that accrues to prime contractors. The government awards these firms a management fee

---

[76] Frederick T. Moore, *Military Procurement and Contracting: An Economic Analysis*, RAND Memorandum RM 2948-PR (Santa Monica, Calif.: The RAND Corporation, June 1962), pp. 32-33.

[77] The Armed Services Procurement Regulations forbid the services from determining a profit rate on each of several individual elements of cost, but various factors such as the total effort of the contractor and the amount of subcontracting are weighed. A contractor might obtain 10 to 11 percent if the programs include no subcontracting and, according to conflicting testimony, anywhere between 3 and 6 percent if subcontracting constituted the bulk of the effort. U.S., Senate, Permanent Subcommittee on Investigations of the Committee on Government Operations, *Pyramiding of Profits and Costs in the Missile Procurement Program*, 87th Cong., 2d Sess., 1962, pp. 499, 831, 832, 835, and 841.

[78] On the other hand, subcontractors are able to diversify and work on many systems. This policy protects these firms against cancellations and cutbacks.

[79] This conclusion was reinforced by statements made at a 1962 Industry-Air Force conference. At that time, the make or buy regulations and the requirements to employ small businesses were denounced by some industry representatives. Firms wanted the right to keep more of the contract for themselves. *Aviation Week*, May 14, 1962, p. 28. Moreover, firms would also have the option of deciding which portions of the contract they would retain for themselves. For Raytheon's decisions on the Hawk missile, see *ibid.*, December 11, 1961, p. 81.

or profit which is a percentage of the total value of their subcontracted work. This fee is in addition to (1) the reimbursement for
administrative and supervisory costs incurred in managing the program, and (2) the fees associated with these expenses.[80] Fees obtained on the subcontracted portion of the contract must be considered as profits, but the rationale for their existence should be
examined.

It has been suggested by a former Assistant Secretary of the Air
Force that these fees must be given to induce the prime contractors
to subcontract a portion of their work.[81] Prime contractors have
argued that subcontracted work and material cost are the same, as
both are subject to markup,[82] or that such fees are justified because
money is often advanced to subcontractors.[83] A more reasonable
argument is that these prime firms perform a management function
for which they expect substantial compensation.[84] Douglas, as a
subcontractor to Western Electric on the Nike missiles, earned fees
amounting to $63.8 million over the life of the contracts. Of this
total, $37.3 million—more than half—were fees resulting from a
percentage of the cost of the subcontracts.[85]

It is reasonable to compensate a firm for its management activities, but it has been suggested that it should be done explicitly in
the form of a management fee rather than implicity as a percentage
of the value of the subcontracted work.[86] A reasonable estimate of
the market price of such services can be obtained, for the manage-

---

80 See *Pyramiding of Profits and Costs . . .*, Pts. 1-4. The size of the fees in relation
to the prime contractor's efforts, the procedures in negotiating these fees, and the
justification of the profits are examined in detail in these hearings.

81 U.S., Senate, Subcommittee of the Select Committee on Small Business, *Hearings, Role of Small Business in Defense Missile Procurement*, 85th Cong., 2d Sess.,
April 29-May 1, 1958, pp. 73-74.

82 U.S., House, Committee on Armed Services, Special Subcommittee on Procurement Practices of the Department of Defense, *Hearings Pursuant to Section 4, Public Law 86-89*, 86th Cong., 2d Sess., April 25-June 9, 1960, p. 240.

83 *Role of Small Business in Defense Missile Procurement*, p. 35. However, con-
tradictory evidence in *Aircraft Industry Hearings*, p. 12, indicates that this practice
has been very limited in scope.

84 *Aviation Week*, October 23, 1961, p. 89.

85 The originally negotiated fees were based on a weighted average of fees associated with various activities with the fee on the subcontracted portion substantially
lower than on the in-house work. However, in billing its prime contractor, Douglas
did not apply the separate fees to each of its bills, but instead marked up all of its
bills, regardless of source, by the composite fee.

86 *Ibid.*, June 11, 1962, p. 28.

ment companies have been performing this service for a fee averaging 10 percent of their costs.[87] In any event, the explicit compensation to the management companies has been much lower than the fee General Dynamics earned on one Atlas subcontract. The company awarded a $102 million subcontract and spent an additional $3 million to supervise and manage the contract. For this, it earned a $5.4 million fee.[88] It is, therefore, not surprising that firms are much interested in becoming prime contractors.[89]

SUMMARY AND CONCLUSIONS

It is possible to conclude that coalitions arise when firms, weak in one area, join forces with other firms, having strengths in this area, to bid for prime contracts. An examination of the competitive effects of coalitions vis-à-vis those of its alternatives enabled us to conclude that coalitions were preferable to the alternatives. Finally, the economic benefits accruing to prime contractors were investigated, with the conclusion that the prime firms gain economic advantages not realized by subcontractors.

---

[87] However, this might be an underestimate of the true market value of these services, for Thompson-Ramo-Wooldridge yielded this function to the Aerospace Corporation. However, TRW's decision may have been influenced by the knowledge that some of the prime contractors were receiving a much larger return for comparable services. In addition, the prime contractors were able to develop and manufacture systems, while TRW was excluded from this market.

[88] *Pyramiding of Profits and Costs* . . . , Pt. 3, *The Atlas Program*, p. 592. If the expenses would have been the same for the management companies as for General Dynamics, the former would have earned only $300,000 (10 percent of the $3 million expenditures).

[89] This was further illustrated on the Nike program, when the Army desired the breakout of a particular item. Western Electric, which was the prime contractor, opposed this procedure, and suggested that its fee be reduced instead to 3 percent from 6 percent. *Pyramiding of Profits and Costs* . . ., Pt. 2, *The Nike Program*, p. 477.

7.

BARRIERS TO ENTRY INTO MISSILES, SPACECRAFT, AND ROCKETS

The large electronics firms which were developing and manufacturing the critical electronic guidance-and-control systems were able to enter the aerospace industry with relative ease. However, the airframe and aircraft-engine companies faced considerable barriers in becoming missile, spacecraft, and rocket-engine producers.

Before proceeding to a consideration of the magnitude of these entry barriers, it is important to note that these conditions of entry cannot be analyzed in the usual manner. In the typical industry, the advantage an established firm holds over a potential competitor may be measured by the extent to which the former can raise prices above average costs without inducing entry.[1] There is no price competition in this industry. Consequently, this generally operational measure is not applicable. In this industry, with its emphasis on cost-plus contracts, entry is based not on the price of a product, but on a firm's ability to develop and produce a new product, that is, its technical skills and scientific know-how. Moreover, one must distinguish clearly between the two possible ways of entry.

Since the use of cost-plus contracts eliminates the scale barriers that may exist otherwise, firms may enter at a very small scale. This usually occurs at the subsystem or even component level where a new company enters as a producer of specialized products. The only requirement is that the firm convince some procuring agency that

---

[1] Joe S. Bain, *Industrial Organization* (New York: John Wiley, 1959), p. 237. See also Bain's *Barriers to New Competition* (Cambridge: Harvard University Press, 1956), p. 4.

it has a "better mouse-trap." If this new idea has merit and some promise of future application, it is usually supported, and the firm is in the industry.[2] Entry at a small scale must thus be considered "easy." The main barrier to be overcome with this scale of entry is meeting potential buyers and convincing them of the quality of the product.

Entry as a prime systems contractor is a different matter. Here, a potential entrant competes with established firms for the large systems contracts. Since price differentials are not likely to be an important consideration in the government's choice of contractor, the technical skills of the firm are fundamental. Thus, the advantages of an established firm over a potential entrant could be measured by the latter's cost of acquiring the technical skills necessary to compete for new contracts. This barrier is likely to be substantial.

The Entry of Aircraft Companies into Missiles

One of the interesting findings concerning this industry is the ease with which firms made the transition from the manufacture of airplanes to the production of missiles. All missile and satellite space frames have been manufactured by former aircraft manufacturers, but not all these companies entered this new area with the same degree of ease. It was noted previously that the electronics firms became prime contractors for the smaller air-to-air missiles in the mid-fifties when the missile program was expanded. However, the bulk of early research and development work on missiles was performed by the aviation companies.[3] Convair had a 1946 study contract for a missile which eventually evolved into the Atlas. Douglas' work on the Ajax antiaircraft missile,[4] WAC Corporal rocket, and Aerobee sounding rockets all started at about this time.[5]

---

[2] If the government's budget were reduced the conditions of entry might be more difficult.

[3] *Aviation Week*, September 16, 1957, p. 21.

[4] U.S., Senate, Permanent Subcommittee on Investigations of the Committee on Government Operations, *Pyramiding of Profits and Costs in the Missile Procurement Program*, Pt. 1, *The Nike Program*, pp. 14 and 21. The Nike evolved from the M-33 anti-aircraft system which used a high explosive shell rather than a guided missile. Moreover, the prime contract for this system was awarded to Western Electric, which selected Douglas in the late 1940's to do the research and development on the airframe, which was to carry Western Electric's guidance package. *Ibid.*, pp. 15 and 21.

[5] David C. Cooke and Martin Caidin, *Jets, Rockets and Guided Missiles* (New York: McBride Co., 1951) pp. 133-135; Kenneth W. Gattland, *Development of the Guided Missile*, 2d ed. (New York: Philosophical Library, 1954), p. 177. It should be noted that Aerojet was also working on the Aerobee Rocket.

The Martin Company's Viking rocket was the result of interest in performing further experiments after all the captured German V-2 rockets had been utilized. Rather than build the new rockets in the same configuration as the V-2's, Martin in the late forties was selected to redesign the rocket.[6] Boeing began working on the BOMARC antiaircraft missile in 1951,[7] and North American received the Navaho and Northrop the Snark contracts in the forties.[8] Of course other projects can be cited, but these are sufficient to indicate the extent to which the aircraft firms had entered the missile sector of the industry at an early stage of its development.

It is necessary to note that a few other companies—not aircraft manufacturers—were beginning to do some work on missiles. General Electric began a study in March, 1946, on a short-range collision interceptor weapon.[9] This later evolved into the Thumper Program, an antimissile system to cope with weapons like the V-2. Similarly, General Electric started working on the Hermes missile in November, 1944. The project was originally intended to develop a rocket-powered missile which would be similar to the German antiaircraft rockets, but different missiles were developed as the program advanced.[10]

The purpose of our discussion was not to chronicle the historical progress of our missile program, but to demonstrate that firms in the aircraft industry had attained a position in the missile program at an early stage of its evolution. Nevertheless, the industry was not completely enthusiastic about these developments, and the Air Force was forced to stimulate interest in the guided-missile program.[11]

---

[6] Gattland, *op. cit.*, p. 180.

[7] *Pyramiding of Profits and Costs . . .*, Pt. 4, *The* BOMARC *Program*, p. 782.

[8] In North American's *1955 Annual Report*, p. 20, a note indicates that the company had received a contract in 1945 for the development of a missile weapon system. This system was later identified as the Navaho.

[9] *Pyramiding of Profits and Costs . . .*, Pt. 4, *The* BOMARC *Program*, p. 782.

[10] *Aviation Week*, March 8, 1954, p. 26.

[11] One utilized technique was to call the Matador, one of this country's first operational missiles, "a pilotless aircraft." Martin Caidin, *Rockets and Missiles, Past and Future* (New York: McBride Co., 1954), p. 162. The Matador was also unique because this was one of the first procurement actions in which specifications were not issued at the time of the contract. The company could experiment to determine the optimum configuration. Moreover, Martin ostensibly went into avionics at this time because it felt that the avionics industry was not inclined to undertake the research and development of missile guidance systems which were to be produced only in limited quantities. *Ibid.*, pp. 163-164.

Further evidence about this lack of enthusiasm for missile work is the refusal of some aircraft manufacturers to undertake missile study contracts.[12] The rationale for these refusals was that the firms, uncertain about the possibility of ultimate production, did not want to commit their skilled manpower to these contracts.[13] The traditional attitude was that research and development contracts were merely the foot in the door for higher-profit production contracts.

This attitude should be examined in more detail to determine the reasons for the firm's behavior. A concern might refuse a profitable missile study contract if the resources which would be applied to this project could be used more profitably elsewhere. It was shown in Chapter 1 that with the curtailment of war production, facilities were in excess supply. This, therefore, could not have been the limiting factor.[14]

However, a shortage of skilled scientific personnel would be the crucial variable. An engineer, for instance, could be employed either on a low-profit-rate missile study from which no future production was expected or on a higher-profit-rate production project. If engineers were in short supply, they would naturally be employed on the latter project. This analysis holds only if the firm could not easily obtain more engineers so that both projects could be staffed. However, available evidence does not indicate a shortage of aeronautical engineers in the immediate postwar period.

Despite forecasts that serious shortages of skilled scientific personnel would prevail in the postwar period,[15] the aircraft companies, at least, did not experience them. A shortage of or excess demand for engineers presumably would be reflected in the number of advertisements of job openings appearing in the newspapers.[16] This would be particularly true if the ads appeared in a

---

12 Merton J. Peck and F. M. Scherer, *The Weapons Acquisition Process: An Economic Analysis* (Cambridge: Harvard University Press, Division of Research, 1962), p. 408. Even in the 1950's it was necessary to sell contractors on the desirability of developing a complex missile system. *Pyramiding of Profits and Costs . . .* , Pt. 4, *The* BOMARC *Program,* p. 782.

13 Peck and Scherer, *op. cit.,* p. 408.

14 However, the companies may have felt that additional and different types of facilities would be required, and they were not willing to invest their capital in such risky ventures.

15 *The New York Times,* October 6, 1946, p. F-1.

16 The idea for using this measure came from Erik Lundberg, "Business Cycle Experiences in Sweden with Special Reference to Economic Policy Issue," in Erik

newspaper distant from the source of the job. Thus, when California aircraft firms advertise in *The New York Times,* it could be argued that the number of engineers available in California is insufficient to meet the demand.

In 1957, the number of square inches of advertising space bought by the California aircraft companies in *The New York Times* Sunday edition fluctuated between 447 square inches and zero.[17]

TABLE 30

CALIFORNIA-BASED AIRCRAFT COMPANIES' ADVERTISEMENTS FOR ENGINEERS
IN *The New York Times,* 1957

Month	Square inches[a]
January	403
February	447
March	412
April	336
May	199
June	137
July	138
August	184
September	18
October	0
November	28
December	54

[a] Samples of Sunday editions.

These figures provide reference points. One would expect the advertisements for aeronautical and avionics engineers to fluctuate widely because the level of activity within the industry varied considerably in 1957. The peak was hit in March followed by cutbacks, cancellations, and stretchouts in the summer and fall months. The demand for engineers, as reflected in the advertisements in *The New York Times,* closely paralleled the fluctuations in production.

The purpose of this discussion was to point out that changes in the demand for engineers are reflected in the number of advertisements. In the last quarter of 1962, the activity of the aerospace industry was again at a high level with a consequent increased need

Lundberg, ed., *The Business Cycle in the Post-War World,* Proceedings of a Conference held by the International Economic Association (New York: St. Martin's Press, 1955), p. 58.

[17] The number of square inches was based on a sample of the *Times'* Sunday issues, with the figures calculated for the first Sunday in every month. The measurements were based on the total amount of advertising appearing in the classified, financial, and sport sections of the paper.

for engineers. In this period the California companies bought no less than 116 and as much as 360 square inches of advertising space in the Sunday *Times*. However, in 1946, 1947, and 1948, the period in which we are primarily interested, the space bought in the Sunday *Times* by these manufacturers was virtually nil. In the issues sampled, there were no ads in either 1946 or 1947. About half of the 1948 issues had ads, but eight square inches was the maximum amount. These data would seem to indicate that there was no serious shortage of scientific personnel.[18]

There may have been other compelling reasons why firms did not hire more engineers in order to accept the study contracts. They may have expected that a study contract would be short-lived. Costs would be incurred to hire the new engineers who would be laid off at the contract termination. A firm would not want to expand its working force to obtain a temporary contract if these expenses were not reimbursable. Alternatively, a firm might act in the same manner even if costs were reimbursable, if they were raised above that of its competitors. Hiring expenses, however, are reimbursable costs for government contracts. There is some evidence indicating that firms are worried about the overhead rates, but there is no evidence that study contracts were refused for this reason.[19] On the other

---

[18] This conclusion is corroborated by I. Hirsh, W. Milwitt, W. J. Oakes, and R. A. Pelton, "Relation of Utilization to the Shortage of Scientists," *IRE Transactions on Engineering Management*, Vol. EM-5, No. 3 (September 1958), pp. 73 ff. They quote surveys which indicate that there was a surplus of engineers in the immediate postwar period. There is one qualification which weakens the conclusions reached from this survey of the employment ads of *The New York Times*. It is possible that the California firms at that time might not have considered *The New York Times* a suitable medium for employment ads. Even in the war these companies did not advertise in this paper over their own names. Instead, their jobs were advertised through the U. S. Department of Labor. (See *The New York Times*, August 10, 1941, and September 7, 1941.) It is possible that with workers frozen to their jobs in wartime, companies realized the futility of attracting distant sources of labor. If the magnitude of the ads is any indication, the demand for labor of even the eastern aircraft companies was unsatisfied during the war. However, the California shipyards and McDonnell aircraft considered the *Times* a proper medium. Moreover, many aircraft companies used unsigned ads merely indicating that travel was required. These might have been the California companies. In any event, there was a distinct postwar decline in *all* advertising in the *Times* for aircraft engineers, designers, and so on. Thus, it is not likely that our conclusions are invalid.

[19] Another possibility, which cannot be verified, is that companies refused the smaller study contracts because they feared that they would become ineligible for the larger production contracts at a time when awards were being spread among the firms in the industries. As previously indicated, the Air Force desired to protect the position of the aviation firms.

hand, previous ICBM projects had been canceled and neither the government nor its scientific advisors were confident that an ICBM could be developed successfully.[20] This may have been the main reason for the firms' unwillingness to accept missile projects. However, the real reason for this reluctance cannot be discovered without examining each company's files.

The development of the hydrogen bomb and the emphasis on missiles induced the airplane firms to accept missile contracts sooner or later. There is some difference in the technology of the two segments of the industry, yet the airplane manufacturers had the technical experience and facilities necessary to become missile producers. The technology differs in that the manufacturing process for missiles is characterized by the fabrication of a few relatively large parts, such as the fuel tank which comprises most of the airframe structure of a ballistic missile, whereas an airplane is composed of many small parts.[21] With the exception of some necessary renovations, the existing airplane plants were suitable for missile production. The high bay areas, required for the tail sections of airplanes, were not used, and air conditioning and dust-free areas had to be added.[22] With the Air Force reversing its policy of providing the industry with production facilities, large expenditures for new missile-producing plants were required of the aerospace firms. Martin's Denver and Convair's San Diego plants were both built with company funds. Each cost approximately $25 million.[23]

THE ENTRY OF AIRCRAFT COMPANIES INTO SPACECRAFT

Many former aircraft companies are also participating in the space program. The frames for the new space rockets are similar,

---

[20] U.S., House, Subcommittee of the Committee on Government Operations, *Hearings, Organization and Management of Missile Programs*, 86th Cong., 1st Sess., February 4-March 20, 1959, pp. 5 and 18.

[21] *Aviation Week*, September 1, 1958, pp. 41-42. In addition, the quality-control standards are much higher and more crucial in a missile and spacecraft than in an aircraft. *The New York Times*, Western Edition, October 4, 1963, pp. 1 and 7 and *Aviation Week*, June 17, 1957, p. 70.

[22] *Aviation Week*, April 29, 1957, p. 28. In fact the space capsules can also be built in the former aircraft plants. For instance, the Apollo is fabricated in the same area in which the BT-13 trainer had been assembled during World War I. The difference is that the trainer was mass produced, while the capsule is hand tooled to exacting tolerances. *The New York Times*, Western Edition, October 10, 1963, p. 7.

[23] U.S., House, Subcommittee of the Committee on Appropriations, *Hearings, Department of Defense Appropriations, 1963*, 87th Cong., 2d Sess., p. 577.

with some exceptions,[24] to the boosters for missiles. Consequently, it is not surprising to find the former airframe companies manufacturing the Saturn, Centaur, and Agena rockets. Moreover, as previously noted, the frames for all satellites and spacecraft have been fabricated by these same companies. This is true regardless of the type of company which holds the prime contract.

It was also observed that the Air Force had divided its prime missile contracts between the airframe and electronics firms, with the latter obtaining the smaller missiles in which the electronics components were the critical items. The airframe firms, in turn, received the larger ballistic missile contracts. A similar development has occurred in the space program, for NASA has awarded all manned-capsule contracts to the aircraft companies.[25] Both NASA and the Air Force have awarded the unmanned satellite contracts to the electronics companies or to the electronics divisions of the airframe companies.[26] These satellites are primarily electronic systems housed within a space frame, and it was natural to award such contracts to the electronics companies. With the expansion of our space program, several companies, such as General Electric and RCA, re-entered the industry which they had left because of the loss of missile contracts.[27] In addition, some other electronics firms were new entrants to the industry. In 1960, eleven companies had prime contracts for spacecraft or satellites, with the number increasing to seventeen by the end of 1963. In 1960, only three of these companies were not involved in missile or aircraft production; in 1963 this number was six.

Since missile- and space-frame contracts have been awarded

---

24 Cyrogenic fuels and clustered engines were not used in the missile program.

25 NASA has announced three manned space programs, requiring four capsules. McDonnell was awarded the contracts for the Mercury and Gemini capsule. North American has the prime contract for one of the modules of the Apollo program and Grumman has another. Similarly, the Air Force awarded its DynaSoar system to Boeing. This too is designed to be a manned spacecraft.

26 The contracts for three military satellites, Discoverer, Midas, and Samos, had been awarded to Lockheed's Electronics Division. An exception was NASA's award of OSO to Grumman. Moreover, the advanced version of the OSO satellite was awarded to Republic Aviation. The prime contract for the earlier version of this satellite was held by an electronics firm.

27 One final point to consider is that re-entry vehicles such as nose cones have been developed by firms which previously were not in the industry. The two major contractors in this segment have been Avco and General Electric. Neither had any prime missile contracts but they became associate prime contractors for these re-entry vehicles.

only to former airframe manufacturers, a necessary but not suffi-cient condition for obtaining such contracts was expertise in the production of aircraft. This implies that the skills obtained in the former sector may be applied in the newer areas. An additional re-quirement for obtaining the prime missile contracts was a strong electronics capability. It is true that one can attribute to the elec-tronics weaknesses of some airplane companies their inability to attract missile and space contracts; yet other requirements also had to be met before such contracts could be obtained. These factors must be considered part of the barriers to entering this industry.

The minimum requirements for successful entry can thus be de-termined from an analysis of the behavior of late entrants into the industry. Grumman was one such company, for it experienced difficulties in obtaining missile and space contracts,[28] until it re-ceived the Lunar Excursion Module (LEM) contract for the Apollo project in November, 1962.

In order to understand these additional entry requirements, we might analyze Grumman's problems. It had received only one con-tract for any space activity, the Orbiting Astronomical Observatory Satellite (OAO).[29] The LEM contract is for the craft which will take the astronauts to the moon and back from the Apollo module, which will be placed in the moon orbit. This contract was the cul-mination of the company's efforts to obtain a spot in the lunar pro-gram. Grumman had spent $2 million of its own funds for the necessary research and for the preparation of proposals.[30] In addi-tion, in 1962 the company was building a $5 million space center, thus completing a $12 million four-year program for additional re-search facilities.[31] Included in these facilities were an environ-mental testing area and an electronics system center. During this expansion program the company built a high-vacuum environ-mental chamber, obtained a centrifuge for the OAO project, and opened a stabilization facility also needed for the OAO.[32]

---

[28] It had left the missile field on its own accord, but by 1957 was attempting to re-enter the field. It made proposals and worked on several teams, but to no avail, and in 1960 it was one of the few airplane companies which still had not received prime missile or space contracts. *Aviation Week*, January 21, 1957, p. 23.

[29] *Missiles and Rockets*, November 12, 1962, p. 46.

[30] *Aviation Week*, October 8, 1962, p. 68; *Missiles and Rockets*, November 12, 1962, p. 12.

[31] *Ibid.*, September 24, 1962, p. 49.

[32] *Ibid.*, December 10, 1962, pp. 30-31.

It seems obvious that airplanes on one hand and satellites and spacecraft on the other both contain systems housed within air or space frames. Yet the research, developing and testing, and manufacturing processes of the two types of systems are distinctly different. Entry into the satellite and spacecraft segment of the industry requires the construction of new facilities to enable completion of the required research. Since the governmental agencies no longer provide funds for these facilities, those laboratories must be financed privately. In addition, the technological knowledge required at the time of contract competition must be readily available, for it is impossible to obtain this knowledge within the time allotted for the preparation of technical proposals.[33] The minimum expense necessary to enter this sector of the industry can then be estimated. Entry into the space program cost Grumman a minimum of $14 million, composed of the $12 million for facilities and the $2 million spent for research and the preparation of the proposals. Other data indicate that this figure may be an estimate only of the minimum expenditures necessary to attract space contracts.

By the end of 1963, there were to be twelve operational space-chamber facilities in the United States. Three were at NASA laboratories with another at the Jet Propulsion Laboratory which is closely associated with NASA.[34] The cost of a complete NASA Laboratory for testing and evaluation was approximately $15 million.[35] The costs for aerospace firms having such aerospace labs start at this minimum level and in some cases are considerably higher.[36]

Republic spent $13 to $14 million on facilities alone.[37] Moreover, the company announced in 1959 that to broaden its space and

---

[33] *Ibid.*, March 25, 1963, p. 63. It was stated that the lead time required for bidding on a proposal has risen by a factor of 3 or 4. This is attributable to the pace of technological developments which require more research.

[34] *Ibid.*, May 20, 1963, p. 59.

[35] *Ibid.*, January 15, 1962, pp. 26-27.

[36] The difference in costs may reflect the number and types of testing facilities included within the laboratories. Some firms may have included the smallest number of facilities in the laboratories consistent with attaining a space-age capability. There are no easily accessible data indicating the extent of the differences among the various space centers. The only data available indicate that STL's complex, which cost $30 million, also includes manufacturing facilities designed for the assembly, integration, and testing of spacecraft. *The New York Times,* Western Edition, October 23, 1963, p. 11.

[37] *Missiles and Rockets*, March 21, 1960, p. 14; and May 8, 1961, p. 40; *Aviation Week,* January 21, 1963, p. 13.

missile activities it was undertaking a four-year research and de-velopment program estimated to cost $35 million.[38] General Elec-tric had originally contemplated a $14 million space technology center,[39] but the final cost of its Valley Forge laboratory was $45 million, to which the government contributed $6 million.[40] Space Technology Laboratories, a division of Thompson-Ramo-Woold-ridge, long active as the Air Force's system manager for the develop-ment of our ballistic missiles, embarked upon the construction of a $30 million space technology center.[41] This facility was necessary when the company yielded its status as a management company for the Air Force and started competing for space contracts. McDon-nell, which already had attained a prominent position in the space age with its Mercury and Gemini capsules, nevertheless started building a $21 million space center.[42] There have been predictions that the cost of space facilities may ultimately reach $100 million.[43]

Some data would indicate that entry might be possible at a some-what lower cost. Douglas, which had already established itself in the missile industry and had contracts for the S-IV and S-IVB stages of the Saturn booster, began construction of a $2 million lab for advanced research in aircraft, missiles, and space systems. This lab was to occupy only 10 acres in the 245-acre area available for Douglas' Space Systems Center.[44] Thus the ultimate cost to Douglas was likely to be many times $2 million. North American Aviation planned a $10 million aerospace laboratory which included an acoustical facility and an environmental test chamber.[45] North American also built a 110,000 square foot science center costing $6

38 *Ibid.*, June 29, 1959, p. 47.

39 *Space Aeronautics*, July 1960, p. 265.

40 Walter Guzzardi, Jr. "G.E., Astride Two Worlds," *Fortune*, June 1962, p. 258; U.S., House, Subcommittee on Manned Space Flight of the Committee on Science and Astronautics, *Hearings, 1963 NASA Authorization*, Pt. 2, 87th Cong., 2d Sess., March 6-April 10, 1962, p. 441.

41 *Missiles and Rockets*, November 6, 1961, p. 39, and March 19, 1962, pp. 28 ff.

42 *Ibid.*, August 27, 1962, p. 38.

43 *Ibid.*, May 20, 1963, pp. 21-22. Boeing's research and development center re-quired an *initial* expenditure of $15 million. Additional facilities were expected to be added in the future. *The Wall Street Journal*, February 5, 1964, p. 24.

44 *Missiles and Rockets*, December 24, 1962, p. 37; *The Wall Street Journal*, Decem-ber 12, 1962. Another source indicates that the final cost of Douglas' space-systems center will approach $75 million. *The New York Times*, Western Edition, November 14, 1963, p. 11.

45 *Missiles and Rockets*, March 13, 1961, p. 43.

million.[46] It is not certain whether this is part of the mentioned facility or an addition to it. If it is an addition, North American's investment is in the neighborhood of $16 million, an investment comparable to that of other firms.

These are estimates of the cost of the facilities required for successful entry as a prime contractor. The cost to subsystem manufacturers which specialize in a particular area or to prime manufacturers who want to establish only electronics capability is much lower. In limiting themselves in this manner the firms would probably forego many prime space contracts. The cost of constructing even such limited facilities may run as high as $5 million.[47]

These data yield estimates only of the cost of facilities and scientific equipment. Since an effective research program is a fundamental requirement for entry into the space program, the amount of company-funded research required to demonstrate this technical competence also must be included in any overall estimate of the cost of entry. It is difficult to obtain estimates of the magnitude of these company-financed research programs, but some qualitative observations are available.

Among such data is Ling-Temco-Vought's announcement of their projected $10.5 to $13 million expenditure for company-sponsored research and development.[48] Republic Aviation stated that in the ten years before 1963 it had spent $25 million on research and development, exclusive of any funds committed to its space research center.[49] It had spent $3 million for personnel and equipment for research on the pinch plasma engine, for which it had a $2 million contract.[50] Similarly, it had a $100,000 study contract for a second generation Orbiting Solar Observatory (OSO) and had committed half a million dollars to the project.[51]

---

46 *Ibid.*, March 18, 1963, p. 39.

47 This is the sum that Minneapolis-Honeywell expended in establishing an Aeronautic Division Research Center. See *ibid.*, July 2, 1962, p. 32; and May 8, 1961, p. 46. There is at least one piece of evidence indicating that a company may obtain a prime space contract without having all mentioned in-house facilities. Fairchild's Stratos satellite was tested at the General Electric space facility because the former company did not have laboratories. *Ibid.*, February 17, 1964, pp. 22-23.

48 *Ibid.*, April 9, 1962, p. 37.

49 *Aviation Week,* January 21, 1963, p. 113.

50 *Ibid.*

51 *Ibid.* Similarly, it spent $750,000 on Apollo studies, but received only the Project Fire re-entry vehicle contract. (This contract is intended to study the Apollo re-entry environment by measuring the heat effect of re-entry at high speeds. *Ibid.*, December

Another qualitative estimate of the effort necessary to attain technical competence can be gained by analyzing the struggles of Boeing before it obtained the contract for the SIC stage of the Saturn booster. According to industry observers it took Boeing three years to attain this capability.[52] Since Boeing was developing the Minuteman missile for the Air Force, it was felt that booster development was a logical area for expansion. In early 1959 it bid unsuccessfully for NASA's Scout booster. After this loss, Boeing "studied." It prepared preliminary design studies. However, when the Defense Department and NASA decided to use liquid hydrogen upper stages for rockets, Boeing was hurt. It obviously had not prepared for this contingency and had no experience in cyrogenic fuels. Despite a hasty effort to develop techniques for handling cyrogenic fuel problems, Boeing failed even to obtain study contracts. The company's entry into this sector of the industry stems from its successful proposal that NASA finance a study of the problems of the clustering of large-scale solid rocket boosters. This contract enabled the company in 1962 to obtain the SIC assembly contract, for that stage consists of a cluster of rocket engines.[53] It is obviously impossible, without company data, to make an estimate of the magnitude of Boeing's research costs, but they probably represent a sizable investment by the company.

All data indicate that a substantial research and development effort is required to attain the technical competence which is rewarded with a contract. All cost estimates presented so far have been the entry costs for firms with the technical knowledge associated with aircraft production. The cost of similar research programs is higher for firms not already in the aircraft industry than for firms which are. The barriers to entry may thus be substantial. In addition, existing firms have a definite advantage, for they have been allowed to include a considerable portion of these company-funded research expenses in indirect costs. Every firm includes such expenses in its overhead burden, yet the advantage accruing to firms already in the industry is that these expenses are allocable to gov-

---

17, 1962, p. 53). This is one of the few nonspacecraft re-entry vehicles not developed by either General Electric or Avco. Recently Chrysler also was awarded a contract for a nonspacecraft re-entry vehicle.

52 *Missiles and Rockets,* April 30, 1962, pp. 26-27.

53 However, the engines use a liquid fuel.

ernment cost and incentive-type contracts.[54] The government thus reimburses these firms for research costs, whereas firms without government contracts have to bear the burden themselves.[55] The Air Force and several of its contractors agreed to cost-sharing formulas which were applied to each company's funded research. The share paid by the government varied between 40 and 70 percent, depending upon the company and program.[56]

Predictably, the number of internally funded research projects increased as companies began to realize that their future depended in part on their ability to originate ideas which were salable to the government.[57] A second aspect of these self-sponsored research efforts is that companies are better prepared to enter management competitions, with the contracting agencies thus obtaining more data on which to judge the competing proposals. Both factors portend an increase in the technological progressiveness of firms in the industry.

General Dynamics expanded its research for the first reason. In 1962, after failing to obtain space contracts for which bids were submitted, its management announced that the funds to be allocated to the research and development activities of its Astronautics Division would be doubled.[58] There are other examples of com-

---

54 *Aviation Week,* February 22, 1960, p. 29.

55 However, company-initiated development programs ceased to be fully allowable items of expense. In the past the government allowed companies to allocate their development but not their research expenses for a reimbursement proposal. This may have been appropriate when companies brought prototypes to the government, and the government wanted to reimburse the contractors for this expense. In this situation, the development costs were indirect costs but fully reimbursable, and thus they were financed directly with defense funds. The government, however, had no control over the direction of the company's efforts and usually did not even get the patent rights. Now, however, the important task of the industry is to attempt to solve the difficult problems associated with missile and space research. Research expenses should be treated as a cost to the company for, in a rapidly changing technological situation, the firm must keep abreast of these developments just to stay in business. With this in mind the Armed Services decided that it would be appropriate to share the cost of company-initiated research and reduce their support of company-initiated development programs.

56 *Aviation Week,* May 16, 1960, p. 23. Thiokol noted that 60 percent of its 1962 funded research expenses were reimbursable for cost-type contracts. *The Wall Street Journal,* January 28, 1963.

57 This is one reason for allowing part of the funding to be private costs, for if the research is successful the company will profit by obtaining a contract. This should be considered a necessary cost of staying in business.

58 *Missiles and Rockets,* October 22, 1962, p. 39.

panies expanding their internally financed research and development activities for similar, though not as urgent, reasons. For instance, Air Research worked on integrated power supply and environmental control systems for spacecraft.[59] Minneapolis-Honeywell expanded its work in microelectronics;[60] Douglas worked on recovering multi-engine boosters;[61] Boeing conducted studies on an antisatellite weapon system; and Goodyear invested its own funds in studying a thirty-foot experimental inflatable space station.[62] These are samples of the type of work aerospace companies began investigating with their own funds.

Evidence of the second reason for financing research activity also exists. After NASA had awarded North American Aviation a study contract for a space station, Boeing, Lockheed, Martin, and General Dynamics all started intensive company-funded studies to be ready for the upcoming competition.[63] With such research efforts, the ensuing research and development contracts do not go automatically to the firm holding the study contracts. North American won the Apollo competition even though study grants defining the problems had been awarded to General Electric, Martin, and General Dynamics.[64]

Another factor which increased research activity was the realization that the economic potential of a system might be larger than the dollar magnitude of the original contract. This difference stems from the fact that the function of a developed system might be expanded. Consequently, a larger number of items might be procured than was originally contemplated. This possibility of "growth" has become more pronounced since the advent of the period in which the cost of research and development has risen so rapidly. In many cases it is probably cheaper to modify an existing system than to develop a new one designed specifically to complete a given assignment. This possibility of modifying and expanding

---

[59] *Aviation Week*, November 7, 1960, p. 62.
[60] *Ibid.*, February 27, 1961, p. 69.
[61] *Ibid.*, May 28, 1962, p. 23.
[62] *Ibid.*, June 25, 1962, p. 26, and August 20, 1962, p. 99; development of the space station is likely to be the next large space program upon completion of the lunar project.
[63] *Ibid.*, November 12, 1962, p. 57.
[64] *Ibid.*, October 31, 1960, p. 31.

developed systems naturally places a premium on firms obtaining the first contract. The rivals thus are encouraged to undertake increased in-house research activity in order to be prepared for the management competitions.[65]

It is difficult to generalize about the level of the entry barriers prevailing in this segment of the industry, for two opposing trends are observed. First, entry barriers seem to be low, for the electronic firms easily entered the industry and obtained a position in both missiles and satellites. On the other hand, these firms were all established companies and prominent in commercial electronics. Moreover, most of these companies had held electronic subsystem contracts before their entry into the industry.[66]

In addition, entry into the frame-fabrication sector of the industry cannot be considered easy. Before 1956 the Air Force provided much of the industry's facilities and, according to some observers, sought to protect the position of the existing firms. New firms were thus effectively blocked from entering because they were unlikely to receive contracts from the government. No new airframe firms entered after Temco's entry in 1946. The government no longer has an overt policy of protecting the industry, but the magnitude of the costs required for entry into the space program can be measured from the immense expenditures required even of existing firms. The cost of a minimum-size space laboratory begins at $14 million. In addition, the immensity of research and development expenditures would also preclude a firm's entry as a prime contractor.

---

[65] Many examples of systems whose "growth" was considered can be cited. Among the possibilities considered for expanding the Titan III were the use of new upper stages or propellants; the uprating of the rocket engines; the reduction of weight; and increasing the length of the Titan II stage. *Missiles and Rockets*, February 17, 1964, p. 9. The possibility of using the Apollo module for other than manned lunar expeditions has also been considered. *Aviation Week*, February 24, 1964, p. 23, and *Missiles and Rockets*, July 8, 1963, p. 9. For other examples concerning the Atlas, Titan II, and Minuteman missiles, see *Aviation Week*, July 15, 1963, p. 35; November 11, 1963, p. 23; February 10, 1964, p. 19; and March 2, 1964, p. 25. Also, *Missiles and Rockets*, July 1, 1963, p. 7, and July 22, 1963, p. 9.

[66] It is difficult to determine precisely what the entry costs would be for a new electronics firm, but one suspects that they probably would be high enough to prevent entry as a prime system contractor. This, of course, would not prevent firms from entering the industry as subcontractors which manufacture specialized subsystems.

Entry into Rocket Work

The aircraft manufacturers participated in missile work at a very early stage in the latter's development, but the aircraft-engine producers and firms engaged in rocket research and development did not. In the period immediately before the Air Force's shift in emphasis toward missiles, there were between eleven and fifteen manufacturers of airplane engines.[67] It is now known that of these firms only General Electric was also active in the manufacture of rocket engines, and this company did not retain its foothold in the industry. In 1950, the four leading companies engaged in the manufacture of aircraft engines were Curtiss-Wright, General Electric, General Motors, and United Aircraft.[68] Although in 1957 Continental Motors replaced General Electric on the list of the four largest manufacturers of military engines, our analysis will focus on these firms for they continued to be among the largest shippers of military engines up to 1957.[69]

It is not unreasonable for engine manufacturers, especially the producers of jet engines, to become producers of rockets, because

---

67 *Aviation Week,* March 2, 1953, pp. 230 and 234; March 14, 1955, pp. 234-240, and April 1, 1957, p. 26.

68 Federal Trade Commission, *Report on Industrial Concentration and Product Diversification in the 1,000 Largest Manufacturing Companies; 1950,* 1957, p. 247. They accounted for 54 percent of the Census Industry's (3722) Employment. *Report of the Federal Trade Commission on Changes in Concentration in Manufacturing, 1935 to 1947 and 1950,* 1954, p. 146. By consulting trade journals it was possible to derive an estimate of the concentration ratio of military-engine sales accounted for by these four firms. According to *Aerospace Facts and Figures, 1962* (New York: McGraw-Hill, 1962), p. 94, 9,361 military-aircraft engines were delivered in 1950. The manufacturers of the various engines were identified and each company's percentage of sales was computed. One difficulty arose because the firms which produced the T-33 and O-190 engines could not be identified. The total sales of these engines was 725, but these sales are nevertheless included in total sales; the identified engine sales of each firm were expressed as a percentage of this figure. The percentages are probably understated, but this rough estimate indicated that General Electric had 29.5 percent of the sales, General Motors 24.3, United Aircraft 21.1 and Curtiss-Wright 9.7. The concentration ratio of these four firms was 84.6 percent. The firms accounted for 91.8 percent of the deliveries of engines whose manufacturers were known.

69 The manufacturers of all military-aircraft engines delivered in 1953 and 1957 could be identified. The percentage of the 1953 sales accruing to each company was General Electric 36.2, Curtiss-Wright 23.2, United Aircraft 19.8, and General Motors 14.2—total 93.4. In 1957 the percentages were United Aircraft 53.7, Curtiss-Wright 21.5, General Motors, 9.1, and Continental Motors 6.2. General Electric, the fifth firm, accounted for 2.9 percent.

the operating principles of jets and rockets are similar. In fact, jet propulsion has been defined to include the operation both of the conventional jet and of the rocket. In principle, jet propulsion is "a means of locomotion whereby a reaction is imparted to a device by the momentum of ejected matter." In rocket propulsion the ejected matter is stored within the device, while in duct propulsion "the surrounding fluid is ducted through the device and accelerated to a greater momentum by mechanical or thermal means prior to ejection."[70] The rocket is considered the simplest form of the jet engine.[71] However, the production of a liquid-propellant rocket engine requires some of the most advanced engineering techniques and materials.[72]

Despite the similarity in technology, why were these companies not actively engaged in rocket research? One possible explanation is that they did not foresee the decline of aircraft and the expansion of missiles.[73] If published statements are any indication of a management's thoughts, Curtiss-Wright did not begin to worry seriously about the possible decline of aircraft until the end of 1957.[74] United Aircraft's *Annual Report for 1957* indicated that the company realized the development of a major shift in defense.[75] However, the company concluded "that the missile will not displace manned aircraft in the foreseeable future, and most probably never will do so."[76] Since a small market for missiles was forecast, these firms were naturally hesitant to make a large commitment in this field. Despite these optimistic predictions about aircraft needs, by

[70] George P. Sutton, *Rocket Propulsion Elements* (New York: John Wiley, 1956), pp 1-14, *passim*.

[71] Cooke and Caidin, *Jets, Rockets and Guided Missiles*, pp. 172-174. Moreover, representatives of the Pratt and Whitney Division of United Aircraft, which held the Centaur contract, testified that the technology of jets and rockets is similar. U.S., House, Subcommittee on Space Sciences of the Committee on Science and Astronautics, *Hearings, Centaur Program*, 87th Cong., 2d Sess., May 15-18, 1962, p. 125.

[72] John Humphries, *Rockets, and Guided Missiles* (New York: Macmillan, 1956), p. 17.

[73] General Electric was active in both areas of propulsion rockets and jet engines. All remarks pertaining to management's ability to predict must necessarily exclude General Electric. However, General Electric lost its position in the rocket field. There is no published explanation for this failure. Furthermore, it also lost its position in the jet-engine area.

[74] The first reference to the possible adverse effects of a decline in aircraft production were found in its *Annual Report for 1957*, p. 8.

[75] United Aircraft, *Annual Report, 1957*, p. 3.

[76] *Ibid*. However, the company was beginning to work on missiles problems, though not heavily. In 1958 the company formed a Missile and Space Systems Division.

the summer of 1957 it was apparent that there would be a sharp cutback in military jet-engine procurement.[77] By this time, rocket capabilities had been established by firms which were not manufacturers of jet engines.[78]

The companies which lost these engine sales were not able to offset the decline by increased rocket sales. Of the four higher producers of engines, General Motors and General Electric stood to suffer least, for their entire defense effort accounted for only 5 and 20 percent respectively of total 1957 sales. Since engine sales are only a part of total defense sales, the loss of this business would presumably reduce profits but no great harm would be inflicted upon the company. However, both Curtiss-Wright and United Aircraft heavily depended on the sales of aircraft engines. These firms might be expected to attempt to enter the new area. United Aircraft did become a rocket producer but only at considerable expense; Curtiss-Wright still does not make rocket engines, and has lost its pre-eminence in the industry.[79]

At the time of this change in emphasis from aircraft to missiles some rocket-engine manufacturers failed to survive even with the increased emphasis on rockets. In 1957 there were two types of rocket-engine or motor manufacturers—producers of liquid-fueled engines or of solid-fueled motors. The companies which in 1957 had the dominant position in the rocket sector of the industry were the Rocketdyne Division of North American Aviation, Thiokol Chemical Corporation, and Aerojet-General Company, a subsidiary of General Tire and Rubber. These companies became engaged in rocket-propulsion research before the increased emphasis on missile development. North American Aviation had worked on liquid-fuel rocket engines since 1946 and in 1955 had established

---

[77] *American Aviation,* July 1, 1957, p. 21.

[78] A similar situation occurred in the early history of the jet engine. Most of the development was undertaken by firms which were not primarily piston-engine producers. (See R. Schlaifer, *Development of Aircraft Engines* (Cambridge, Mass.: School of Business Administration, Harvard University, 1950), pp. 466 ff.; Peck and Scherer, *op. cit.,* p. 199.

In this case, North American Aviation's management had recognized the full potential of the rocket engine as early as 1955, for it was then that the company established a separate division, Rocketdyne, to design and develop rocket engines. North American Aviation, *Annual Report, 1955,* p. 20.

[79] The company expanded in a different direction. It built up its electronic capability and also started making motor cases. *Missiles and Rockets,* May 22, 1961, p. 9, and June 26, 1961, p. 24.

the Rocketdyne Division.[80] This company's interest in rocket propulsion began with the Navaho missile, but it also had developed engines for the Hermes A-2 and Redstone missiles and held contracts for the propulsion units of the Atlas, Thor, and Jupiter missiles.[81]

Thiokol started working on solid propellants in 1948, and in 1950 fired the General Electric RVA 10, proving that large solid-propellant motors could be developed. This was followed by the Hermes motor in 1952, and a new solid-fueled rocket motor for a follow-on version of the Matador missile, the Mace.[82] In 1956, the company's motors were used for the X-17 project, which subsequently led to the Polaris and Minuteman missiles.[83]

Aerojet-General attained its position in this sector of the industry as the result of its World War II development of jet-assisted take-off (JATO) propellants and rockets.[84] JATO was a solid-fueled rocket, and by 1948 Aerojet was the dominant manufacturer in this area. It also expanded into high-thrust liquid-assisted take-off engines (ATO). The purpose of the Aerobee rocket contract, awarded to Aerojet, was to advance the state of knowledge of liquid propellants. Subsequently, this was the major rocket of the atmospheric sounding program.

In 1957, Rocketdyne was active only in liquid-fueled and Thiokol only in solid-fueled rockets, but Aerojet was active in both. It had contracts for many of our major missiles including Titan and Vanguard.[85] These were the major companies, but not the only

---

[80] *Aviation Week*, November 25, 1957, pp. 86 ff.

[81] Gattland, *op. cit.* (see n. 5), pp. 156 and 260. The Hermes project itself experienced several reorientations and finally became a program for the development of many experimental missiles and rocket engines and motors. In addition to the North American engine, General Electric developed a liquid-propellant engine under this program and Thiokol joined General Electric in proving that large solid-propellant motors could be developed. *Ibid.*, p. 154; *Aviation Week*, March 8, 1964, p. 26; a letter to the author from R. O. Day, Advertising Manager of Thiokol Chemical Corp., dated January 16, 1963; and *Missiles and Rockets*, March 6, 1961, p. 13.

[82] *Aviation Week*, November 5, 1962, p. 115.

[83] Most of these data concerning the corporate history of Thiokol were obtained from the mentioned letter from R. O. Day.

[84] General Tire and Rubber felt that its investment in Aerojet was justified since there was a close relationship between the chemistry of these propellants and that of rubber.

[85] Most of these data were derived from the *Annual Reports* of General Tire and Rubber.

ones, operating in this area. Others active in rocket-engine development were General Electric, Reaction Motors, Marquardt Aircraft, Grand Central Rocket Company, Hercules Powder, and several other firms in a minor way.

Reaction Motors, which received its first financial support in 1947 from Laurance Rockefeller,[86] had some of the earliest rocket contracts awarded. It had the first contract for the rocket engine of the Convair 774 (Atlas) missile, and it also had worked on the Viking, and the Bell and Douglas series of supersonic aircraft, the X-1 to X-3.[87] Furthermore, in 1953 Reaction Motors had entered a joint venture with Mathieson Chemical Company and had expanded into solid-propellant research, although its main interest remained in liquid-propulsion systems.[88] For some reason the company could not establish itself and merged with Thiokol.[89] This enabled the latter to obtain some liquid-propulsion capabilities to add to its experience in solid fuels.[90]

General Electric's work on rocket engines began with the Hermes project in which an engine of less than 20,000 pounds thrust was developed.[91] General Electric's work in this direction continued with its selection as the manufacturer of the first stage rocket engine for the Vanguard Project.[92] It was required to modify the Hermes engine so that the required 27,000 pounds of thrust would be developed.[93] After the completion of the Vanguard Project, a modi-

---

[86] Peck and Scherer, *op. cit.*, p. 204. Reaction Motors had been active in rocket-powered flights since 1943. *Missiles and Rockets*, September 26, 1960, p. 12.

[87] Gattland, *op. cit.*, pp. 157 and 182.

[88] *Ibid.*, and *Aviation Week*, January 20, 1958, pp. 34 ff.

[89] The financial resources of Reaction were meager. Just before its merger with Thiokol the value of its assets was $5.844 million. Its sales in 1957 were less than $24.5 million.

[90] *Aviation Week*, February 3, 1958, p. 37 and August 4, 1958, p. 37.

[91] *Missiles and Rockets*, July 1957, p. 117.

[92] The entire Vanguard Project was given low priority and the intention was to use as many "off-the-shelf" items as possible. The satellite project was also designed to minimize interference with the research and development efforts for the ballistic-missile programs. *Ibid.*, and *Time*, October 21, 1957, p. 22.

[93] In 1958, Rocketdyne's Thor engine was rated at 165,000 pounds of thrust, thus indicating the small scale of General Electric's engines. Moreover, the company's selection by the Navy to do the research necessary to modify the Hermes engine implies that General Electric's research role in large-scale military rocket engines had a low priority, if it even existed. The fact that Aerojet was selected to construct the second-stage engine cannot be interpreted in the same way, for Aerojet had merely to adapt the Aerobee main engine into a second stage.

fied version of General Electric's Vanguard engine was selected as the rocket for the second stage of the Vega booster.[94] Even this engine's thrust was small in comparison with that of other boosters developed simultaneously.[95] This was the last rocket engine that General Electric developed although it continued bidding on rocket contracts.[96] Its failure to expand within this area of the industry might be attributed to its inability to compete for the more powerful liquid boosters. It is impossible to determine whether this is the result of lack of technical know-how[97] or of management's decision to refrain from developing a large-scale rocket-engine capability.[98]

Marquardt Aircraft's rocket research program was originally financed—in 1948—by General Tire. When the latter company sold its interest in 1950, financing was undertaken by Laurance Rockefeller, and was subsequently taken over by Olin-Mathieson in 1953.[99] Except for the ramjet engine developed for the BOMARC missile, the company did not achieve much of a rocket capability, and as the BOMARC program neared completion in 1960, it sought to merge with other companies and moved partly into electronics.[100] Among the possible merger partners were Thiokol, General Electric, and United Aircraft.[101] Since discussions with Thiokol

---

[94] *Aviation Week,* June 22, 1959, pp. 120-122; *Missiles and Rockets,* March 7, 1960, p. 30 and June 20, 1960, p. 20.

[95] In 1960 this Vega engine had a thrust of more than 30,000 pounds. The Atlas had a thrust of 360,000 pounds and the Titan of 380,000 pounds.

[96] *Missiles and Rockets,* February 15, 1960, pp. 10-11.

[97] For the reasons behind the Vega project cancellation see *Aviation Week,* December 21, 1959, pp. 18-19 and June 27, 1960, pp. 62-68. One reason was that the Agena B was a superior booster.

[98] Some other companies had received large-scale rocket-engine contracts many years previously. To overcome this lead, and to develop the same competence that these companies had, presumably would have entailed considerable entry costs. The company, instead, started working on nozzles for solid and liquid rockets, large-scale power systems, ion engines, and pulsed plasma propulsion. *Missiles and Rockets,* September 26, 1960, p. 44, and July 9, 1962, p. 16. *Aviation Week,* October 22, 1962, p. 61.

[99] Peck and Scherer, *op. cit.,* p. 204. Olin received a 50-percent interest in the company.

[100] *Aviation Week,* August 1, 1960, p. 78. In fact, in 1960, electronics accounted for 10 percent of the company's sales. For acquisitions that Marquardt made in an attempt to enter the electronics area, see *ibid.,* September 15, 1958, p. 27, and November 10, 1958, p. 29.

[101] *Ibid.,* April 20, 1959, p. 23 and June 1, 1959, p. 37. It is interesting to note that two of the firms hurt by the decline in aircraft engine demand, and which theoretically should attempt to enter the rocket engine field, were attempting this through mergers. This suggests that the attempt to establish a rocket-engine capability independently must be expensive. This topic is discussed in more detail below.

failed, and nothing ever developed with the other firms, Marquardt retained its corporate identity.[102]

Hercules Powder had produced all rocket propellants during World War II and the Korean War, yet it had attained only a small role in the rocket program by 1957.[103] It had not received any major rocket contracts by that date, but obtained some subsequently.[104] Part of Hercules' success in entering the industry must be attributed to the experience obtained in managing the Allegheny Ballistic Laboratory for the Navy where the propellant for the second stage of the Polaris was developed.[105]

Bell Aircraft, later a division of Textron known as Bell Aerospace, was also one of the original firms producing liquid-fuel rocket engines. It had originally obtained some experience with the X-1 supersonic plane. Bell decided that in working with missiles and liquid-fuel engines it would focus its attention on the whole system rather than to the rocket chambers alone.[106] Bell had received engine contracts for its Rascal missile and for the Nike,[107] and later announced that it was to make the engine for the air-to-surface missile to be carried by the B-58.[108] This last engine was adopted and eventually became an upper-stage rocket known as the Agena. This was the first engine ever restarted in space.[109] In addition the company had obtained considerable experience in the

---

102 The sales of the company declined more than 25 percent between 1960 and 1961, but increased slightly between 1961 and 1962. The company then expanded into other areas, including storable liquid-fuel and hybrid rocket engines. Part of the latter research was conducted in conjunction with Grand Central Rocket Co. NASA also awarded a plasma propulsion contract to the company. *Aviation Week*, May 9, 1960, p. 84; *Missiles and Rockets*, November 7, 1960, p. 23 and September 3, 1962, p. 9. Marquardt also obtained the reaction control engine for the LEM. *Ibid.*, December 17, 1962, p. 9.

103 *1963 NASA Authorization*, Pt. 3, pp. 1653-1654. The company worked on a solid-fuel rocket motor for the Vanguard project. This motor was installed in the last Vanguard which was flown.

104 *Ibid.* These include the Altair and Antares stages of the Scout booster, the second stage of the Polaris, and the Minuteman third stage. Also see *Missiles and Rockets*, June 6, 1960, p. 29; February 26, 1962, p. 25; and July 2, 1962, p. 20.

105 *Ibid.*, October 31, 1960, p. 36 and November 28, 1960, p. 22. As a consequence of its research, Hercules became the leader in double-base propellant technology. *Ibid.*, June 6, 1960, p. 30.

106 Bell Aircraft Co., *Annual Report for 1953*, p. 20.

107 *Ibid.* for 1954, p. 8.

108 *Ibid.* for 1957, p. 7 and *ibid.* for 1958, p. 2.

109 *Missiles and Rockets*, February 8, 1960, p. 34; July 18, 1960, p. 68; December 19, 1960, p. 34; and July 30, 1962, p. 67. The Agena is also the object with which the Gemini spacecraft will rendezvous.

use of fluorine, which at one time was considered useful for high-energy, upper-stage applications.[110] The decision to use liquid hydrogen rather than fluorine in the upper stages of all large boosters hurt Bell.[111] This action, plus Bell's original decision not to specialize in rocket chamber work, and its later avowed intention to avoid the big booster field[112] may explain why the company has not become a major producer of rocket engines. In addition to the Agena, Bell currently has a contract for another take-off engine for the LEM.[113]

Grand Central, a firm interested in solid-fueled propulsion motors, was founded in 1955,[114] and by 1957 had developed the third-stage engine for the Vanguard.[115] The emphasis on big solid rockets required large resources with the consequence that Grand Central was forced to seek outside financial assistance. It first ceded a majority interest to Tennessee Gas Transmission, from which it obtained financial backing, and then in 1958 became an affiliate jointly owned by the FMC Corporation and Tennessee Gas.[116] Finally, Lockheed bought Grand Central in a two-stage transaction. In 1960 it obtained a 50 percent interest in the company,[117] and in 1961 it acquired the company and changed its name to Lockheed Propulsion Company.[118] This marked Grand Central's exit from the industry and Lockheed's entry.

Among firms with minor activity in this area are Atlantic Research and Goodrich. Atlantic Research has conducted solid-propellant research for the Arca, Archer, and Iris research rockets, and

---

110 *Aviation Week*, September 1, 1958, p. 23; September 19, 1960, p. 34; and December 26, 1960, p. 18.

111 Its only competitor in this area was Rocketdyne. Even though there was not much competition in this area, interproduct competition existed (that is, fluorine-versus liquid-hydrogen-fueled rockets).

Bell had also been hurt by the cutbacks in 1958.

112 *Aviation Week*, April 24, 1961, p. 34. As a division of Textron, Bell might not have been able to command sufficient capital to expand in this area.

113 *Missiles and Rockets*, December 17, 1962, p. 9.

114 *Aviation Week*, February 8, 1960, p. 31.

115 On the final shot of the Vanguard project, an Allegheny Ballistic Laboratory solid-propellant motor was substituted for the GCR solid third stage. *Ibid.*, September 23, 1959, p. 32.

116 *Ibid.*, January 27, 1958, pp. 33-34; October 26, 1959, p. 91; February 8, 1960, p. 31.

117 *Ibid.*, February 8, 1960, p. 31.

118 *Ibid.*, May 21, 1962, p. 34; and *Missiles and Rockets*, May 28, 1962.

for the Navy's Terrier rocket.[119] It has expanded somewhat since it received a specialized study contract from the Air Force in 1962[120] Goodrich has been active in the small-rocket motor market since 1952 and has expressed its intention to continue working primarily in this area.[121]

A company desirous of entering the rocket-engine field may do so in several different ways. Merger is one possibility. This is the path chosen by Lockheed and the means used by Thiokol to obtain a foothold in the liquid-fuel rocket engine field. However, the number of companies which could be bought was limited because the number of firms originally in the industry was small. There are three other techniques through which a firm can enter the industry: It could create its own staff and develop its know-how about existing technology to the point where it could compete with extant firms for new business; it could bypass existing technology and concede new contracts associated with this technology to the existing firms, which could be accomplished by advancing the state of the art substantially, thus creating a new generation of engines; the risk and expense of entry could be shared by forming an alliance or joint venture with another firm. All three approaches were followed by companies in this industry, with each approach tailored to individual needs.

Before proceeding to the analysis of entry paths other than mergers, it is pertinent to discuss two topics relating to mergers. First, the merger route is not necessarily an inexpensive means of entering the industry. It was estimated that Lockheed would have to spend $40 million to establish itself in the big solid-fuel rocket field.[122] Half this amount had been committed in the two years subsequent to Lockheed's association with Grand Central Rocket, but the company had lost the 120-inch competition which was the only large solid-propellant contract awarded before 1963. However, the company had received other contracts such as research support for the 120-inch motor, the Apollo launch-escape rocket, and a sub-

---

119 *Missiles and Rockets,* October 16, 1961, p. 44.
120 *Ibid.,* April 30, 1962, p. 34. It was even invited to submit bids for the large solid-fuel booster competition held in 1963. *Aviation Week,* January 21, 1963, p. 37.
121 *Missiles and Rockets,* June 5, 1961, p. 29.
122 *Ibid.,* May 28, 1962, p. 34.

contract from General Dynamics for work on the rocket for the Mauler.[123] The competition for the large solid-propellant motor-development program was held in 1963. This program was divided into four packages. Lockheed was placed in the big booster field when it was awarded the contract for Package IV, which involved the static firing of a 156-inch single-segment motor.[124]

Actually, this large solid-propellant competition illustrates another point about the prevailing barriers to entry into the rocket industry. An entering firm is uncertain about future demand, for there is no proved method of forecasting the direction of government procurement actions. Within a year of this big competition in solid-propellant rockets, there was speculation that the Department of Defense would curtail if not discontinue this program. Several heavy investors in solid-propellant rocket facilities would have been hurt by such a cutback, but this threat did not materialize.[125] Nevertheless, our conclusion is that uncertainty of the future, which is not limited to the rocket-engine field, when coupled with large expenditures for new facilities may impede entry into the industry.

Thiokol's merger with Reaction Motors also requires further elaboration, for it enabled Thiokol to attain a liquid-propellant rocket capability to complement its solid-propellant experience. This attempt to attain expertise in both areas might stem from a fear that developments in one area could render the other type of rocket obsolete, for the two are substitutes. With a capability in both areas, technological developments in either area could be exploited without jeopardizing the position of the company. The fact that Rocketdyne moved into solid-propellant rockets[126] increases our confidence that this hypothesis is true. Subsequent to the successful entry of United Aircraft into both solid- and liquid-fuel rockets, all major rocket manufacturers were active in both areas.

United Aircraft was the only firm to enter the industry by creat-

---

123 *Ibid.*, p. 35. However, the annual billings of the rocket division were only in the neighborhood of $2 million. This probably did not take into account the newer work on projects such as the Apollo escape rocket. Moreover, Lockheed later received a subcontract from Hughes to develop a solid-fuel rocket motor for an air-to-air missile. *Aviation Week*, October 8, 1962, p. 98.

124 *Ibid.*, April 22, 1963, p. 33. The value of this contract was estimated at $6 million. *Ibid.*, July 1, 1963, p. 23.

125 *Missiles and Rockets*, July 8, 1963, pp. 16-17; July 15, 1963, p. 9; August 26, 1963, p. 16; and February 19, 1963, p. 38.

126 *Ibid.*, May 16, 1960, p. 25; *Aviation Week*, April 1, 1963, p. 23.

ing its own staff and developing its technical competence to the point where it could compete with the existing firms for large current contracts. A large percentage of the company's sales is in propulsion systems. With the decline of aircraft-engine sales, the firm considered that its most advantageous course was to create its own technical staff, enter the industry, and try to overcome its competitors' lead. The alternative would have been to await the management competitions for the next generation of rocket engines, thus bypassing present contracts. This policy would have meant that the staff of United Aircraft would have been allowed to dwindle, with the added possibility that its technical skills might also be diminished. This decision would have been extremely risky, for while waiting the company could be hit by financial difficulties, and thus could not be certain of being in existence when the competition for the next generation of rocket engines began. The company must have concluded that entering the industry immediately was its most feasible decision. However, it had neither liquid- nor solid-fuel rocket experience, and it attempted to enter both areas simultaneously.

United Aircraft had some experience in using and storing liquid hydrogen and had undertaken studies on the application of liquid hydrogen to aircraft propulsion.[127] On the basis of this experience, the company's Pratt & Whitney Division was awarded an Air Force contract in 1958 to develop a liquid-hydrogen engine for the Centaur rocket.[128] This contract enabled the company not only to enter the rocket-engine field but to shift the cost of acquiring its technical knowledge about liquid-hydrogen rocket engines to the government. Since a liquid-hydrogen engine is an improvement over the conventional liquid-oxygen rocket engine, the former might therefore be considered a second generation liquid-fuel rocket engine. This point is important, for the Pratt & Whitney Division did not meet Rocketdyne and Aerojet head-on in the competition for the conventional liquid-oxygen engines, but sought to develop the newer rocket engines.

The difficulties which Pratt & Whitney encountered in the development of this liquid-hydrogen engine have been well docu-

---

127 *Centaur Program Hearings* (as cited in n. 71), pp. 28 and 111. *Aviation Week,* October 23, 1961, p. 27.

128 *Ibid.,* November 10, 1958, p. 26.

mented.[129] If the company had not had a government contract, it would have borne a considerably larger share of the cost of developing the engine, and perhaps all the cost of obtaining the experience necessary to undertake such development.[130] If this were so, the company *might* have been unwilling to enter the liquid-hydrogen field, and had it entered nonetheless, its entry costs would have been considerably higher. However, the government absorbed these costs, and the company solved its technical problems and had its rocket accepted for space flight. As a result, the company is now established in the industry, is considered a major liquid-fuel rocket-engine producer, and is also one of the three firms which now have liquid-hydrogen experience.[131] This points up that barriers to entry may be reduced if a company obtains a government contract when it makes a technical breakthrough. Scientific knowledge is a neces-sary, but not sufficient, condition to enable a company to enter the industry. Contract acquisition enables a company to shift a large portion of the entry costs, and, in addition, permits it to acquire additional scientific knowledge.[132] Thus a firm which wishes to enter the propulsion sector of the industry faces high but not in-surmountable barriers.

An estimate of the monetary magnitude of these barriers can be obtained since United was forced to develop its solid-fuel capabili-ties with its own funds.[133] Between 1958 and 1959 it established a subsidiary, United Technology Corporation (UTC), which under-

---

129 See the *Centaur Program Hearings* and *1963 NASA Authorization*, Pt. 4, pp. 1956 ff. Several explosions occurred on the test stand. They all stemmed from the same cause, and the data which would have enabled the company to diagnose the problems were available after the first explosion. However, the company misinter-preted the data. *Centaur Program Hearings*, pp. 8 and 115.

130 The misinterpretation of the data pertaining to the rocket *may* have been en-tirely the result of the company's inexperience in this area. If this *were* true, then the government, in paying for the development of the rocket, also paid for the company's learning processes.

131 The other firms are Aerojet which has the M-1 engine, and Rocketdyne which has the J-2 engine for the Saturn. *Aviation Week*, October 15, 1962, p. 37, and *Missiles and Rockets*, February 26, 1962, p. 22.

132 When a company obtains a government contract it also gains access to the work that other firms have performed for the government. This eliminates the need for the newer company to duplicate all scientific experiments and assists it in overcom-ing any technological leads which the older firms may have obtained. *Aviation Week*, July 4, 1960, p. 23.

133 *Ibid.*, December 18, 1961, p. 30.

took research in solid fuels.[134] For the first two years of its existence UTC did not receive a major contract and was financed primarily by funds from the parent company.[135] The magnitude of United Aircraft's contributions toward UTC's research and development expenditures from 1958 to the receipt of its first large contract, would be a minimum estimate of the monetary scale of the entry barriers. It is estimated that United spent more than $30 million before UTC established itself in the industry by winning the 120-inch solid-fuel motor competition.[136] UTC spent $16 million on facilities, $17.5 million for research and development, and the parent company allocated an additional $8 million for more facili-

---

[134] When UTC was founded, it was thought of as a sophisticated research group which would make scientific advances, and subsequently a production organization would be established. The idea was not to undertake a two-year research project to advance to the industry's technological level, for the latter would be advancing too. *Missiles and Rockets*, July 16, 1962, p. 33. Moreover, its original major interest, according to industry observers, was in storable liquid-fuel rockets of less than 25,000 pounds thrust. This statement was made just after UTC had been awarded a NASA contract to study the feasibility of a conical-shaped solid-fuel rocket engine. *Ibid.*, August 1, 1960, pp. 32-33. In 1962 and 1963 the company was engaged in hybrid liquid-and-solid-fuel research and was also working on thrust reduction techniques and variable thrust upper-stage liquid-fuel engines. All projects were company-sponsored and funded. *Aviation Week*, November 5, 1962, p. 27; and February 17, 1964, p. 75. *Missiles and Rockets*, March 5, 1962, p. 10; July 16, 1962, p. 34; August 6, 1962, p. 25. *The Wall Street Journal*, May 26, 1964, p. 8.

[135] *Aviation Week*, April 10, 1961, pp. 56 ff. The company received several government contracts which assisted its entry. There was a 1960 NASA contract ($186,000) to study the feasibility of a conical-shaped solid-fuel rocket motor. In 1961, UTC received a contract for the development of a 70,000-pound-thrust flight weight segmented solid motor. This was a cost-sharing contract. There are also two references to Air Force assistance, but no explicit mention is made of the purpose of the contracts. *Missiles and Rockets*, February 1, 1960, p. 11; June 6, 1960, p. 15; June 13, 1960, p. 35; March 20, 1961, p. 16; April 24, 1961, p. 21; December 18, 1961, p. 15; and July 16, 1962, p. 33.

[136] *Missiles and Rockets*, July 16, 1962, p. 33. Another reference indicates that between 1958 and 1960 United Aircraft had committed $79 million of its own funds to research and development. These estimates are consistent, for a portion of the larger amount was spent on entering the weapons system and liquid-fuel rocket-engine sectors of the industry. United's Missile and Space System Division, organized in 1958, had to be financed with company funds for one year until the first contracts were obtained. Nevertheless, the company still spent $40 million for research and development in each of the years 1960 through 1962. A large percentage may be attributable to the company's research effort, for the company developed a 96-inch solid-fuel rocket motor preparatory to entering the 120-inch competition. *Aviation Week*, June 30, 1958, p. 18; August 3, 1959, p. 34; March 13, 1961, p. 216; December 18, 1961, p. 30; and May 14, 1961, p. 33. The chairman of United Aircraft explicitly stated that a large portion of the company's research and development funds went to UTC. *The Wall Street Journal*, March 4, 1964, p. 21.

ties. As further indication that these figures are of the correct order of magnitude, both Aerojet and Thiokol have recently reported the cost of their new large solid-fuel rocket-motor plants. Exclusive of the price of land, the estimated costs of the facilities are $10 to $11 million.[137] Aerojet's land expenses are estimated to be an additional $9 million.[138]

In the 120-inch competition, UTC "gambled" by going directly to a flight weight motor whereas its competitors took the safer course of constructing heavy boiler-plate research motors.[139] This approach was selected despite the company's inexperience in making cases and nozzles and in casting solids. Moreover, the cost was three to four times that of developing boiler plates. One possible explanation for this procedure is that UTC felt it had to make a *dramatic* presentation to overcome its inexperience in the rocket field. It succeeded and entered the industry by beating the leaders in the competitive arena,[140] thus proving that entry as a major firm was both possible and expensive.[141]

In an area in which technological progress is rapid, one firm need not duplicate the efforts of others in order to enter the industry. It may follow a second path and attempt to bypass the present competition by working on ideas which will eventually make the present generation of equipment obsolete. In this industry if a firm develops a novel idea and obtains government support it may bypass present competition with relative ease. A form of this approach was used by Pratt & Whitney Division of United Aircraft in entering the liquid-hydrogen rocket-engine field.

---

137 *Missiles and Rockets*, January 14, 1963, p. 19; April 22, 1963, p. 15.

138 *Aviation Week*, April 29, 1963, p. 54. Aerojet also reported that it invests about $25 million a year in its space program. (This must include both facilities and research and development.) *The Wall Street Journal*, March 28, 1963, p. 17. The cost of a facility for high-pressure liquid-propellant rocket-engine research cost United's Pratt & Whitney Division $4 million. *Aviation Week*, April 8, 1963, p. 98.

139 *Missiles and Rockets*, July 16, 1962, pp. 32 ff. For the major problems that UTC has faced in its actual development efforts, see *ibid.*, January 20, 1964, pp. 34 ff. It has had to develop some new approaches in working on the motor.

140 The other firms were Aerojet, Bell Aero Systems, Rocketdyne, and Thiokol. Aerojet and Thiokol were well established in this field. *Aviation Week*, May 21, 1962, pp. 98-99. Similarly, NASA's objective of increasing the number of solid-propellant manufacturers was also satisfied by the selection of UTC. *Ibid.*, April 16, 1962, p. 28. One might wonder if this objective might not have influenced the choice of UTC.

141 The more common practice is to enter by the "bootstrap" method, where a firm grows slowly by first obtaining a small government contract and then building on that.

It is difficult to obtain a valid theoretical explanation for the observation that successive generations of aerospace propulsion systems generally have been developed first by firms not actively engaged in producing the preceding generation of systems. This was as true in the transition from piston to jet engines as from aircraft engines to rocket systems. One possible explanation is that the technology of existing systems is still evolving. This requires that the existing major companies commit their most qualified personnel to current contracts. Little emphasis can thus be placed on germinating and developing ideas for future generations of equipment. Besides, these firms may underestimate the pace of technological progress, or may be so committed to their present ideas[142] that they may not realize how quickly the present generation of propulsion systems is becoming outmoded. Through the impact of technological progress there has been considerable movement into and out of the propulsion area of the industry.[143] This sector may then provide a perfect example of Schumpeter's creative destruction.[144] However, it should be recognized that in addition to the novel idea, the new competition is stimulated by the availability of reimbursement-type contracts, in which the risk is at least partly assumed by the government.

It is therefore not surprising that the aerospace firms were actively interested in competing for rocket-engine contracts designed

---

142 It should be realized that it is impossible for a firm to investigate all of a set of possible new develoments. By chance, the path that a new firm is pursuing actively may have been one of the paths rejected by the present leader. This is just a case of betting on the wrong horse and does not tell anything about the technological progressiveness of existing firms. This is especially true since the outcomes of research and development are uncertain. However, there *may* be some correlation between the degree of certainty of the research and development policies which are pursued and the company's position in the industry. For instance, Rocketdyne, which was attempting to establish itself in the solid-fuel rocket-motor field, produced its solid propellants with the first new process developed in fifteen years. The company reduced costs by 10 percent while increasing performance by 20 percent. *Missiles and Rockets*, July 2, 1962, pp. 16 ff.

There have been some discussions of the path a firm should follow in conducting its research program if it cannot explore every possibility. See C. M. Mottley and R. D. Newton, "The Selection of Projects for Industrial Research," *Operations Research*, VII, No. 6 (November-December 1959), pp. 740-751; and O. L. Davies, "Some Statistical Considerations in the Selection of Research Projects in the Pharmaceutical Industry," *Applied Statistics*, XI, No. 3 (November 1962), pp. 170-183.

143 Peck and Scherer, *op. cit.*, p. 197.

144 J. A. Schumpeter, *Capitalism, Socialism, and Democracy* (New York: Harper, 1942), p. 84.

to replace or supplement the present generation of rocket-propulsion systems. Included were rockets to be powered either by plasma-arc jet or ion engines. There were eleven competitors in the plasma-arc competition and six for the latter.[145] The second group was composed mainly of electronics firms.[146] Entrants in the arc-jet competition included existing rocket-engine manufacturers such as Rocketdyne and Aerojet; firms such as Westinghouse, General Electric, Avco and Curtiss-Wright which previously had manufactured aircraft engines but had not entered the rocket-engine fields; and two airframe manufacturers, Republic and General Dynamics. Obviously, the existing rocket-engine manufacturers were interested in maintaining their position while the others were attempting entrance at an advanced stage of industry development, by obtaining contracts in an area still unexplored and not dominated by an existing firm.

At least one company was successful in entering in this manner. Space Technology Laboratories won back-up contracts for an LEM engine and for the vernier engine for the Surveyor spacecraft because the company advanced the state of the art in deep-throttling engines.[147] These developments took two years and were self-financed. After successfully demonstrating these techniques the company received the contracts.

Other technological advances were not associated with new en-

---

[145] *Aviation Week,* April 18, 1960, p. 30.

[146] Thompson-Ramo-Wooldridge, Raytheon, Goodrich, Hughes Aircraft, Armour Research, and International Telephone and Telegraph. Shortly thereafter, United Aircraft announced its entry into the electrical rocket propulsion field, and Douglas acquired a subsidiary to perform research in electrical, nuclear, and high energy chemical propulsion systems. See *ibid.,* September 7, 1959, p. 23; October 31, 1960, p. 73; November 7, 1960, p. 30; and April 29, 1963, p. 33. Also *Missiles and Rockets,* April 25, 1960, p. 47 and September 3, 1962, p. 9. In 1960, Avco and General Electric were chosen for studies to prove the feasibility of pulsed plasma propulsion. In 1962, Marquardt also received a NASA contract to study plasma propulsion. Douglas subsequently announced that its propulsion subsidiary, Astropower, would specialize in various electrical propulsion systems, nuclear propulsion, solid-state devices, and SNAP. It would undertake only limited chemical propulsion efforts. *Ibid.,* February 13, 1961, pp. 30-31. Aerojet was able to obtain a position in the ion engine field because Electro-Optical, which had such a contract, sold a minority interest to the former company. *Ibid.,* February 8, 1960, p. 39. For further discussion about possible next-generation rocket engines see *Aviation Week,* September 23, 1963, p. 73; October 21, 1963, pp. 64-65; November 25, 1963, p. 32; January 6, 1964, pp. 65 ff.; January 27, 1964, pp. 77 ff.; February 3, 1964, pp. 54 ff.; February 10, 1964, pp. 54 ff; and February 17, 1964, pp. 78 ff. Also *Missiles and Rockets,* February 10, 1964, pp. 24-25.

[147] *Ibid.,* June 3, 1963, p. 24; *Aviation Week,* June 3, 1963, p. 30.

trants. For instance, the development of storable liquid-fuel rocket engines was achieved by the existing firms.[148] If the hybrid solid-liquid-fuel engine is developed successfully, other firms may enter in the future, but up to this point existing companies have performed much of the research.[149] Eventually an entirely new concept, such as air-breathing rocket engines, may replace the big boosters.[150] Whether this results in new entrants cannot be determined as yet.

The third and final means of entrance to the industry was through joint ventures. This path was chosen mainly by chemical companies which had interests in entering the propulsion field and, therefore, joined forces with some aerospace firms.[151] North American Aviation and Phillips formed a jointly owned subsidiary, Astrodyne, to specialize in solid-propellant research. For North American this was particularly suitable since it had no solid-fuel capability at that time. It later purchased Phillip's half of Astrodyne,[152] and is now active but has not yet become a major factor in solid-fuel rocket motors.

This was an inexpensive mode of industry entrance for the chemical companies. Originally the government had supported the engine makers with money to produce propellants,[153] but with the chemical companies themselves in the field, the Air Force saw no reason to support both groups. With the know-how and facilities of

---

148 The Reaction Motor Division of Thiokol received contracts to develop prepackaged liquid-fuel engines to replace the solid-propellant units in Sparrow III and Bullpup. *Ibid.*, November 24, 1958, p. 62. Aerojet worked on a storable propellant version of Titan. *Ibid.*, October 1959, p. 68. For other references see *ibid.*, June 22, 1959, p. 121, and July 27, 1959, p. 30; *Missiles and Rockets*, November 7, 1960, p. 23.

149 As early as 1960, Grand Central and Marquardt engaged in hybrid research. *Aviation Week*, May 9, 1960, p. 84. A hybrid engine was successfully developed and tested. *Ibid.*, October 8, 1962, p. 67. NASA accelerated its research program on hybrids. Until 1962, a total of $2 million had been committed to this program. In 1962, an additional $3 million were spent. All major propulsion firms were interested in this program. *Missiles and Rockets*, November 5, 1962, pp. 14 and 43; *Aviation Week*, November 12, 1962, p. 23. United Aircraft announced that it had developed such a hybrid rocket successfully. *The Wall Street Journal*, May 26, 1964, p. 8.

150 *Missiles and Rockets*, April 8, 1963, p. 12.

151 Among such ventures were Phillips Petroleum and North American Aviation; Aerojet and Stauffer Chemical; and Thiokol and Callery Chemical. *Aviation Week*, January 20, 1958, pp. 34 ff. The last two combinations were particularly interested in developing boron-based high-energy propellants. Another combination involved Hooker Electrochemical and Foote Mineral. See *ibid.*, March 10, 1958, p. 43.

152 *Ibid.*, July 20, 1959, p. 28.

153 This was appropriate since a solid-fuel rocket motor is said to consist of the working parts plus the propellant. *Ibid.*, September 12, 1960, p. 23.

the chemical companies available, alliances were suggested as the appropriate solution,[154] but there is no evidence that any of these joint ventures were successful.

The chemical companies have continued to take an active interest in rocket-propellant research. This may be attributable partly to their belief that synthetic chemicals would replace petroleum fuels in liquid-fuel rocket engines.[155] This was first investigated by Rocketdyne, but numerous chemical and petrochemcial firms have also begun research. These firms have analyzed the propulsion characteristics of many types of propellants, including solids, high-energy liquids, monopropellants, and storable liquids.[156] In addition, Union Carbide has received a contract to perform research on a new method of fabricating solid-fuel motors.[157]

Summary and Conclusions

In the first half of this chapter we concluded that despite the ease with which some of the electronics firms entered the missile industry, entry into the missile and spacecraft sections of the industry was difficult. The entry of the electronics companies was comparatively easy because these firms had had some earlier subsystem contracts. The major barriers to entry are the cost of facilities, with a minimum-size space laboratory costing $14 million, and research and development. Immense expenditures for research are required to obtain new contracts even for existing firms. Such expenditures must be still larger for new entrants.

In investigating the rocket-engine section of the industry, we discovered that the major manufacturers of jet engines were not the principal producers of rocket engines and motors although United Aircraft did eventually enter the industry. After examining the various techniques toward entrance that a new firm may select, the conclusion was drawn that entry into rocket-propulsion systems on

154 *Ibid.*, January 20, 1958, pp. 34 ff.

155 *Ibid.*, March 23, 1959, p. 30; and December 5, 1960, p. 38.

156 *Ibid.*, September 22, 1958. p. 28; November 3, 1958, p. 34; November 10, 1958, p. 63; February 9, 1959, p. 34; July 27, 1959, p. 30; December 14, 1959, pp. 68 ff.; July 4, 1960, p. 23; July 25, 1960, p. 23 and February 17, 1964, p. 31, also *Missiles and Rockets*, June 25, 1962, p. 15. Firms active in this area included Wyandotte Chemical, Phillips Petroleum, Stauffer Chemical, American Cyanamid, Dow Chemical, Standard Oil of New Jersey, Minnesota Mining and Manufacturing, Allied Chemical, Callery Chemical, Hercules Powder, Olin-Mathieson, DuPont, Union Carbide, and Shell Oil.

157 *Missiles and Rockets*, June 25, 1962, p. 15.

a major scale is expensive and impeded but not impossible. Between 1957 and 1963 only two firms joined Aerojet, Rocketdyne, and Thiokol as major propulsion manufacturers. These are United, which is active both in solids and liquids, and Hercules, which achieved its position in the solid-fuel motor field. In addition, Rocketdyne and Thiokol added solid- and liquid-fuel capabilities, respectively, and Lockheed received its first major contract in 1963. These were not the only firms in the industry, for companies such as Bell, Marquardt, and STL had attained a somewhat limited position in the field by 1963, but had not yet obtained big booster contracts.

Finally, it is important to determine the fate of the aircraft-engine companies which failed to obtain rocket-propulsion contracts. Curtiss-Wright, General Motors' Allison Division, and General Electric were all active in manufacturing rocket-motor cases for large solid-fuel rocket motors.[158] Though these firms had not obtained contracts for rocket-propulsion systems, they were still active in the aerospace industry, although in a different area and capacity.

---

[158] *Ibid.*, May 2, 1960, pp. 38-39; October 3, 1960, p. 38; November 14, 1960, pp. 22-23; November 21, 1960, p. 19; June 26, 1961, p. 24; September 11, 1961, pp. 24-25. *Aviation Week*, December 17, 1962, p. 87. For the possibility that shipbuilders would also manufacture casings, see *The Wall Street Journal*, April 2, 1963, p. 1. General Electric was also a producer of nozzles for rockets. This had become a major subcontracting item with the dollar value of the contracts approaching the value of motor case contracts. *Aviation Week*, April 8, 1963, p. 23.

8.

THE PERFORMANCE OF THE AEROSPACE INDUSTRY

An examination of the performance of an industry is customarily based on "the efficiency of the organization of the industry in terms of the scales of plants and firms, the relation of price to cost as reflected in the profit rate, and the size of selling costs in relation to sales revenue." [1] These criteria are important for most industries, but they are not totally applicable to the aerospace industry. There are special additional factors applicable only to the industry under investigation; these are the basis upon which we shall have to judge the performance of the aerospace industry.

Traditional Measures of Performance

Let us first examine the reason for discarding the customary measures of performance. The efficiency of an industry is determined both by the market organization and by the internal organization of firms. [2] The government's procuring agencies have often interfered in the former, for, as has been noted above, contracts are often awarded to firms merely to keep facilities and staffs employed and to prevent the firms from going out of existence. This interference with the market mechanism may perhaps have resulted in an optimal organization of the industry, but this result should not be attributed to the industry. Nor should any failures on this

---

[1] Joe S. Bain, *Industrial Organization* (New York: John Wiley, 1959), p. 341. The technical progressiveness of firms in the industry has been accepted as a traditional measure of performance, but Bain excluded this variable.

[2] *Ibid.*

score be debited to the private firms. This was a public policy which is not in the province of our analysis. Even the internal organization of firms is affected by an extraneous factor—political pressure. Companies in the industry do not have complete freedom to choose where to produce and which plants to use. They often submit bids indicating that production will take place in an area of substantial unemployment.[3] These firms might not have chosen to use these particular plants had it not been the intent of public policy to award contracts to labor-surplus areas.[4]

On the other hand, the scientific personnel of these companies are among the industry's scarce resources, and the manner in which they are used may reflect on the firm's ability to economize. Data indicate that average wages for aerospace production workers and nonsupervisory employees have increased by a larger percentage than those for all manufacturing even for durable-goods production.[5] Since there has been a shift in emphasis from production to research, with a concomitant decline in the number of production workers required, an increase in wages larger than for all other manufacturing industries cannot be attributed to excess demand. This is especially true in view of the fact that the major differential in wage-rate increases occurred between 1953 and 1959.[6]

If this difference in wage-rate increases cannot be ascribed to excess demand, what is the cause? One possibility is the presence of an environment in which firms are not concerned with costs and will give workers whatever wage increases are needed to prevent strikes. This is a possibility, but the data are confounded because the government itself has often intervened in the collective-bargaining process in order to prevent strikes.[7] Moreover, the data pertain-

---

[3] Two recent illustrations are the TFX competition in which Boeing chose to use its Wichita, Kansas, plant and Ling-Temco-Vought's bid for the Army Missile B. This Texas-based company indicated that it would develop and produce the missile in the Warren Ordnance Plant near Detroit. *Aviation Week*, November 1962, p. 25.

[4] The social and private-welfare problems are beyond the jurisdiction of this paper.

[5] Merton J. Peck and F. M. Scherer, *The Weapons Acquisition Process: An Economic Analysis* (Cambridge: Harvard University Press, Division of Research, 1962), pp. 520-521.

[6] *Ibid.*, pp. 522 ff.

[7] *Aviation Week*, June 5, 1961, p. 37; September 24, 1962, p. 39; December 24, 1962, p. 22; and May 6, 1963, p. 36. Also U.S., Senate, Permanent Subcommittee on Investigations of the Committee on Government Operations, *Hearings, Work Stoppage at Missile Bases*, 87th Cong., 1st Sess., April 25-June 1, 1961.

ing to executive salaries do not support the former view, for executive pay declined when aerospace profits fell.[8]

The most that can be concluded is that it is impossible to judge whether the industry has made an optimal utilization of its resources, for this problem was partly removed from its jurisdiction.

The second and third usually considered aspects of performance are also inappropriate here because of peculiar industry characteristics. It would be foolish to judge the industry on the basis of its profit rate, and if it happened to be low, to call it efficient, for a large percentage of the industry's contracts are of the cost-plus variety. Thus, *a priori,* one would expect to find relatively low profit ratios. Finally, since most of the industry's business is with the government, there would be little need to advertise, and the ratio of advertising costs to sales revenue would be irrelevant.

How can the performance of the industry be judged? We must consider its main purpose and must appraise its fulfillment of this function. Our interest has centered on the role of the industry members as contractors to the Armed Forces and NASA, for we have excluded their commercial activity. It is possible to determine if the companies in the industry have performed their work as contractors at the minimum cost consistent with the reliability and delivery time desired by the government. Since technological change has been one of the characteristics of the industry, one can also determine how well the companies adjusted and in turn contributed to this process.

---

8 *Missiles and Rockets,* December 24, 1962, p. 36. There are also some data on the direct employment costs which must be expended to hire salaried specialists. (U.S., House, Subcommittee No. 4 of the Select Committee on Small Business, *Hearings, The Aircraft Industry,* 85th Cong., 2d Sess., June 27-28, 1958, p. 204.) Similar data for other industries were not available, and it was therefore impossible to evaluate these figures. The final piece of evidence concerning the industry's utilization of its manpower is the turnover rate. Firms in the aerospace industry lose between 10 and 20 percent of their workforce every year. *Aviation Week,* June 3, 1957, pp. 247-248; *Missiles and Rockets,* December 10, 1962, p. 30; Peck and Scherer, *op. cit.,* p. 89. The Bell Telephone Laboratories, however, have a turnover rate of less than 4 percent a year. The most logical explanation for this large manpower turnover is the need of companies receiving new contracts for additional personnel. Thus, the personnel of this industry may be considered similar to a band of migratory workers which move from place to place as opportunities develop. Higher wages must be offered to attract this scientific group, and this may account for the observed wage-rate movements.

PROFIT RATIOS AS A MEASURE OF PERFORMANCE

Before we analyze the special factors peculiar to this industry, it is necessary to present and interpret the results obtained from profit ratios. These figures can be calculated readily and in the past have been used at several Congressional hearings to "prove" various theories about the industry. We want to avoid these arguments, but at the same time, some insights may be obtained from an analysis of these data. These ratios have been used to "prove" that the firms in the industry have earned excessive profits. The same figures have been modified and have then been used to "prove" that the earnings of the aerospace firms have been inadequate.

First, it has been noted previously that profit ratios have a multitude of functions, hence each ratio must be interpreted judiciously.[9] One ratio presented to Congress yielded the percentage profit earned on the firms' invested capital.[10] It is hard to determine the theoretical justification for such a ratio except to obtain a high figure. Retained earnings which are invested in the business are ignored. Even if they are taken into account, net worth is certainly not the best basis from which a profit ratio may be calculated. The ratio of net worth to assets may differ between companies, thus yielding results which may, at best, be difficult to interpret.

In any event, the ratio of profits before taxes to invested capital yields very high rates of return. In the 1952 to 1954 period, these rates ranged from 79.9 percent for the Glenn L. Martin Company in 1953 to 802 percent for North American Aviation in 1954.[11] These figures, recomputed as a percentage of net worth, ranged between 34.9 for Douglas in 1954 and 74.1 for Lockheed in 1953.[12] The choice of a different base for the ratio not only reduced the

---

9 H. O. Stekler, *Profitability and Size of Firms* (prepared by the Institute of Business and Economic Research, University of California, Berkeley, 1963), pp. 1-7.

10 U.S., House, Committee on Ways and Means, *Hearings, Extension of the Renegotiation Act*, 86th Cong., 1st Sess., April 27-29, 1959, p. 186. Invested capital in this case refers to that part of net worth which represents the value of the company's capital stock. It excludes retained earnings.

11 *Ibid.*

12 *Ibid.*, p. 196. For similar results for 1955 see U.S., House, Committee on Armed Services, *Report on Aircraft Production Costs and Profits*, 84th Cong., 2d Sess., July 13, 1956, pp. 3105-3109; and Frederick T. Moore, *Military Procurement and Contracting: An Economic Analysis*, RAND Memorandum RM 2948-PR (Santa Monica, Calif.: The RAND Corporation, June 1962), p. 107.

range of the ratios but also changed the company rankings, which were based on the size of the profit ratios. The latter set of ratios is more meaningful, but even these rates of return, since they are calculated on a net-worth base, present difficulties in interpretation. These ratios may be high because of two factors. First, companies might have used debt rather than equity financing or the ratio of company-owned assets to sales might have been exceedingly low. The latter possibility has already been demonstrated and is the result of the large portion of the facilities financed and furnished by the government.[13] It is unfortunate that the current value of the government-furnished property cannot be calculated for each year, but the available data are all based on historical undepreciated cost.[14] If the former possibility had existed, it would have been possible to calculate the rate of return on all resources used by the industry.

The only calculations possible for the major aircraft companies were the rates of return on company-owned assets for selected years between 1950 and 1962.[15] These rates of return computed before taxes on the average assets of the firms are relatively high.[16] Table

---

[13] Another possibility is that very few facilities are required for research-intensive output. However, our discussion of the entry barriers prevailing in the industry indicated that, at least in the past few years, facilities have been required to contract research.

[14] However, for the 1952-1954 period the ratios of original cost of government furnished property to original company investment in plant and equipment was often 2 to 1 and for some companies came close to 4 to 1. Source: *Extension of the Renegotiation Act*, p. 196.

The Stanford Research Institute's study, *The Industry-Government Aerospace Relationship*, presents a considerable amount of financial data on the industry. However, it also excludes the government-owned facilities.

[15] The years were selected on the basis of the information available at the time of computation. In some cases the 1962 data were available, in others they were not. The data for Martin were computed only through 1960, for it was felt that the merger with American Marietta would substantially change the company's activity and the inclusion of 1961's observations might subsequently bias the data. If the 1961 data for Martin-Marietta had been included the rate of return would have risen to 14.9. (It was 14.3 through 1960; see Table 31.) The data for Temco and Chance-Vought were presented only for the years in which these companies existed independently.

It is more difficult to rationalize the choice of the first observation. However, it was felt that the period 1950-1962 was more representative of the level of activity that could be expected to prevail in the future than were the years 1947-1949. Inclusion of the latter years would naturally have lowered the ratios.

[16] The rate of return was computed by adding the profits and interest of each firm for n years, and assets for $n + 1$ years. The fraction was then adjusted by the factor $n + 1/n$. Thus the period average is not a simple average of the yearly observations.

31 presents the levels of the profit ratios for a sample of the prime contractors active in the industry, and Table 32 shows a distribution of the pretax profit ratios for all manufacturing firms for a somewhat similar period, 1947-1954 and 1955-1957. With several

TABLE 31

RATE OF RETURN ON ASSETS AND NET WORTH FOR SELECTED AIRCRAFT COMPANIES
1950-1962

Company	Selected years	Rate of return (percent)	
		on assets[a]	on net worth[b]
Boeing	1950-1961	15.8	39.7
Chance-Vought	1955-1960	15.0	33.3
Douglas	1950-1962	10.6	23.2
General Dynamics	1950-1961	3.8	10.8
Grumman	1950-1961	19.1	36.1
Lockheed	1950-1962	8.4	26.3
Martin	1950-1960	14.3	34.8
McDonnell	1950-1962	18.4	46.6
North American Aviation	1950-1962	17.2	37.3
Northrop	1950-1962	18.0	42.5
Republic	1950-1961	19.7	44.4
Temco	1950-1959	17.2	57.7

a Pre-tax profits plus interest as percent of total assets.
b Profits as percent of net worth.

TABLE 32

RATES OF RETURN ON ASSETS[a] BEFORE TAXES FOR ALL MANUFACTURING CORPORATIONS,
1947-1954 AND 1955-1957

Asset size class (in thousands of dollars)		Rate of return on assets before taxes (percent)	
		1947-1954	1955-1957
(1)	0-25	−3.8	−13.0
(2)	25-50		− 0.1
(3)	50-100	4.8	3.6
(4)	100-250	7.8	6.3
(5)	250-500	10.4	8.0
(6)	500-1,000	12.4	10.0
(7)	1,000-2,500	14.3	11.3
(8)	2,500-5,000		11.8
(9)	5,000-10,000	15.2	12.6
(10)	10,000-25,000	15.7	14.0
(11)	25,000-50,000		13.0
(12)	50,000-100,000	14.9	13.0
(13)	100,000-250,000	14.5	13.3
(14)	250,000 plus		13.1

a Profits before taxes plus interest divided by assets.

exceptions the rate of return of the aircraft companies is substantially higher than the rates for all manufacturing firms.[17]

The companies with the lowest rates of return—Douglas, General Dynamics, and Lockheed—all incurred substantial losses in the development of their commercial jets which were reflected in profit-ratio reductions. General Dynamics' 1961 loss of $168 million was the greatest ever sustained by an American company in any one year. It amounted to a negative return of 20.3 percent on its average 1961 assets.

These results can be used to substantiate neither the hypothesis that the aircraft firms "gouged" the government nor the position that the firms were efficient. If the assets supplied by the government had been company-owned, the rate of return would have been lower.[18] Thus, if this rate is considered as a measure of the profitability of all resources employed by the aircraft firms, it may not be too high. If the firms had owned all their used resources, they would not have received excessive profits, *if* all the assumptions listed in footnote 18 were true. Despite this finding, it may be argued that the aviation companies were overcompensated in terms of the risks they bore in the form of assets owned and committed to the productive process.[19] This overcompensation, however, was not the result

---

[17] Although a rate of return on assets is a more meaningful measure, the rate of return on net worth has also been presented in Table 31 for those who prefer this measure.

[18] In order to estimate the profit ratios which would have resulted *if* the firms had owned all their facilities and *if* the fees would have remained the same, some assumptions must be made. Any adjustment used must take into account two known facts: First, the original cost of government-owned facilities, used by firms, was at one time at least twice and in some cases four times that of the companies' own facilities; second, plant and equipment constitute only a portion of the assets of the firm, so it is unlikely that the ratio of the *value* of government-owned equipment to the total assets of a firm would exceed 2 to 1. If the ratio is less, our estimate would be biased downwards.

To illustrate our procedure, let us assume that a firm, showing a 15 percent rate of return on its assets, had used government-owned equipment with a valuation twice that of the firm's own assets. *If* the firm *had* owned all the equipment, it would have earned appreciably lower rates of return. The 15 percent return on its assets would now be 5 percent. However, owning more of its own assets, it could depreciate these additional assets at the rate of 10 percent per year and include this in its allowable costs. The firm could earn 6 percent on this extra cost, but the extra return would increase the rate to only 5.4 percent. This is composed of the 5 percent previously discussed plus 6 percent on two-thirds of the depreciation which is 10 percent of the value of the assets. Consequently, 6 percent $\times$ 2/3 $\times$ 10 percent equals an extra four-tenths of 1 percent.

[19] Some assets on the books of the companies are inventories for which these firms have already been compensated in the form of progress payments. The inclusion of

of company performance but of the pricing schedule established by government procuring agencies. There seems to be little connection between the levels of the fixed fee allowed in CPFF contracts and the amount of risk accepted by firms. Allowable profits, possibly insufficient if all the capital is firm-contributed, might actually yield very high profit rates when a smaller fraction of the required facilities is owned by the firms.[20]

On the other hand, Jacoby and Weston[21] argue that the earnings of the aircraft industry are inadequate to finance growth from internally generated funds despite the fact that the aircraft firms usually have paid out, in the form of dividends, a lower percentage of their profits than other companies.[22] Moreover, the debt to equity ratio for the aircraft firms is higher than for other manufacturers.[23]

It is worth considering the procedure used to test the hypothesis that the industry earnings are inadequate to generate enough funds for growth. Jacoby and Weston compared the rates of returns of firms in the aircraft industry with the rates of returns of twenty-two other fast-growing companies.[24] Since all companies compete for capital in the open market, and since investors on the margin would expect to obtain equal rates of return (adjusted for risk) from all their investments, it is relevant to compare the rate of earnings of these twenty-two companies with that of firms in the air-

---

this item increases the denominator and lowers the rate of return, thus introducing a downward bias in the observed results.

[20] This conclusion helps to explain the feeling of individuals connected with the aircraft companies about the level of fees. The fees which led to these high returns came in periods when very little capital had to be invested by the companies. They came to accept these very high rates of return as natural and now complain when they must accept lower rates of return because the fee schedule is unchanged while more investment is required. See the testimony by the President of Northrop in U.S., House, Subcommittee on Manned Space Flight of the Committee on Science and Astronautics, *Hearings, 1963 NASA Authorization,* Pt. 2, 87th Cong., 2d Sess., March 6-April 10, 1962, pp. 395-397.

[21] Neil H. Jacoby and J. Fred Weston, "Profit Standards for Renegotiation," in J. Fred Weston, ed., *Procurement and Profit Renegotiation* (Belmont, Calif.: Wadsworth, 1960), pp. 122-158. The authors also have another article dealing with a somewhat similar subject, "Profit Standards," *Quarterly Journal of Economics,* LXI (1952), pp. 244-250. Here they attempt to determine a basic rate of return and raise the question of rewarding differential performance.

[22] Jacoby and Weston, "Profit Standards for Renegotiation," pp. 129 and 133.

[23] *Ibid.* This latter fact explains why the profit ratios of the aircraft firms are so much lower when an asset base is used as compared to the net-worth figure.

[24] *Ibid.,* pp. 153-156.

craft industry. Since these twenty-two companies have to obtain all their financial resources in the open market or through internally generated sources, the aircraft industry, to finance its own growth, should theoretically have to show similar earnings. Although the aircraft industry did not obtain these rates of return, it was not completely self-financed as the government furnished some of their facilities. The analysis of Jacoby and Weston reinforces our previous conclusions that the profit rates of aircraft firms were high considering the percentage of the capital which they contributed, but would have been too low had the firms been required to finance all the facilities used.

Little insight into the performance of the industry is obtained from examination of these profit ratios. Moreover, a preoccupation with profits and profit rates is likely to cause us to miss examining a much more important factor—the level of costs.

Nontraditional Measures of Performance

At best it is difficult to determine how well a company has succeeded in reducing its costs. In a standard market environment, however, there are obtainable insights from which some conclusions may be drawn about efficiency. For instance, the income statements of comparable firms vying in the same market may be compared. This *might* allow us to determine if some of the firms have achieved a minimum attainable level of costs relative to the performance of others in the industry. Yet even here conceptual problems exist, for it might have been possible for even the most efficient firm to have attained a lower level of costs, if it had innovated. In practice it is difficult to evaluate the efficiency of a firm's utilization of resources. Moreover, the environment in which the aerospace firms operate is not competitive, nor are comparable products sold. So, difficult as it may be to judge the efficiency of firms operating in a market environment, it is even more difficult to draw conclusions about efficiency of the aerospace firms.

Among the nontraditional sources of information here chosen to measure performance of the aerospace industry are reports of the American Institute of Management which determine whether companies are well managed. Then the cost overruns experienced by the aerospace firms are compared with similar data for commercial nonaerospace activity. This comparison may allow us to evaluate the efficiency of aerospace firms.

Performance as Measured by the American Institute of Management

The first nontraditional source of information used in this analysis of the efficiency of the aerospace companies was the *Manual of Excellent Managements*.[25] The American Institute of Management lists about five hundred American and foreign companies which it deems to be well managed. The managements of various companies are rated in ten categories of differing weights. Not only are the weights assigned in a manner which cannot be duplicated by an outside observer, but it is also possible to argue that, from an economic point of view, allotting of arbitrary weights is inappropriate. The weights as assigned by the Institute yield a possible maximum value of 10,000 points.[26] The highest value is assigned to executive evaluation which receives 24 percent of the total. Research and development receives 700 points, and 1,300 points are assigned to production efficiency.[27] Furthermore, in evaluating a company's executives, it is difficult at best for an outsider to determine how well executives work together.[28] Thus, even under optimal conditions, this method of evaluating managements is imprecise.

Six of the major aerospace prime contractors are included among these five hundred well-managed companies.[29] The difficulty arises when one attempts to assess these results. From a positive aspect, more than 50 percent of the major aircraft firms were considered well managed even when this decision was based upon criteria and weights which certainly did not bias the results in their favor. On the other hand, these five hundred firms include most of the country's largest concerns, and not to be included within the top five hundred certainly must be considered a minus sign for those ex-

---

25 American Institute of Management, *Manual of Excellent Managements*, 8th ed. (New York, 1962), pp. 12-64, *passim*. Kaysen and Turner were the first to use this source in measuring the performance of any industry or firms. See: Carl Kaysen and Donald Turner, *Antitrust Policy* (Cambridge: Harvard University Press, 1959), p. 10.

26 *Ibid.*, pp. 7-30. The categories and their assigned points are economic function, 400; corporate structure, 500; health of earnings, 600; service to stockholders, 700; research and development, 700; directorate analysis, 900; production efficiency, 1,300; sales vigor, 1,400, and executive evaluation, 2,400.

27 *Ibid.*, p. 7.

28 *Ibid.*, p. 30.

29 Included are Boeing, Douglas, Grumman, Lockheed, North American Aviation, and Northrop. Excluded are General Dynamics, Martin, McDonnell, Republic, and Ling-Temco-Vought. General Dynamics had been included on the list before 1962.

cluded. Perhaps one may disagree with the rankings in several cases. General Dynamics had considerable difficulties with the Centaur program and required outside assistance in the development of the ICBM.[30] In fact, the Centaur program required a reorganization of the company's management concepts.[31] However, the most likely reason for excluding General Dynamics was the enormous loss the company sustained in its commercial jet-development program.[32] Martin, in turn, had difficulties with the construction of the ICBM bases for the Titan I missile, and it too needed outside assistance.[33] McDonnell, whose Mercury capsule and F-4H-1 and F-4B (Phantom) fighters have been considered among the most successful systems produced by the industry, is excluded. So is another company related to the airframe sector of the industry, General Electric. General Electric, long considered one of the best-managed companies in the country, was included in this list until 1960. It probably was excluded in 1961 and 1962 because of its participation in the price-fixing conspiracy.[34]

The best one can do with these data is to say that they yielded no conclusive evidence about the performance either of the aerospace industry in general or the airframe segment of the industry in particular. The weights are arbitrary, and one cannot justify the exclusion of some companies, and the inclusion of others which have experienced similar problems.

PERFORMANCE AS MEASURED BY COST OVERRUNS

A second way to measure the performance of the industry is to compare the original cost estimates for weapon systems with their final costs. One can then compare this ratio of costs for the weapon

---

30 This was when Ramo-Wooldridge became affiliated with the missile program as a management company.

31 U.S., House, Subcommittee on Space Sciences of the Committee on Science and Astronautics, *Hearings, Centaur Program,* 87th Cong., 2d Sess., May 15-18, 1962, p. 9. General Dynamics' Astronautics Division was reorganized from a matrix to a projectized organization.

32 According to the weighting, failure to provide for the safety of the company is heavily penalized. By this scheme the company would not, however, be penalized for its failure to devote some of its own funds to the Centaur. The company considered but rejected this because of the risk. See the *Centaur Program Hearings,* p. 108.

33 *Missiles and Rockets,* June 19, 1961, p. 9. However, Boeing, which is included in the category of well-managed companies, had similar problems with another missile.

34 One must infer this, since Westinghouse Electric was eliminated at the same time.

or space systems developed by the aerospace firms with a similar ratio derived from projects which involved nongovernment work. The hypothesis to be tested is that the accuracy of cost estimates is lower for the aerospace than for other firms. There are several reasons for suspecting this possibility.

The aerospace firms may deliberately bid low in order to obtain the contract.[35] The purpose of the low bid is not to underbid a competitor but to obtain entry to a program by convincing the appropriate government agency that a given project is not only feasible but is obtainable at little expense. The low price might encourage the agency to undertake this project, which might not have been started had its real cost been known.[36]

At a later stage of this system's development, the contractor would show that the funds were insufficient and request an extension of the contract. By this time, the agency might be committed to the project, and might have focused its long-range planning on it. The agency thus is likely to request additional appropriations from Congress and to grant a subsequent contract. Thus, unduly low cost estimates may be used to obtain a contract; once the work has begun, these estimates are revised upwards. At this point, it should be noted that complete separation of contractor and government performance is impossible. Consequently, results ascribed to the behavior of the firms may in fact be attributable to the overall procurement process, including the agencies' previous willingness to accept unduly overoptimistic bids.

A possible second factor contributing to final costs exceeding original estimates is that contractors are not expending their own but public funds. They therefore may not feel the need to minimize expenses, for there is no real economic penalty imposed on firms with overruns. The absence of such a penalty may, in fact, induce overruns. There are opportunity costs involved in overruns, but their significance cannot be estimated. The personnel and

---

[35] Peck and Scherer, *op. cit.*, p. 421. A former Assistant Secretary of the Air Force subsequently became vice-president of Northrop. He indicated that overruns arose because the industry submitted overoptimistic bids which were prompted both by the need for business and the difficulties faced by the military in obtaining program approval. *Aviation Week*, October 28, 1963, p. 91.

[36] Part of the controversy on the TFX revolved around the Defense Department's fears that Boeing was using extremely low estimates. See *ibid.*, May 6, 1963, p. 25. In a similar vein the Air Force argued that the X-20 (DynaSoar) program should not be canceled because it was too far along. *Ibid.*, December 16, 1963, p. 30.

equipment committed to the project cannot be employed else-where until the task is completed. Consequently, if the firms had other uses for these resources, the profits foregone would be counted as opportunity costs.[37]

The widespread prevalence of these overruns should be noted, for in many instances the final costs of a weapon or aerospace system have exceeded the original estimates by several hundred percent. As examples of low estimates used to obtain contracts, Peck and Scherer report on two contracts in which the estimated costs rose 65 and 75 percent in two-and-one-half to three months.[38] This re-sult is attributable to many factors, among which the industry's inefficiency or deliberate overoptimism *may* be included. How-ever, one cannot attribute these results to either of these factors until all other possibilities have been analyzed and ruled out. One possibility is that the magnitude of the job may have changed be-tween the beginning and end of the project. This, in turn, would have affected the cost level. This is not to imply that there is no substance to the complaint that low bids are used to obtain the con-tract, and that prices are subsequently revised drastically. However, this contention by itself is not a proof, and, if it is true, it must be substantiated.

Recent NASA and Defense Department experiences probably can be used to lay the foundation for verifying this assertion. Re-visions in estimated costs between the time when a bid is submitted to and accepted by NASA, and the time when the contract becomes definitive have often been substantial.[39] Contractors frequently asserted that changes in the contract requirements caused these re-vised costs.[40] For instance, the accepted bid for the Apollo capsule was $368 million; the definitive contract was for more than a billion dollars, an increase of 200 percent.[41] One firm working on the guid-ance and control system for the Apollo project found that its costs had risen 150 percent above its original estimates. The explanation

---

[37] Unless there is a shortage of skilled personnel, facilities are the factor more likely to limit the firm's ability to undertake new projects.

[38] Peck and Scherer, *op. cit.*, pp. 414-415.

[39] *Aviation Week*, February 4, 1963, p. 99, and January 28, 1963, p. 58.

[40] It is difficult to believe that changes in the specifications always raise costs, for there must have been *some* changes which simplified procedures.

[41] *Ibid.*, January 28, 1963, p. 58.

was that both new and modified items were wanted.[42] NASA, however, must believe that its required changes are not the only factors responsible for this escalation, for it has issued new regulations which stipulate that the original estimate is to be used in negotiating a contract. If any deviations from the contract are required, they will be priced and negotiated separately.[43] Thus, contractors will no longer be able to claim that NASA's changes have caused cost increases.

A recent example of suspected underbidding for a Department of Defense contract was the TFX (F-111). Boeing included thrust reversers in its design proposals and priced the items at $14,500 each with an eventual drop to $8,500 because of the learning curve.[44] This price was quoted despite the fact that the then-current price for thrust reversers installed in the Douglas DC-8 was $95,000 apiece. Pratt & Whitney had estimated that the thrust reversers would cost $100,000 each.[45]

It is thus plausible to believe that the aerospace firms have used the "low bid" as a device to obtain a particular contract. It is therefore appropriate to question whether or not all cost estimates are inherently low, or if this bias is a characteristic peculiar to the aerospace industry. Marshall and Meckling's[46] and Peck and Scherer's studies provide a limited amount of data concerning the extent to which final figures have exceeded original cost estimates.

Marshall and Meckling provide several sets of cost estimates for advanced military aerospace projects, and all indicate a substantial degree of underestimation of cost. Production-cost factors, which are the ratio of final production cost to the earliest estimated costs, were tabulated for twenty-two military systems. These systems consisted of nine fighter planes, three bombers, four cargo and tanker planes, and six missiles. The production-cost factor for the fighters was 2.4 (i.e., 240 percent of the earliest estimated costs), for the bombers 4.5, for the cargo and tanker planes only 1.3, and for the

---

42 *Missiles and Rockets*, October 22, 1962, p. 12.

43 *Aviation Week*, February 4, 1963, p. 99.

44 *Ibid.*, April 15, 1963, p. 30.

45 *Ibid.*

46 A. W. Marshall and W. H. Meckling, "Predictability of the Costs, Time, and Success of Development," in *The Rate and Direction of Inventive Activity* (National Bureau of Economic Research, 1962), pp. 461-475.

missiles 17.1.[47] In order to show the dispersion of these ratios, the cost factor for each of the systems is presented in Table 33. This sample does not seem to yield atypical results, for more recent projects such as Mercury and Gemini show a similar pattern. The former had a cost factor of 3, and the estimated costs of the latter at a time when it had not even had its maiden flight were already double the original figures.[48]

There are many possible reasons for the errors in these cost estimates. The level of costs changes when the specifications change; consequently any error may be the result both of misestimating the

TABLE 33
PRODUCTION COST FACTORS FOR TWENTY-TWO
WEAPON SYSTEMS

Fighters	Bombers	Cargos/Tankers	Missiles
5.6	8.7	1.7	57.6
3.6	3.5	1.6	20.7
3.1	1.5	1.0	11.1
2.1		1.0	10.3
1.9			1.5
1.5			1.3
1.4			
1.2			
1.2			

SOURCE: Marshall & Meckling, *op. cit.*, p. 467.

cost of the original design and of failing to take into account design changes. Though seemingly uncorrelated, there is a relation between these two errors, for if a firm has difficulties in achieving the technical breakthrough necessary to complete the weapon system as originally designed, a new approach may be required.[49] Thus, overoptimism in predicting the technical advances required to bring a weapon system to function could lead to design changes. The more advanced the project, the greater the likelihood that the original configuration will not be final. However, this is a factor which should have been taken into account in the original proposals.

---

[47] *Ibid.*, p. 467.

[48] *Aviation Week*, May 6, 1963, p. 22. Other data indicate that the Mercury cost factor was only 2.

[49] Naturally, the costs which have already occurred must be included in the final figures. The actual costs of "the" successful approach will, therefore, include all these costs resulting from "false starts."

There are two additional factors not under the firm's control which could cause the actual cost to differ from the original estimate. These are price changes and changes in the number of items of the system required.[50] Marshall and Meckling adjust the cost factors of each of the mentioned systems for these influences. The final factors are 1.7 for fighters, 2.7 for bombers, 1.2 for tankers and cargos, and 4.1 for missiles.[51]

Marshall and Meckling argue that cost estimates of equipment resembling commercial equipment (i.e., cargos and tankers) are quite accurate because they do not tend to push the state of the art to its limit.[52] The argument is that the degree of technological advance required to complete a project determines the extent of the overrun. The data indicate that there is a correlation between the degree of technological advance and the adjusted production-cost factors. For those projects in which only a small amount of technological change was required, the adjusted cost factor was 1.4; it rose to 1.7 and 3.4 when medium and large technological advances occurred.[53] Peck and Scherer obtained similar results, for the development-cost factor (slightly different from the production-cost factor) of the advanced weapon (not all aerospace) systems which were included in their sample was 3.2.[54]

It is important to devise a standard against which these data may be judged. The only data available are crude but do yield meaningful results. Peck and Scherer obtained both development cost and time factors for some *advanced* commercial research and development projects. It may be argued that even the most advanced commercial research and development project does not require the technical breakthroughs needed for advanced military and aerospace systems. Nevertheless, if we make the necessary assumptions,

---

50 Actually, changes in the number of items procured may be correlated with the extent of the overrun, for if a fixed sum has been allocated to a given project, cost increases limit the number that may be purchased.

51 Marshall and Meckling, *op. cit.*, p. 469.

52 *Ibid.*, p. 462.

53 *Ibid.*, p. 472.

54 Peck and Scherer, *op. cit.*, p. 22. Moreover, the time-slippage factor for the projects analyzed by Marshall and Meckling was 1.5; for those analyzed by Peck and Scherer, it was 1.36. *Ibid.*, and Marshall and Meckling, *op. cit.*, p. 473. An official of the Defense Department quoted that a survey of twelve defense projects yielded cost factors of 3.2. *Missiles and Rockets,* June 3, 1963, p. 10. It is not clear if the two samples are identical or different.

it is possible to use these commercial data as standards against
which the aerospace industry's performance may be judged. The
necessary assumption is that development (or production) cost and
time factors are constants between projects which require the same
degree of technological advance. It is thus explicitly assumed that
a firm which is seeking to make a technological breakthrough in its
commercial area will underestimate its research and development
time and expense by the same proportions as would an aerospace
firm in developing a new system for the government. It is thus explicitly assumed that the time and cost factors are independent of
the *level* of research and development expenditures.[55]

The average development-cost factor of the advanced commercial systems was 1.7, the corresponding time factor was 1.4.[56] This
would seem to indicate that overoptimism in terms both of cost
and time of delivery is a universal phenomenon.[57] It is important
to note that all calculated *time* factors, both for commercial and
military systems, are of the same order of magnitude. The time
factor of the military projects which Peck and Scherer investigated
was 1.36, and for those analyzed by Marshall and Meckling 1.5.
The commercial data of Peck and Scherer yielded a figure of 1.4.
This conclusion reinforces our belief that the cost factors of the
military projects can be compared with a standard established by
privately financed commercial projects.

On this basis one must conclude that although the average advanced commercial project exceeded its original costs by only 70

---

55 On the other hand, there may be economies or diseconomies of scale associated
with a research and development organization. The opportunity to hire specialists
would provide economies, and the aerospace companies have been able to use such
specialists. However, the research departments of these firms may have reached the
point where diseconomies appear. There is no evidence to substantiate either the
absence or presence of economies or diseconomies of scale.

56 Peck and Scherer, *op. cit.*, p. 433. A prepared statement by Homer E. Newell of
NASA which was to be presented to a 1964 hearing before the House Committee on
Science and Astronautics gave similar data for some NASA projects. The figures
indicated that the average cost factor was 2.1 and the average time factor 1.6. However, these included figures for the Ranger project which were obviously low, for the
respective numbers of this project were 1.0 and 1.1. There has been considerable discussion of the Ranger project and its delays and overruns, but the mentioned NASA
data refer only to the first five Ranger satellites.

57 For some illustrations of the way costs have behaved in the atomic power plant
area see *Business Week*, October 12, 1957, pp. 48-50. For other evidence concerning
the variability of cost estimates see Armen A. Alchian, *Reliability of Cost Estimates—
Some Evidence*, Project RAND Memorandum, RM-481, October 30, 1950.

percent, the advanced aerospace military projects had a mean over-run of 240 percent. Moreover, these latter data take into account the price and quantity adjustments made by Marshall and Meck-ling for the mentioned aerospace systems. The cost factors of com-mercial projects were not adjusted in this manner. Consequently, if this had been considered, the comparison with Marshall and Meckling's data would have been even more unfavorable to the aerospace systems.[58] It is possible to conclude that firms working on military research and development contracts have experienced per-centage overruns considerably larger than those encountered in commercial endeavors.

This result may be caused by at least three factors: the extreme overoptimism of the firms; the absence of a cost minimization stimulus; a possible perpetual change in the specifications or scope of the project. This implies that military aerospace weapon systems are more likely to undergo such changes than advanced commer-cial projects,[59] for we have compared their cost factors. The data are thoroughly intermixed, and it is impossible at this time to separate them into these principal components.

If the large overruns are attributable to the perennial overopti-mism of aerospace firms eager to obtain contracts, the blame should not be absorbed entirely by the contractor. If this is a repetitive phenomenon, the procuring agencies should have become aware of this tendency, and, if unaware, they must be considered less than well informed buyers. If they did know, they gave tacit agreement for reasons that could not be determined. Similarly, if the overruns

---

58 Reconstruction of Marshall and Meckling's data (Tables 1, 2, 3, pp. 467, 469, 472) indicates that the following projects were considered to have made large tech-nological advance: Fighters 1, 7 and 8; Bombers 1 and 3; and Missiles 1, 2, 3, 4 and 6. The mean unadjusted production-cost factor for these projects is 11.9. If the first missile project with a factor of 57.6 is excluded, the mean is still 6.9, an overrun of 590 percent.

59 For evidence that advanced commercial projects do not experience that many reorientations, see Marschak's study of Bell Telephone Laboratories' development of the TH relay system. It required an expenditure of $15 million and was considered one of the laboratories' most complex systems. Thomas Marschak, "Strategy and Or-ganization in a System Development Project," in *The Rate and Direction of Inven-tive Activity*, pp. 509-548. However, a contradiction appears, for a change in a sys-tem's specifications should also theoretically increase the development time, yet the time factors of the military and commercial projects are comparable.

On the other hand, the original specifications for the Apollo capsule were de-pendent upon earth-orbit rendezvous. When lunar orbit was selected, a design change in the capsule was required. *Aviation Week*, July 22, 1963, p. 111.

had been due to perpetual change in the procuring agency's specifications, these agencies should have determined if their research
and development policies are the most productive.[60] It is at least
possible that some portion of these overruns is attributable to the
performance of the aerospace firms themselves.

It is difficult to obtain any evidence that a firm operated ineffi-
ciently, and therefore even more difficult to attempt to determine
what percentage of the cost-estimate variations is attributable to
inefficiencies. One can, however, draw some inferences about efficiency, for it has been noted that the aerospace companies want
incentive-type contracts in order to improve their cost controls.[61]
The implication is that the firms realize that there are inefficiencies inherent in their operations, but as long as they are not rewarded for removing them or penalized for retaining them, nothing
will be done. Although it is impossible to obtain precise data about
these inefficiences, inferences may be drawn from a study of the
firms' development policies about some of the industry's practices.

PERFORMANCE AS EVIDENCED BY DEVELOPMENT POLICIES
AND THE QUALITY OF THE DELIVERED PRODUCT

In Chapter 6 we noted that prime contractors had economic opportunities not available to subcontractors. Included among these
advantages was the possibility of retaining a large share of the contract for itself. If this opportunity was abused by unnecessary subsystem development, the costs of developing the system itself were
not minimized. While the data do not prove this point irrefutably,
they do point in this direction.

For instance, there is a case study of subcontracting which seems

---

[60] This is the crux of the argument for those analysts who favor the development
of prototypes before committing funds to a large-scale system effort. In the case of
the Saturn rocket it was argued that some of the problems resulted from the lack of
a proper program definition before the actual work was undertaken. *Ibid.*, November 18, 1963, p. 106.

[61] Herbert Solow, "North American: A Corporation Deeply Committed," *Fortune*,
June, 1962, p. 178. On the other hand, Boeing did not want to accept incentive-type
contracts for the BOMARC. U.S., Senate, Permanent Subcommittee on Investigations of
the Committee on Government Operations, *Pyramiding of Profits and Costs in the
Missile Procurement Program* Pt. 4, BOMARC *Program*, 87th Cong., 2d Sess., May 22-25,
1962, p. 690. The company was persuaded to accept such a contract, and it proved to
be financially profitable.

to imply that excessive costs were incurred in developing part of the ground-support system for the B-58.[62] An investigation of the choice of the ground-support airconditioning equipment for this bomber suggested that Convair may have developed an unnecessary item.[63] For nontechnical observers it is impossible to judge whether this development was indeed necessary. If it were not, and this is possible, excessive costs would have been incurred. Convair subcontracted the development of this ground support to another of its divisions—which could not receive a profit on this subcontract.[64] The important consideration is not the level of profits but the level of costs necessary to perform a given task. Because the author was restricted to unclassified data, and because he does not possess expertise in electronics and military-systems analysis, an evaluation of possible unnecessary system developments was not feasible. On the other hand, testimony by Air Force representatives indicate that the entire ground-support-equipment (GSE) program was under constant scrutiny to prevent excessive developments where acceptable items were already available.[65]

Although it cannot be proved conclusively that aerospace firms have undertaken unnecessary development projects, there is considerable evidence of their overdeveloping or "gold plating" their product (i.e., introducing at considerable expense technically unnecessary refinements).[66] This "gold plating" may also be due partly to Defense Department and NASA demands for reliability and

---

62 U.S., Senate, Select Committee on Small Business, Report on Excessive Cost of the Ground Support Air-Conditioning Equipment for the B-58 Bomber Program, *Case Study in Subcontracting by Weapon System Contractor*, Report No. 1947, 86th Cong., 2d Sess., September 16, 1960.

63 The report indicated that several slightly different carts used for ground support were available and could have been modified. However, it had been announced previously that Convair was applying the weapon-system concept even to the ground-support problem, for it was designing the B-58 support equipment specifically to the needs of the bomber. *Aviation Week*, September 15, 1958, p. 119.

64 As previously noted, when a firm subcontracts to one of its subsidiaries, the subsidiary does not obtain a profit for its work.

65 U.S., Senate, Subcommittee of the Select Committee on Small Business, *Hearings, Role of Small Business in Defense Missile Procurement*, 85th Cong., 2d Sess., April 29-May 1, 1958, p. 67. These hearings also cite an example of an Air Force contracting company which planned to develop special materials-handling equipment for transporting its missile. The Air Force suggested that this equipment be replaced with its standard equipment. Other contractors also changed their plans and shifted to the standard equipment with a consequent reduction in costs.

66 Peck and Scherer, *op. cit.*, p. 477.

maximum performance.[67] However, this demand for reliability is similar in many respects to the oft-noted concern of engineers with maximum performance from a system (be it electronic, mechanical, military, and so on) regardless of cost and may have been the stimulus for this "gold plating." Unlike civilian operations, where engineers are forced to compromise with their performance criteria in order to achieve more reasonable costs, there had been little movement in this direction within the aerospace industry.[68]

During World War II, when the emphasis was supposedly on maximum production, a conflict over a similar problem developed.[69] At that time both the aircraft and automobile companies were assembling planes. Although their airplane production lines had been established by the aircraft firms, the automobile companies wanted to use their own effective mass-production techniques. The aircraft companies, accustomed to coddling each individual airplane through the production process, refused to allow the design to be frozen and insisted that design changes be made midstream. This procedure may have been compatible with the limited-quantity production before the war but certainly was not efficient for mass production.[70] Thus, we note a tendency on the part of the aerospace companies to give low weights to cost factors in making their design and manufacturing decisions.

---

[67] Since the country's deterrent strength is based in part on missiles, it is necessary to convince any possible enemy that the missiles are reliable. Second, with unmanned operations no one can correct an error which may result from an electronic malfunction. Moreover, the safety of our manned space flights depends on the reliable operations of all systems. Finally, a malfunction in a component may result in the destruction of a very expensive spacecraft or rocket. A computer program error resulted in one such accident. The production costs of our boosters run as high as $7.5 million for the Centaur and $20 million for the Saturn C-1. Ranger and Surveyor spacecrafts cost between $7½ and $15 million each. See *Missiles and Rockets*, March 6, 1961, p. 9, and *1963 NASA Authorization*, Pt. 4, pp. 1822 and 1929.

[68] Peck and Scherer make this same point in a slightly different manner when they note that different value systems prevail for commercial and for military research and development projects. In the latter the contractors have maximized quality at the expense of costs and delivery time, whereas in commercial development projects the emphasis is more on the costs and time aspects. Peck and Scherer, *op. cit.*, pp. 293-295. It was previously noted that in some recent competition the government has insisted that the contractors include within their proposal an analysis of possible trade-offs. Similarly, North American's first task in constructing the Apollo capsule is to insure reliable operations. Meeting time and cost schedules command lower premiums. See *Aviation Week*, July 22, 1963, p. 124.

[69] Peck and Scherer, *op. cit.*, p. 479, and *Aviation Week*, December 9, 1957, p. 26.

[70] With a return to small production runs, the previous techniques of production may again be applicable.

With this emphasis on performance, a rating of "superior" quality is expectable, but both the Department of Defense and NASA have criticized aerospace workmanship. The Navy specified that only high-quality components should be included in the Polaris A-2. Contractors received prices three times those charged for "normal" parts, yet the rejection rate on these parts reached 56 percent.[71] Despite this high rejection rate, the Navy had to convince Lockheed, the prime contractor, to conduct reliability tests. Lockheed then started in-house environmental testing, and by making suppliers aware of the problem, reduced the component rejection percentage to 36 percent.[72]

In its 444-page report on the Mercury project, NASA was quite critical of the industry's performance and noted the many defects of the system.[73] Some of the cost overruns previously noted can now also be explained, for "time and money were expended in Mercury to rectify cases where improper materials were found in the systems because someone had failed to follow the approved materials list."[74] NASA's attempt to temper the tone of its report,[75] by stating that this project provided a lesson about the new quality standards required for the space age, is at best an indictment of the industry's quality standards which were not revised in conformity with the new aerospace requirements. On the other hand, it should be recognized that some of these failures cannot be attributed to the industry since a new environment of unknown characteristics was being explored. However, NASA's criticism of the Mercury team is not an isolated example of its concern about the quality of the industry's work. It had previously expressed its hope to boost systems reliability by awarding more incentive contracts.[76] Under

---

71 *Missiles and Rockets*, April 8, 1963, p. 33.

72 *Ibid.*

73 Some of the defects were: "spare parts that were 50 percent defective, capsules with more than 500 defects, batteries with holes in them, electronic parts improperly soldered, valves improperly installed, gas-pressure regulators that were not clean, and breathing oxygen and water that was contaminated." *The New York Times*, Western Edition, October 4, 1963, p. 1. On the last Mercury flight, the explosive charges used to jettison the retropack straps were defective. The charges which were designed for ground testing and had less power were mistakenly substituted for the flight charges. *Aviation Week*, July 1, 1963, p. 75.

74 *The New York Times*, Western Edition, October 4, 1963, p. 7.

75 *Ibid.*, October 5, 1963, pp. 1 and 5; October 10, 1963, p. 7.

76 *The Wall Street Journal*, September 30, 1963, p. 24. The space agency also announced that it would supervise its suppliers more closely.

the terms of these contracts, firms would be rewarded for meeting specified performance criteria.

The Centaur program provides another example of the design difficulties of the industry.[77] Not only did General Dynamics use incorrect engineering designs on the weathershield between the nose fairing and the Centaur stage, but it also used the same standards on the Centaur bulkhead as were used for the Atlas.[78] Even though the Atlas leaked kerosene across its bulkhead insulation,[79] the same bulkhead was used despite the fact that liquid hydrogen presents more problems than LOX.[80]

Part of the technical-performance problems of the industry may be attributable to its pragmatic research and development approach. The F-1 engine, to be used in the first stage of the Saturn booster, displayed combustion instability.[81] The contractor, North American, could not cope with the problem because there was no basic knowledge about this phenomenon. Similar problems in the past were solved by modifying the injector and then testing the engine's performance. If the instability disappeared, the problem was solved; if not, the procedure was repeated.[82] Finally, the industry's failure to produce sufficiently durable and reliable components has long been recognized, but in the past this has been attributed to time pressures imposed by budgetary limitations.[83]

To improve the industry's performance in these areas, the

---

[77] It was also observed that boosters which were shipped by NASA's Huntsville facilities required less change and double checking than similar rockets delivered by private contractors. *1963 NASA Authorization,* Pt. 2, p. 523.

[78] *Centaur Program Hearings,* pp. 51, 90-91, and 97.

[79] The A which was supposed to launch our first astronaut, John Glenn, leaked as did one selected for the Ranger III flight. *Missiles and Rockets,* February 5, 1962, p. 10.

[80] General Dynamics testimony on this point is interesting. See *Centaur Program Hearings,* p. 97, "We have definitely in this particular case, if I might say so, *gambled* at a very low weight and found that we have to correct ourselves. Now we have under fabrication bulkheads which have greater wall thickness at the point of welding so that we are confident we can overcome this problem." (Emphasis supplied.)

[81] *Missiles and Rockets,* June 4, 1962, p. 10; *Aviation Week,* February 4, 1963, p. 26 and May 27, 1963, p. 48.

[82] *Ibid.,* May 27, 1963, p. 48. One must also wonder about the government agencies' failure to support basic research in this area. Lately there may have been a change in this approach, for Martin, in rectifying the Titan II oscillations, developed several theories which may prove useful in solving similar problems in other boosters. *Ibid.,* February 17, 1964, p. 33.

[83] U.S., House, Subcommittee of the Committee on Government Operations, *Hearings, Organization and Management of Missile Programs,* 86th Cong., 2d Sess., 1960, pp. 59-60.

Defense Department recommended that the aerospace firms reconsider their design philosophies by adopting value-engineering techniques. The use of value engineering entails an examination of the
design and manufacturing process both of individual parts and of
the entire system in order to determine if alternative designs or
production methods would reduce costs. The Defense Department
is so intent on instilling cost consciousness in the industry that it
has offered very attractive terms to the participants. The cost of the
value-engineering team would be charged to the Defense Department, but any savings effected would be split evenly between the
firm and the government.[84] The Pentagon hopes to reduce costs by
$100 million annually through this technique alone.[85]

There are many indications that costs can be reduced through
value analysis. The production cost of the Bullpup missile fell 70
percent between production of the first missile in 1959, and the end
of 1962.[86] The Martin Company attributed this saving entirely to
value engineering, but a great part may be credited to the learning
curve and competition from a second source. As another example,
after General Electric became the second source for the Sidewinder
missile it instituted value engineering,[87] and managed to reduce the
cost of one part from $45 to $2 while improving its reliability.[88]
This evidence would seem to indicate that costs of the aerospace
firms can still be reduced. More important, industry observers have
indicated that many firms are reluctant to accept and use value
engineering.[89]

Unfortunately, cost-reduction campaigns are often tardy, and

---

[84] *Aviation Week*, December 3, 1962, p. 117. In addition, the government indicated
that the absence or presence of value-engineering departments would be a factor
taken into account in rating the capabilities of defense contractors.

[85] *The Wall Street Journal*, May 22, 1963, p. 9, and May 31, 1963, pp. 1 and 10. As
one example of the reduction in costs which is attributable to the elimination of
either gold-plating or excessive development, Secretary of Defense McNamara cited a
subsystem for the Minuteman missile. When hydraulic devices were substituted for
electronic mules for the missile silos, there was a saving of nearly a half million
dollars per missile site. *Aviation Week*, July 15, 1963, p. 33.

[86] *Ibid.*, December 3, 1962, p. 118.

[87] General Electric is considered to be one of the first firms to introduce value-engineering.

[88] *Ibid.*, April 9, 1962, p. 94. There are also some other references which would
indicate that considerable sums of money could be saved through value-engineering.
See: *Missiles and Rockets*, November 13, 1961, p. 42, and September 3, 1962, p. 39;
The Wall Street Journal, May 31, 1963, p. 1.

[89] *Missiles and Rockets*, April 8, 1963, pp. 27 ff.

many times are merely a response to political pressures. Close to a billion dollars *might* have been saved if value engineering had been applied to the original design program for the Minuteman missile,[90] but this was not done. It is fruitless at this stage to second-guess this decision. However, it is interesting to note the time at which Boeing, the major contractor for the Minuteman, began a cost-reduction campaign. The Air Force defended the missile program against the attacks which followed large overruns.[91] Nevertheless, within a month after this attack, Boeing appointed a cost-reduction committee whose purpose was to lower both in-house and suppliers' costs. Total savings of $60 million were to be projected by this committee, with a $44 million in-house reduction and the remainder from the suppliers.[92]

On the basis of this evidence, it is possible to make the following conclusions: It is conceivable that prime contractors have taken advantage of their position and have engaged in excessive development. There are indications that there has been "gold plating," without resultant increased reliability. In fact, both the Department of Defense and NASA have complained about the absence of dependable components. Finally, it has been demonstrated that value engineering is likely to reduce costs, thus indicating that costs are not at the lowest attainable level. Moreover, there are also reports that the aerospace firms are reluctant to adopt these procedures.

A Comparison of the Development of Relay and Telstar

Another mode of aerospace industry performance evaluation is by contrasting similar and comparable projects performed under private as against government financing. Since the projects are similar, one would theorize that both the costs and the elapsed time of development should be comparable. Any great discrepancies would then require explanation. The Telstar and Relay satellites, designed to be experimental low-level space communication satellites, are the only aerospace programs sufficiently similar to be used for this purpose. Both weigh approximately the same, 170 to 172 pounds, and though the designs differ somewhat, they are strictly

---

90 *The Wall Street Journal,* May 31, 1963, p. 10.
91 *Missiles and Rockets,* May 13, 1963, p. 18.
92 *Ibid.,* June 24, 1963, pp. 40 ff.

comparable.[93] Telstar was financed privately by American Telephone and Telegraph; RCA was NASA's prime contractor for the Relay project.

The bases for comparison of the two programs are their respective costs and development time.[94] The difficulties with this comparison are that (1) the company confidential data are available only in sketchy form, and (2) the precise time at which the research and development effort started is not easily determined. Thus, a comparison between the two projects cannot be perfectly precise, but enough data are available to warrant this analysis.

To determine the respective starting dates for the two companies, a brief history of the Telstar and Relay projects is necessary. In formulating its plans for the exploration of space, NASA had decided that communications satellites would be included within its jurisdiction. These programs included passive communications satellites, such as Echo, and the active satellite systems, such as Relay and Syncom.[95] Relay is a low-altitude satellite, Syncom is designed for high-altitude communications. The communications satellite program started very slowly and at first focused on the passive system, Echo.[96] The early lack of emphasis on the entire communications program can be noted from Table 34 which shows the program costs for NASA's communications satellites.

NASA's bid requests for the Relay project did not go out until January, 1961. In the meantime, probably as early as August, 1960,[97] American Telephone had started a small basic research and development effort on an experimental communications satellite system. This effort was of a comparatively small magnitude and re-

---

93 The Relay satellite used redundant circuits, but Telstar was constructed from highly tested reliable components. However, ideas about design were exchanged between the two programs.

94 Most of the following information was obtained from conversations with officials at RCA and AT&T.

95 The distinguishing feature between the active and passive systems is that the latter are merely reflectors of signals whereas the former receive a signal and have the electronic equipment necessary to transmit the signal in any desired form.

96 The first active repeater satellite was the Army's project Score. In this program a transmitter was put in an Atlas missile, and Christmas (1958) greetings from President Eisenhower were broadcast to the world.

97 This date came from the proposed project schedule included in "Supplemental Agreement No. 1 to the Cooperative Agreement between the National Aeronautics and Space Administration and the American Telephone and Telegraph Co. dated July 27, 1961," March 2, 1962.

quired expenditures of less than $2 million annually. Included in this effort was the research on the Bell Telephone Labs horn antenna at Holmdel, New Jersey. This was used in the Echo experiment, and therefore should not be included as part of the satellite communications systems effort.

In October, 1960, NASA offered to provide at cost any facilities required for launching a private company's communications satellite. Several weeks later it withdrew this offer and suggested that

TABLE 34

ESTIMATED FLIGHT PROGRAM COSTS FOR APPROVED
COMMUNICATIONS SATELLITES[a]

Fiscal year	Costs (in millions of dollars)
1959	1,000
1960	1,500
1961	29,903
1962	43,727
1963	40,110

SOURCE: *1963 NASA Authorization*, p. 2093.

[a] Echo I and II, Relay, Syncom, and Rebound.

industry wait for Project Relay, for there was too much risk for private industry.[98] American Telephone and Telegraph obviously disagreed, for later in 1960 the Bell Telephone Laboratories seriously started a research and development effort on the experimental satellite which was to become Telstar. This work also enabled the company to bid on Relay. AT&T obtained an FCC license to use specified frequencies for communication experiments with this satellite. On March 22, 1961, two days after the Relay bids were due, the company announced that regardless of the outcome of the Relay bids, it was going to proceed with its own satellite.[99] The Relay contract was awarded to RCA in May, 1961, and on July 27 of that year NASA and AT&T signed an agreement whereby NASA would provide the launching facilities at cost to enable Telstar to get off the ground. Thus, two competing low-altitude communications satellite systems were created. Telstar I was launched on July 10, 1962; Relay I was first orbited in December, 1962.

---

[98] *Aviation Week*, April 17, 1961, p. 104. In December 1960 AT&T offered to merge Project Relay and its own efforts. It offered to build the satellite on any cost basis that NASA determined. NASA refused this offer.

[99] *Ibid.*

To evaluate the comparative development time, beginning dates must be established. Obviously, RCA's effort must be dated from the time it won the award, for all work before that time must be considered as merely preparatory to submitting the proposal. Thus June 1, 1961, would be considered the starting date. The first satellite was delivered to NASA in mid-November, 1962. The research and development time was 17½ months or 3½ months longer than specified in the original contract. However, part of this delay may be attributed to major changes in the system. One factor which the contractor could not have foreseen was NASA's insistence that the satellite provide for telephone experiments, for these were not included in the original specifications. The other major changes seem to involve events which should be expected in the course of any development effort. These included an increase in the complexity of the coder, tube problems, and a basic change in the way the satellite would be stabilized in space.[100]

It is difficult to pinpoint precisely the date on which AT&T *seriously* started developing Telstar. It should not be considered as early as the summer of 1960, when the first experiments with communication systems started, for they were a minor effort and included research on the Holmdel antenna also. Nor should the date be set as late as July 27, 1961, when the NASA-AT&T agreement was reached, for construction of the Andover antenna which was required for the experiment had begun on May 29, 1961. It could be as early as December, 1960, or January, 1961, when FCC approval for the experiments was obtained. With the first space craft delivered to NASA for launching around May 1, 1962, a development time of 16 to 16½ months is indicated. This estimate of the time required for developing the satellite is slightly longer than figures used by informed industry sources. They stated that Telstar was built in 15 months.[101]

We may conclude that the development time of the two satellites was comparable, with Relay requiring 17½ months and Telstar 15 to 16½ months depending on which estimate is used. Second, part of the longer development time for Relay may have been due

---

100 The original specifications called for a satellite weighing 85 pounds; the final satellite actually weighed 172.

101 *Ibid.*, December 3, 1962, p. 95. The original agreement between NASA and AT&T had specified mid-April 1962 as the date of the first launching.

to RCA's being forced to reconsider its approach when the telephone experiments were included. However, it should be noted that RCA, a company with some experience in developing space satellites, required as much or more time to develop a satellite as a company with no previous experience in the field. The evidence seems to be sufficient to prove that RCA did not out-perform AT&T, but the evidence is not sufficient to prove that AT&T did the better job. This evaluation does not profess to compare the operating characteristics and performances of the two communication systems. Lacking expertise, it is impossible for the author to perform this evaluation. Moreover, industry spokesmen have not ascribed an overall superiority to one or the other system. Consequently, no conclusions about the comparative operating performance can be reached.

Imprecise as our estimates of time of development are, the cost data are even less precise. Yet if we want to compare the two systems, the cost of performing these similar tasks must be considered. According to figures provided by AT&T, less than $20 million were spent from 1960 through December 31, 1963, on the research, development, design, and construction of the Telstar satellites. This figure should be considered an estimate, for it is composed of two components: the expense of fabricating the satellites, and some portion of the $33 million spent on research, development, and design for the entire satellite program.[102] This latter figure includes both the $4 million spent on fundamental studies and basic research on the entire satellite system including the antenna, and also the research on the Holmdel antenna used in the Echo experiments. It is thus virtually impossible to determine the exact percentage of the $33 million which is attributable only to Telstar. Even if it were possible to derive such an estimate, there is a conceptual problem, for the development of a communications system composed of an antenna and satellite involves joint costs. To which element are

---

[102] Originally AT&T provided data that the total expenditure of $33 million had been spent by December 1962. However, later information from the company indicated that the 1963 expenditures on this project were insignificant and that these figures were still of the proper order of magnitude if carried through 1963.

The chairman of the board of AT&T indicated that the company had spent approximately $15 million for Telstar experiments. *The New York Times*, Western Edition, March 19, 1963, p. 5. However, it is not certain that this figure measures the same variables as are included in our estimate.

these costs assigned? Furthermore, these cost data are overestimates relative to any cost estimates that could be obtained for Relay, for they would include the expenses AT&T incurred in its preparations for the Relay bid, whereas similar costs incurred by RCA were not included in the latter's figures.

These technical points should not be dwelled upon, for the Relay cost data are difficult to interpret and not strictly comparable to the AT&T Telstar data.[103] NASA indicated that approximately $37.9 million was spent on the Relay project from its inception through November 30, 1963.[104] A breakdown of this figure indicated that $13.7 million was spent for the spacecraft, $15.6 million for ground operations, and $8.6 million for launch vehicles. To make the Relay data comparable to Telstar figures a minimum requirement is that the $8.6 million expended for the launch vehicles be subtracted from the project's total expenditures. When this cost is eliminated, an estimate which is comparable to the Telstar cost theoretically would be obtained. The figure is $29.3 million, which could be compared with AT&T's expenditure of less than $20 million. However, it is possible that the Relay data include expenditures for functions not encompassed in the Telstar experiments. For instance, NASA requested appropriations of more than $2.1 million for the command and control stations and almost $3.7 million for ground station operations.[105] It is not clear what portion of these expenditures should be excluded to make the data comparable with the Telstar figures. Thus it is not at all clear by what margins, if any, the combined RCA-NASA Relay expenditures exceeded those of AT&T on Telstar. Since the data are so imprecise, no conclusions about the comparative costs of the two projects can

---

103 RCA received a CPFF contract for approximately $5 million. The estimated costs were $4,640,000 and the fee was $350,000. The original bid had estimated costs at $3.25 million. *The Wall Street Journal*, May 19, 1963, p. 5. Delivery of the first satellite was scheduled for July 1962.

104 These data were contained in letters from the House and Senate Committees on Appropriations. Both letters were dated January 10, 1964. A letter from Roland L. Callaghan, NASA's Assistant Administrator for Legislative Affairs, to Representative Jeffrey Cohelan indicated that $44.9 million would eventually be spent on the Relay project. This included $15.2 million for the spacecraft, $19.7 million for ground operations and support, $8.8 million for the launch vehicles, and $1.2 million for data analysis.

105 U.S., House, Subcommittee of the Committee on Appropriations, *Hearings, Independent Offices Appropriations for 1964*, 88th Cong., 1st Sess., p. 379.

be drawn.[106] Thus the only finding about the two projects is that there was no significant difference between the projects in the elapsed development time.

PERFORMANCE AS MEASURED BY GENERAL ACCOUNTING OFFICE REPORTS

The periodic reports of the General Accounting Office (GAO) concerning excessive costs in contracting might be considered another source of aerospace-industry performance evidence. The GAO is Congress' watch dog on the spending practices of the executive branch of the government.[107] Therefore, a typical GAO report on excessive costs is more likely to be a critique of governmental contracting procedures than a comparison of the actual costs of production with costs which theoretically could have been attained had the contractor used an alternative manufacturing process. Excessive costs, therefore, merely refer to costs which are higher than they should have been under the existing conditions because the government used an improper procedure.

Between 1958 and 1962 there were approximately fifty such GAO reports dealing with the aerospace industry.[108] According to the GAO findings, costs have been only 1 percent higher than they should have been had proper practice been observed. Moreover, it was the largest contracts which were audited, in areas where errors were likely to be of the most consequence in absolute terms. Thus, although these reports drew much attention in Congress, they inflicted little damage on the reputation of the aerospace industry.[109]

---

106 However, it is known that the Relay spacecraft cost at least $13.7 million. The lowest estimate for the total cost of the Telstar experiment including the spacecraft was $15 million. (See footnotes 102 and 104 above.) On the basis of this evidence, it is unlikely that any findings which could have been obtained if comparable data had been available would have favored the Relay project.

107 This authority stems from the Budget and Accounting Act, 1921 (31 U.S.C. 53) and the Accounting and Auditing Act of 1950 (31 U.S.C. 67). The critique of Air Force procurement practices can be noted in U.S., House, Committee on Armed Services, *Weapons System Management and Teams System Concept in Government Contracting*, 86th Cong., 1st Sess., 1959, pp. 348-349.

108 Some of these reports are listed and discussed in *ibid.*, pp. 384-428, 625-641, and 703-708. Also in U.S., House, Committee on Armed Services, Special Subcommittee on Procurement Practices of the Department of Defense, *Hearings Pursuant to Section 4, Public Law 86-89*, 86th Cong., 2d Sess., April 25-June 9, 1960, pp. 64-70.

109 There is some evidence that the prime contractors have not been diligent in monitoring the costs of their subcontractors. This would indicate a lack of concern

Major focus was on the contracting procedures of the executive branch of the government, to which excessive costs were attributed. For instance, the GAO noted that the government made the transition from cost-plus to fixed-price contracts too early in the development process. Because costs were not yet precisely determinable, the contractor obtained high profit rates.[110] If there were cases in which losses were incurred as a result of the same procedure, they have not been documented.

Another type of report dealing with the same general class of data involved General Electric, but again attention was focused on the role of the government.[111] In this transaction General Electric leased back five government-owned, General Electic-built test engines which were unsuccessful entrants in the Air Force turbofan engine-design competition won by Pratt & Whitney. General Electric was to use these engines in its commercial jet-engine development program, and in return for a nominal leasing fee of $24,000 was to provide the Air Force with all derived data at no cost. GAO found the rental fee inadequate, as General Electric would otherwise have had to spend about a million dollars for similar equipment. The fact that the Air Force failed to exact a maximum rental fee from the company cannot be used to evaluate the performance of the aerospace industry.[112]

A second type of GAO report deals with overestimates in the target pricing of incentive-type contracts. If the contractor succeeds in attaining lower actual costs than the established target figure, these savings are shared in some specified ratio between the government and the contractor. The effectiveness of these contracts in

---

about costs. See *Weapons System Hearings*, p. 348; U.S., House, Procurement Subcommittee of the Committee on Armed Services, *Procurement Study*, Pt. 1, 86th Cong., 2d Sess., 1960, p. 112.

110 For example, see *Weapons System Hearings*, pp. 463-476. The reason for these "excessive" costs is obvious. If the company is forced to accept the risk of a fixed price contract, it will estimate costs in such a way that errors are most likely to be in its favor.

111 General Accounting Office Report, B-133328, *Examination of the Leasing of Government-Owned Aircraft Test Engines by the Department of the Air Force to General Electric Co.*, Cincinnati, Ohio, June 1961.

112 Another example of Air Force purchasing procedures which led to excessive cost can be noted. Through sole source procedures the Air Force contracted for one part with two separate companies, unintentionally paying one company $3 more per item than it paid the other. U.S., Senate, Subcommittee of the Select Committee on Small Business, *Hearings, Government Procurement, 1960*, 86th Cong. 2d Sess., April 5-8, 1960, p. 393.

reducing costs depends, as noted above, upon the accuracy of the target costs. If the target costs are overestimated, the contractor obtains "savings" which are the direct result of this estimate. The GAO reports note several instances in which the target costs were overestimated, for the price estimates for subcontracted components were substantially higher than pretarget cost negotiation prices.[113]

It is impossible to determine whether these overestimates were deliberate efforts to obtain higher company profits, were genuine mistakes, or included risk premiums to cover possible price changes. These data can therefore not be used to evaluate the performance of the industry, but should make us wary of statements which imply that incentive-type contracts may yield lower costs.[114]

In a similar vein, Boeing once refused to accept a $5 million refund from Ford, one of its subcontractors. The reason for this hesitancy is not known, but the facts themselves are interesting.[115] GAO had expressed the opinion that Boeing's price redetermination of the Ford subcontract was made too early. Consequently, Ford was able to obtain a fee of 28.9 percent instead of the contemplated 10 percent.[116] Boeing replied to GAO's findings on November 3, 1955,

---

113 For examples, see *Weapons System Hearings*, pp. 384-428 and 704-708. The Air Force itself had noted discrepancies between costs current at the time of negotiation and the estimated prices submitted in the bids. *Aviation Week*, January 19, 1959, p. 35.

For the difficulties in estimating costs see David Novick, "Costing Tomorrow's Weapons System," *The Quarterly Review of Economics and Business*, III, No. 1 (Spring 1963); and a series of memoranda published by the RAND Corporation (Santa Monica, California). These memoranda include David Novick, *System and Total Force Cost Analysis*, RM 2695 (1961); G. H. Fisher, *Military System Cost Analysis*, RM 2975-PR (1961); J. W. Noah, *Identifying and Estimating R & D Costs*, RM 3067-PR (May 1962); and J. M. Calmer and R. W. Smith, *Aircraft Airframe Cost Estimating Techniques*, RM 3375-PR (November 1962).

114 In 1962, a law requiring that all price estimates be certified for their accuracy was enacted. *Aviation Week*, August 13, 1962, p. 30; September 3, 1962, p. 23.

Moreover, an argument has been advanced that the use of multiple incentive fees may not yield results which coincide with the procurement agencies' preferences. This might be the case in which a schedule of fees was established and the firms chose some procedure which would maximize their potential fees. See Neil S. Weiner, "Multiple Incentive Fee Maximization: An Economic Model," *Quarterly Journal of Economics*, LXVII, No. 4 (November 1963), pp. 603-616. Also *Missiles and Rockets*, January 20, 1964, pp. 24-25.

115 The entire history of this transaction is documented in U.S., House, Subcommittee for Special Investigations of the Committee on Armed Services, *Report and Hearings, Boeing Airplane Co.-Ford Motor Co.: Purchase Order Subcontract on AF 33-600-5148*, 85th Cong., 1st Sess., August 14, 1957.

116 *Ibid.*, p. 2322. The date of the first tentative report was October 19, 1955.

and defended its methodology for redetermining the price.[117] At this time Boeing did not mention a possible refund, although an intradivisional memorandum dated November 4, 1955, indicated that Ford had telephoned and proposed that a $5 million refund be made.[118] There are indications that Boeing was at first reluctant to accept this refund,[119] but by January, 1957, it was accepted and transmitted to the Air Force, although no records corroborate this fact.[120]

In contrast to Ford's willingness to make a refund, General Motors in a similar case refused to do so. General Motors had a fixed-price contract to manufacture 599 F-84F jet fighters.[121] It supposedly earned $17 million in excess profits because the price was redetermined too early. However, it felt that there were no legal or moral grounds requiring it to refund the money.

Other GAO reports yield some data which indicate that the aerospace firms are not producing at the lowest possible costs. The value of a contract is often redetermined at some specified point in the production process (i.e., when x percent of the items are complete, and so on). At this juncture, far enough along in the production process, costs usually can be determined accurately and a firm price negotiated. The evidence indicates that after this redetermination the actual costs of completing the contract are often lower than the estimates made at the time of redetermination.[122] One can infer that when a firm's own profits are at stake it can find methods to reduce costs further.[123] At other times there may be less concern with minimizing costs.[124]

---

117 *Ibid.,* p. 2358.

118 *Ibid.*

119 *Ibid.,* p. 2346.

120 *Ibid.,* p. 2349.

121 See *Aviation Week,* August 26, 1957, p. 31; U.S., House, Committee on Armed Services, *Hearings, Study of Air Force Contract, AF 33(038)-18503, General Motors Corporation: Buick-Oldsmobile-Pontiac Assembly Division,* 85th Cong., 1st Sess., 1957.

122 Price redetermination often occurs after the contract has actually been completed. The estimated price can be based only on costs through the redetermination point.

123 In a report on Westinghouse Electric (B-132963) GAO noted that at the 40-percent mark estimated cost would be $14.8 million; the actual costs were $13.9. *Weapons System Hearings,* p. 625. Similarly, McDonnell Aircraft was able to produce some F-3H airplanes for $6 million less than anticipated. *Ibid.,* pp. 62-67. (GAO Report B-132936.) The Boeing-Ford and General Motors cases cited above provide similar data.

124 Similarly, there are fears that firms which receive as a profit fee 2 percent of

Various GAO reports analyze excess costs resulting from the improper procurement procedures. Most of these reports focus on the contracting procedures of the government and therefore shed little light on industry performance. Any information purveyed about the industry's behavior can be considered only as inferential. A weak conclusion which may be inferred from these GAO reports is that the aerospace firms are probably not always producing at minimum attainable costs. This hypothesis is tested directly in the following section.

PERFORMANCE AS MEASURED BY THE DECREASE IN PRICES RESULTING FROM COMPETITION

The most useful information about the performance of the industry can be obtained through a comparison of the prices charged by a sole-source contractor before competitive bidding and the prices resulting at the first competitive stage. This yields an estimate of the higher costs incurred by the government as a result of sole-source procurement. In measuring these differences, care must be exercised, for the data might be misleading.

There are two methods for measuring these price differences: to compare the prices charged by the sole-source contractor before the competition with the price resulting from competitive bidding; and to compare the bid submitted by the previous sole-source contractor in the subsequent competition with the actual price resulting from the competitive bidding. Both methods yield biased estimates, but the direction, although not the degree, of bias can be determined for both. The first method overestimates the extent of the saving resulting from competitive bidding because part of the savings might be attributable to the purchase of larger quantities or to the application of the learning curve to follow-on production. Thus not all savings between a previously negotiated price and the subsequent competitive price can be attributed to the competitive process. The second method probably underestimates the extent

---

the value of subcontracts may not have incentives to keep down the cost of subcontracts. *Weapons System Hearings*, pp. 137-176. For a similar view expressed by the GAO, see General Accounting Office, "Examination of the Pricing of Certain Components of Corporal Missiles under Department of the Army negotiated Fixed-Price Subcontracts awarded by Gilfillan Bros., Inc., . . . to Motorola, Inc., . . . Report B-125027," June 1961.

of the saving resulting from a competitive process, for the sole-source contractor, knowing that he is now engaged in a competitive process, may take this into account and reduce his price.[125] The extent of the true saving resulting from competition then must lie between these extreme measurements.

Let us now consider the data available to measure the extent of the saving resulting from the competitive process. One set of voluminous data must be discarded because it does not lend itself to analysis. The army listed a number of items which it broke out from the prime contract and awarded in some form of competitive bidding.[126] In comparing item prices, the tabulation listed the unit price at the time of the last sole-source procurement and the price at which the *last* competitive purchase was made.[127] Between the time of the last source procurement, and the time of the last competitive purchase many years may have elapsed, and the prices may not be comparable. The relevant data to permit a meaningful comparison would have been a list of the prices charged for these components at the time of the first competitive purchase. It is unfortunate that the only complete list available does not contain this relevant information. Since these data are unavailable in such complete detail, a summary of fragmentary data including hearsay testimony of experts must be used.

When aeronautical spare parts were procured competitively rather than from a single source, significant savings were obtained. A group of 1,214 items was procured competitively for the first time at a saving of $300,000. Since the total value of these contracts (after the savings) was $1½ million, 38 percent of the previous cost was saved.[128] This figure is fairly close to similar estimates made independently at other times by other government officials. These other

---

125 The price may have been reduced in any event because of the application of the learning curve. Price reductions due to competitive pressures are over and above those resulting from "learning."

126 This competitive bidding included the negotiated form as well as the advertised.

127 *Government Procurement, 1960* (as cited in n. 112), pp. 411-600.

128 U.S., House, Subcommittee of the Committee on Appropriations, *Hearings, Department of Defense Appropriations, 1963*, 87th Cong., 2d Sess., p. 511. These data refer to the period July 1, 1961 to January 31, 1962. A GAO report dated January 29, 1960, indicates a saving of 40 percent is possible through competition. *Government Procurement, 1960*, pp. 68-69.

estimates indicate that when competitive rather than sole-source procurement is used, savings range from 30 to 75 percent.[129] These data use the first measure mentioned above—the extent by which prices decline when competitive bidding is substituted for sole-source procurement. It must be remembered that this method over-estimates the extent of the savings attributable to competitive procurement. The saving is more likely to be closer to the 25 per-cent figure which Secretary of Defense McNamara mentioned in 1963.[130] Similar evidence also exists for aerospace procurements of other than spare parts.[131]

Although many firms may reduce the government's cost for a par-ticular item by 70 percent, some of these bids may be overly opti-mistic. Bidders may be unaware of some of the procedures necessary in manufacturing and may bid very low the first time, but as soon as these firms incur losses and discover errors, prices will probably rise. The experience of Hoffman Electric with an Air Force TACAN navigational device may be typical. Hoffman's winning bid for the contract was half the previous price.[132] However, the company had to use certain reliability procedures in manufacturing this item. Perhaps because of its lack of familiarity with these tech-niques the company lost $8 million on this $40-million contract.[133]

Using the other method of comparison whereby the quotations submitted by the original prime contractor are compared with the winning bid, we obtain somewhat lower estimates of the saving resulting from competition. In a procurement for the Sidewinder missile, 15 percent was saved; for the Terrier 18 percent; and for others, cited by the Navy, as much as 25 percent.[134] Another ex-ample is provided by the subsystems of the Army's Nike missile. The trailers for the system were originally purchased at $10,300

---

[129] *Ibid.*, p. 494; *Aviation Week,* February 13, 1961, p. 87 (the figure here was 30-40 percent); and U.S., Senate, Subcommittee of the Select Committee on Small Business, *Hearings, The Role of Small Business in Government Procurement, 1961,* 87th Cong., 1st Sess., April 25-26, 1961, p. 36. *Department of Defense Appropriations, 1963,* p. 553 (a saving of 30-50 percent was indicated).

[130] *The Wall Street Journal,* March 29, 1963, p. 6, and July 12, 1963, p. 5.

[131] See *Government Procurement, 1960,* pp. 45-50 (mentioning examples of price reductions amounting to as much as 50 percent); *Department of Defense Appropria-tions, 1963,* p. 23; *Pyramiding of Profits and Costs . . .,* Pt. 1, pp. 81-90 and 95-97.

[132] *Aviation Week,* January 19, 1959, p. 100.

[133] *Ibid.,* March 13, 1961, p. 216.

[134] *Procurement Practices, Hearings* (as cited in n. 108), pp. 273-275.

from Fruehauf, but when the contract was placed competitively the price dropped to $5,300. Fruehauf's bid for this contract was $9,178.[135] In any event, it must again be emphasized that this method of estimating savings leads to underestimates. Consequently, a figure as high as 25 percent would be representative of the advantage that may be gained through competitive procurement.

These illustrations are not isolated pieces of evidence presented to Congress in an effort to convince the legislators of the military's sincerity to cut costs, for other data reinforce this conclusion. Whenever possible the Navy has made it a practice to select second sources for those missiles, such as the air-to-air Sidewinder, which are produced in large volume. The history of Sidewinder procurement illustrates the extent to which competition is beneficial.

Between 1956, when the second source for Sidewinder was selected, and 1962, the cost of the missile guidance and control system dropped 70 percent.[136] Philco received the original contract in 1955, and General Electric was selected as the second source in 1956. At that time it received a contract to produce a pilot quantity in order to establish its production procedures,[137] but beginning in 1957 the two companies competed for their respective shares of the market.

It is interesting to observe the trend in the price of this missile system after the entry of General Electric. Philco's 1956 price was only one-third of its 1955 price. General Electric's 1956 price was higher than Philco's but still less than Philco's 1955 price.[138] The drop has continued, and in 1962 was only one-seventh of the pilot quantity price, and one-third of the 1956 price.[139] It is difficult to determine the extent of the decline which would have occurred without competition, but it would probably have been less. The Navy obviously feels that the competition from a second source is very beneficial, for it has selected a second company for both the

---

135 *Pyramiding of Profits and Costs* . . ., Pt. 1 (as cited in n. 61), pp. 84-87. This is an indicated saving of 42 percent calculated by a method which underestimates the savings.

136 *Aviation Week,* April 9, 1962, pp. 89 ff. The guidance and control systems are the major cost elements of such a missile.

137 The Navy reimbursed both companies for the tooling expenses incurred.

138 *Ibid.,* p. 89.

139 *Ibid.,* p. 93.

Bullpup, an air-to-surface missile which is also mass produced, and the shipboard inertial navigation system (SINS) for the Polaris submarines.[140]

To judge the influence of competition on a firm's efforts to reduce costs, another example must be considered, namely the influence exerted by interproduct competition. The Martin Company had the prime contract for the Titan I ICBM. In reporting on the progress of its missile program it noted that by the time 50 percent of the required missiles were assembled, the number of man hours required for each was reduced from 75,000 to 19,000.[141] This was a 75 percent reduction in the number of labor hours required, but the total decrease in costs may not have been of the same magnitude.[142] This information cannot be obtained without access to company data, but the total saving was probably substantial.[143]

It is important to determine the reasons which may have contributed to this reduction in cost. First, the experience gained through increased volume production would have tended in any event to reduce costs.[144] Second, the company may have had incentive-type contracts through which it would have shared these savings with the government, but the evidence of such contracts was not available.

On the other hand, the competitive pressure exerted by other missiles vying with the Titan for Air Force funds may have provided this stimulus. The Titan and General Dynamic's Atlas, both first-generation missiles, were developed simultaneously.[145] The success of the Atlas led to proposals that the Titan be dropped. The idea was to rely on the Atlas and then move directly to the Minute-

---

140 Martin was already trying to cut its cost when the Navy announced the selection of a second source, Maxson Electronics. The former company managed to reduce its costs between 70 and 75 percent. *Missiles and Rockets,* February 20, 1961, p. 9; March 12, 1962, pp. 16-17 and June 18, 1962, p. 37. No cost information about the shipboard inertial-navigation-system contracts is available. See *Aviation Week,* May 11, 1959, p. 23 for information concerning award of the contract.

141 *Missiles and Rockets,* August 28, 1961, p. 9. On the second-generation Titan II missiles, the first five missiles required 35,000 man hours per missile.

142 The price of subcontracted electronic components which account for a substantial portion of a missile's costs would not have been affected.

143 Martin stated that in 1962 it had saved $40 million. This was 10 percent of the year's Titan funds. *Missiles and Rockets,* February 4, 1963, p. 41.

144 This is the principle of the learning curve.

145 Both missiles were developed in order to assure the development of *an* ICBM. The Titan was originally considered the backup vehicle.

man.[146] Finally, development of the Atlas was speeded and that of the Titan delayed to make sure that the latter would be an improvement over the former.[147] Titan survived three reviews of its status, with the Budget Bureau recommending its elimination and the scientists favoring its continuation.[148] One of the reasons advanced for continuing the project was the possibility that it would provide competition for the other missiles.[149] It is feasible that Martin's savings on Titan were the result of competitive pressures on the company—such as fear of contract termination. The company thus may have sought to improve its efficiency.

The Titan I cost-cutting evidence seems to lend additional support to the conclusion that competition forces firms to become more efficient. A final point on this subject is the degree of effectiveness of incentive-type contracts vis-à-vis competition in promoting efficiency. It was previously noted that the government's sharing of savings with a contractor through incentive type contracts was a reward to the firm for being efficient; competition, on the other hand, penalizes those who are not. One would theorize that the latter mechanism, since it operates automatically on all decisions and not just on those selected by a firm, is likely to produce better results. The evidence confirms this hypothesis. Secretary of Defense McNamara indicated that the government saves 25 percent when a noncompetitive contract is awarded competitively, but the savings are only 10 percent when an incentive contract rather than a CPFF contract is used.[150] We must conclude that the absence of adequate competition has increased the cost of aerospace products by about 25 percent. Part of this differential may be attributable

---

146 *The New York Times*, September 24, 1958, p. 10, and September 27, 1958, p. 11.

147 U.S., House, Committee on Armed Services, *Hearings, Investigation of National Defense Missiles*, 85th Cong., 2d Sess., 1958, p. 4151.

148 *Organization and Management of the Missile Program*, (see n. 83), pp. 66-67. Unfortunately, one cannot obtain the Air Force evaluations of the missile and thus determine the probability that the project would be canceled. An additional constraint should be mentioned. The Air Force had insisted that Martin build a new missile plant when it undertook the Titan project. *As a conjecture*, is it not possible that the Air Force was afraid to take this contract away from Martin after the company had invested in the plant? (However, there is no evidence to support such a view.)

149 *Ibid.*, p. 67.

150 *The Wall Street Journal*, July 12, 1963, p. 5. This indicates that the savings resulting from incentive contracts is 12½ percent, as the savings are customarily shared 80-20 with the firms.

to the higher level of profits prevailing on sole-source negotiated procurements than occur with competition;[151] the remainder can be considered the result of the firms' failure to take advantage of all cost-reduction opportunities.

Since there is sufficient evidence that competition results in lower prices, it is important to question why the government does not encourage it. For instance, the failure of the government to break out some components after the system has been developed, in order to reap the benefits of competition, should be investigated. Sometimes the developer of the system is retained as the sole supplier because the complete manufacturing drawings and technical data are not supplied promptly enough after development. Then the item cannot be advertised competitively.[152] Thus, the prime contractors' failure to comply with the requirement that adequate drawings be provided prevents the government from obtaining competitive bids.[153] This is another facet of industry performance that should be evaluated, but again inadequate data make this impossible.

PERFORMANCE AS MEASURED BY TECHNOLOGICAL PROGRESS

The final aspect of performance involves a consideration of the technological progress of the industry. There is no doubt that in the past twenty-five years the aerospace industry has adjusted to the changing times. In the early forties the industry was required to change to mass-production techniques, only to find that demand was again curtailed at the end of World War II. The aircraft firms did not seek missile contracts eagerly, perhaps because the potential of these contracts was not recognized. However, when our missiles were required, the aircraft industry was able to make the transition, but only with the assistance of the management companies. The laggard transition from aircraft to a mix of aircraft and missiles may

---

151 Peck and Scherer, *op. cit.*, p. 208. The data indicate that profits are 11.5 percent of sales on fixed-price contracts against 4.9 percent on CPFF. Also see *Procurement Study*, Pt. 2, p. 123; even higher rates of return on fixed-price contracts are indicated there.

152 U.S., Subcommittee on Defense Procurement of the Joint Economic Committee, *Progress Made by the Department of Defense in Reducing the Impact of Military Procurement on the Economy*, 87th Cong., 1st Sess., June 12, 1961, p. 7.

153 It is also possible for the developer to submit incorrect drawings resulting in bidding errors. On one Redstone missile item previously costing $1,640, the low bidder's price was $87.25. It developed that the specification drawings were wrong. *Government Procurement, 1960*, p. 164.

have been the deciding factor that management companies were necessary.[154]

Some experts complained about the length of time required to develop our weapon systems,[155] but the systems were developed and served as an adequate deterrent. In the meantime the aerospace companies were required to make the transition to space-oriented projects, thus contributing to the feeling that the only factor constant in the aerospace industry was change.[156] To be able to adjust to these changes is a partial indication of the progressiveness of the aerospace firms. The industry's performance must be considered more than adequate on this score.[157] The evaluation might have been higher if government prodding had not been required to achieve this result.

Developments in the electronics sector of the industry need not be detailed, for most observers agree that the electronics industry has been very progressive. The magnitude of the aerospace industry's contribution to furthering technological progress in other areas cannot be measured with precision because the author lacks technical expertise and the data are classified. However, one example can be cited. The technique originally used in manufacturing cases for solid-fuel rockets was the roll-and-weld method applicable in the production of airplane parts.[158] This was used only because the airplane companies, which were actively competing for these contracts, knew this technique. After the cases were produced it was discovered that there was greater weakness at the weld than at any other point.[159] It is reasonable to say that either the government or the contractors should have discovered this shortcoming earlier. In the course of developing a new product it is reasonable to expect both the buyer and the competing sellers to question the applicability of an old production technique. Since the specifications of the production contracts for these rocket cases are not available, it is difficult to ascertain why this process was used. In any event, once

---

154 U.S., House, Committee on Science and Astronautics, *Staff Study, Independent Non Profit Federal Research Contractor,* 87th Cong., 2d Sess., October 10, 1963, p. 1.

155 Peck and Scherer, *op. cit.,* p. 427.

156 *The New York Times,* Western Edition, May 7, 1963, p. 13.

157 One exception previously noted was the apparent failure of the aerospace companies to adjust their quality-control procedures to the new requirements.

158 *Missiles and Rockets,* May 2, 1960, pp. 38-39.

159 *Ibid.*

aware of this problem, at least one major aerospace company developed a new production technique.[160] It is obvious that it is difficult to evaluate the industry's performance even in this one respect. It is consequently almost impossible to reach any valid conclusions about the industry's overall performance with respect to technical progress.

Summary and Conclusions

Although many of the measures used to evaluate the performance of the industry were weak or inconclusive, the overall impression is that the industry's performance up to the early 1960's left something to be desired. The data, while imperfect, all point in the same direction, or at least do not contradict this conclusion. For instance, the data indicated that without competition, costs increased by 25 percent. This was somewhat corroborated by the cost factor analysis where the ratios were considerably higher for the aerospace industry than for commercial products. There is some evidence of excessive developments and "gold plating" and a lack of enthusiasm for value engineering. The use of the latter indicates that costs may be reduced without impairing reliability. Furthermore, there is evidence that product quality could be improved. Other data, such as the *Manual of Excellent Management,* the GAO reports, and the Relay-Telstar comparison, yield inconclusive evidence, but do not negate our findings. The aerospace companies *were* able to adjust to technological change, but this conclusion must be tempered, for they had to be prodded to make the transition from aircraft to missiles.

---

[160] Republic announced the development of a weldless motor-case technique. *Ibid.,* May 6, 1960, p. 31. It is not known whether this innovation was the result of a government contract or of the company's own efforts. However, since there has been considerable competition for the rocket-case contracts one would hope that government funds were not used. It would be a sign of the industry's progressiveness if it actively sought to improve the technology. However, it is known that government funds are often substitutes for research activity that the firm would have undertaken in any event. Richard Nelson, "The Impact of Arms Reduction on Research and Development," *American Economic Review, Papers and Proceedings,* LIII, No. 2 (May 1963), p. 436.

9.

CONCLUDING REMARKS

The analysis of the structure and performance of the aerospace industry now enables us to determine which of the economic forces operating in the industry were primarily responsible for the observed behavior. The industry's performance was measured in several dimensions, and although the data for several measures were imperfect, the greater part of the evidence seemed to indicate that performance could have been improved.

It was noted in Chapter 8 that the structure of this industry prevented us from using the traditional objective standards devised for measuring an industry's performance. The main factor which precluded use of data such as profit rates is the absence of a market. As market standards were thus inapplicable, other measures were devised which permit the drawing of some conclusions about the performance of this industry. As a corollary these new measures prevented the making of interindustry comparisons, since they are relevant only to the aerospace industry.

Our conclusion about the industry's performance stemmed primarily from an analysis of its cost overruns, development procedures, and price behavior following introduction of competition. Analysis indicated that cost overruns occur in most research and development activities, hence their mere presence cannot be equated with poor performance. However, the fact that defense-contract overruns exceeded those on nondefense commercial research projects provided some evidence that there was room for improvement. That these overruns were partly attributable to the industry's perennial overoptimism does not lessen their portent.

There was also some evidence that the industry overdeveloped its products. An unduly large percentage of each system may have been developed *de novo,* and excessive costs may have been incurred because the industry "gold-plated" or overrefined its products. Finally, despite these development procedures and expenditures, some data indicate that the quality of the industry's products often did not meet the procuring agencies' expectations.

The most important sources of information about industry performance were data obtained from comparison of prices charged by sole-source contractors before competitive bidding and the prices which resulted when competition occurred. This yielded estimates of the higher costs incurred by the government as a result of sole-source procurement. The data indicated that the prices paid by the government declined 25 percent when competition was introduced. The 10 percent decline in prices when incentive-type replaced cost-reimbursement-type contracts corroborated this evidence.

REVIEW OF ECONOMIC FORCES

It is now possible to review the economic forces which were operating in the aerospace industry and to indicate the effect that each has had on industry performance.

The first factor to be considered was the enormous growth, coupled with several periods of sharp decline, in the government's demand for aerospace products. The growth in demand occurred when airplanes and missiles were needed first to fight a war and then to serve as a deterrent against possible war. In this economic environment the speed with which a weapon can be obtained may outweigh other considerations such as the cost of the system. In time of war or cold war there is likely to be a military demand that a weapon be designed for maximum performance. This demand would again outweigh cost considerations. A crash space program might also place other considerations above cost. Thus, the observed cost overruns might be attributable partly to the increase in demand and the factors which occasioned this demand. Moreover, the gold-plating which occurred might be attributable to the procuring agencies' excessive demands for performance.

The periodic sharp decline in government expenditures for aerospace products also has been partly responsible for the observed performance. Since military strategy originally dictated that a broad mobilization base be maintained, there are some indications that the government's procurement policies were directed at least partly toward assuring the continued survival of the existing firms. However, this policy has never been clearly articulated or consistently pursued. Thus the possibility of sharp declines in military expenditures was ever present, increasing the level of uncertainty facing the airplane manufacturers. Therefore a large part of the industry's required capital expenditure was provided by the government; this reduced the extent of the industry's risk. But this practice varied considerably and is now largely discontinued.

Military planners and the industry were affected by these fluctuations in government expenditures. Consequently the periodic curtailment of expenditures may also have contributed to the high level of overruns in another way. If a procuring agency or even a particular element within an agency felt that it needed a particular program or weapon but could not justify it on the basis of true estimated costs, it might either suggest or sanction the industry's submission of low bids. A low estimate might then convince the appropriate budget officers that the program could be started without violating the monetary constraints. It is possible that the "low" bid was thus used to begin many programs which would never have been started had "true" costs been known. Thus it is seen that demand factors have somewhat affected the industry's performance.

A second factor which may have influenced economic outcomes was change in the composition of industry output. The industry originally was production-oriented, but then a trend toward more research and development and less production was observed. There was even a shift within the production category since missiles and space systems are now manufactured in conjunction with airplanes. Likewise the importance of electronic products has grown within the aerospace industry. Furthermore the shift in output composition led to successful entry into the industry of some electronics companies which received contracts for the smaller missiles. Contracts for larger missiles, however, were still awarded to the former airplane manufacturers. The entry of the electronics firms was important in encouraging technical change in view of the airplane firms' apparent reluctance to accept missile contracts.

Since the specification of the final product is not known when a research and development contract is awarded, a price for the product cannot be determined. Thus the growing importance of research and development expenditures contributed to the elimination of a market environment. In addition, research and development involve uncertainty and risk which both the government and the firms were anxious to reduce. Consequently cost-reimbursement contracts began to be used more frequently. Since firms bear little risk with this type of contract, the incentive to minimize costs may be eliminated. Thus some portion of the cost overruns might stem from the greater use of the cost-reimbursement contracts used to avoid the uncertainties of the research and development process.

The growing importance of electronics output has probably produced conflicting results. On the one hand, the entry of the electronics firms into the industry provided the government with more sources of supply. Similarly, the need for electronics competence forced the airplane manufacturers to expand their in-house capabilities in this area. Both factors were disposed to benefit the performance of the aerospace industry. On the other hand, the growing importance of electronics meant that a smaller percentage of the aerospace dollar was spent on items traditionally produced by the airplane manufacturers. This may have encouraged the airframe firms to seek to develop more subsystems and may have been partly responsible for the observed overdevelopment of systems. It must be remembered that the prime constructors had the opportunities to keep such subsystem work for themselves. Further, the observed overdevelopment of subsystems was also partly caused by the weapon-system form of contracting in which an integrated system was to be produced *in toto*. It is therefore difficult to determine precisely the causes of the observed overdevelopment of weapon and space systems. On balance the changing composition of the industry's output and the increased importance of electronics probably furnished positive stimuli for the industry's performance. These factors provided new sources of supply and encouraged technical progress.

The third and perhaps most important set of forces which would explain the performance of the industry is its structure. Although many firms participate, a large percentage of industry sales is accounted for by a very small number of companies. This concentration is mainly attributable to the use of a single prime contractor for the large weapon and space systems. The concentration may have increased in some sectors of the industry because there have been some exits since missiles and space products have begun to supplant airplanes as the major output of the industry. It has been noted that research and development contracts were not awarded at fixed prices, but the absence of a market environment and competitive forces should be mentioned again. Since World War II, interfirm competition for the right to develop and produce specific-function systems in general has occurred, if at all, only at the onset of the procurement process. After that the system is usually developed and produced by a single firm. Thus there is little direct competition prevailing in the industry. The only effective competition is between two companies chosen to produce different yet similar systems for the same procuring agency, or in interservice or interagency rivalry for a mission. In the latter case the systems of the firms working for each agency would be in competition. Again, there is little competition except for the interservice, interproduct rivalry.

The growing importance of CPFF contracts was noted previously. As these contracts impose little risk on the firm, the absence of a market coupled with these contractual arrangements might explain much of the observed performance. However, this combination might also be expected to encourage entry into the industry, especially in view of the advantages accruing to prime contractors. The uncertainty of future demand and the government's previous policy of protecting existing firms were, on the other hand, barriers to be hurdled by prospective entrants. This may explain why more entry did not occur. Moreover, the barriers to entry at a large scale are very high. For instance, entry into the airframe sector of the industry requires a minimum investment of $14 million for a space laboratory with additional expenditures for research and development. United Technology Corporation was forced to spend $40 million to expand successfully within the propulsion sector of the industry. Since these are estimates of the *minimum* level of expenditure for successful entry, it is not surprising that there were few new entrants.

GOVERNMENT PROCUREMENT POLICIES

Finally it should be noted that the government, as the largest buyer, could have introduced more institutional arrangements which might have induced results similar to those produced by competition. However, the government did not always introduce such safeguards. It can be argued that the government was not a single buyer since several agencies procured aerospace products. However, all agencies were subject to the same basic procurement regulations, and their actions could have been coordinated to obtain the maximum competitive impact.

Noted throughout this book are the fundamental changes in government policies since 1961. These were instituted in the Department of Defense when Secretary of Defense McNamara and Assistant Secretary of Defense Hitch assumed office. The procurement policies of NASA have also moved in the same direction. These new policies probably have made a considerable impact upon the industry's performance, but at the time that this book went to press a complete assessment of the effect of these policies could not be made. It is therefore possible only to recapitulate some of the fundamental changes which have transpired since 1961.

First, the Department of Defense rationalized its entire procurement process when the programming concept was introduced. Under this concept the relation of particular weapon systems is not made on an item by item consideration, but rather the selection is made in the context of how the particular system fits into the overall defense needs of the country. Thus specific programs are defined based on the major missions of the armed forces, and a program package consisting of an interrelated group of planned military systems is prepared. Each proposed system is costed, and its effectiveness is analyzed. The selection of the systems which are to proceed into development is determined from the cost and effectiveness of each. This new concept of procurement also should encourage interagency interproduct competition. Similarly, five-year cost estimates are now used so that low initial outlays are not used to implement programs that would never have been begun had their true overall costs been known. In addition, this will discourage the combined agency-industry use of the low bid to start a new program. Finally, the development policies of the Defense

Department and NASA have been coordinated. This enables the government to procure systems which might be used by either agency.

It has been suggested that fixed-price or incentive-type contracts could be substituted for the cost reimbursement contract. In Chapters 4 and 5 it was noted that since 1961 the use of both incentive and fixed-price contracts has increased with a simultaneous decrease in CPFF contracts. Preliminary evidence presented in Chapter 8 indicated that some improvement in industry performance could be anticipated when incentive and fixed-price contracts were substituted for the CPFF contracts.

In addition, at the time this book went to press, governmental procuring agencies were establishing procedures for evaluating the performance of their contractors. One of the factors to be considered was a comparison of the results obtained with the promised performance contained in the original proposal. The implementation of such a procedure will conceivably reduce the extravagant promises contained in the proposals thereby providing the procuring agencies with better information for deciding between programs and contractors. This policy may also lead to a reduction in the magnitude of cost overruns since judgment of the firms would be partly on their ability to meet the original cost estimates. In a similar vein it was noted in Chapter 8 that NASA recently introduced regulations requiring that the original cost estimates be used in negotiating a definitive contract. Any changes in the specifications are to be priced and negotiated separately.

The government had to make several other changes to insure that the procedures provided the maximum improvement in performance. Before a development contract could be awarded, many uncertainties which faced both the buyer and the seller had to be resolved. Thus there has been an increase in conceptual-design competitions. This also involved the introduction of a program-definition phase designed to establish technical criteria. Moreover, in these design competitions the new procedures required the firms to analyze possible tradeoffs in the various dimensions. This procedure provides the buying agency with additional technical information and also enables the buyer to evaluate the firms' technical competence.

Because some of these institutional arrangements have been introduced comparatively recently, there is still insufficient evidence to measure the extent of industry performance improvement. The evidence available would seem to indicate that some improvement can be expected. Consequently it should be recognized that the industry should not bear the full responsibility for its observed *past* performance, for the procurement process represents an interaction between the government and the selling firms.

The purpose of this study was to investigate the relationship between industry structure and performance. If government procurement actions are accepted as a given part of the structure, then the relationship has been demonstrated clearly. The salient features of the aerospace industry structure are: a high concentration of sales; the absence of competition; a failure on the buyer's part to impose economic incentives on the sellers; and high entry barriers. One would theorize that the performance of an industry with such a structure would not be outstanding. This, indeed, is the case.

The purpose of this study was not to evaluate the efficiency of government procurement policies, still less to survey the management procedure of the various agencies. Consequently, throughout this study government policies were accepted as given, and no detailed recommendations for remedial actions by the government can be presented. It was suggested that a more competitive environment would be desirable, and that the introduction of certain institutional arrangements would produce beneficial results. However, no specific recommendations will be made about the policies which the government should pursue. Also, we have indicated that the arrangements which both NASA and the Defense Department have introduced since 1961 are likely to improve the industry's performance. These policies were designed to remove many of the adverse effects observed throughout this study. The effectiveness of these policies, intended to overcome many of the structural factors which have contributed to the observed performance, however, can be evaluated only at a later date.

APPENDIXES

APPENDIX A: SUPERSONIC COMMERCIAL AIRLINER DEVELOPMENT

In our analysis we have purposely excluded discussions of the airlines and airplane manufacturers. The development of a supersonic airliner, however, will require government participation and is therefore within the province of our analysis. At the time of this writing, no final decision about the supersonic transport (SST) has been made. Consequently any comments made at this stage must be considered preliminary and tentative.

NASA and the Federal Aviation Agency were jointly responsible for any federal commitment that might be made in the development of a supersonic passenger transport. Even before President Kennedy announced that the government and the private firm would share the development cost of the SST, the two agencies were preparing designs and awarding study contracts. NASA awarded Boeing and Lockheed small contracts to study the general design of such an airplane.[1] These studies were for evaluating designs proposed by NASA. At the time of this award the companies were asked to bid on other study contracts to examine the feasibility of the aircraft. Because of the risk inherent in the project, Boeing and North American participated in a joint venture.[2] This team and Lockheed both won cost-sharing contracts for research on the airframes for the plane.[3]

The estimated cost of developing the SST is $1 billion. Proponents of the plane's development advocated that the government assume as much as 90 percent of the development cost, since the aircraft industry was unlikely to assume such a risk. Part of this could be recovered in the form of royalties from the eventual manufacturer of the plane.[4] As

---

[1] *The Wall Street Journal*, January 18, 1963, p. 2.

[2] *Ibid.* Other coalitions included Douglas, McDonnell, and Republic which teamed to bid for a study contract for engines and fuels. *Ibid.*, January 16, 1963.

[3] The total value of the contracts was $3.4 million, with the government contributing $1.8 million. The government's contribution to Lockheed was $950,000. *Ibid.*, April 2, 1963, p. 2.

[4] *Ibid.*, May 17, 1963, p. 4.

soon as Pan American Airlines announced its decision to purchase six Concorde, the British-French supersonic jets which are expected to be flying in 1970, President Kennedy proposed that the United States program begin. He suggested that the government contribute $750 million toward the SST's development.[5]

It is not clear how the benefits subsequent to this development would be shared between the government and the successful aircraft manufacturer. Several companies are willing to participate in the development of the plane, others are reluctant. No company is eager to risk the $250 million it would be required to contribute.

Boeing, Lockheed, and North American agreed to submit bids for the airframes while United Aircraft, General Electric and Curtiss-Wright were willing to bid for the engine contracts.[6] The other airframe companies declined to bid,[7] and the prospective bidders complained that their contemplated 25 percent contribution was beyond their capabilities.[8] However, when Boeing, Lockheed, General Electric, and United Aircraft were selected to produce the designs for the plane and its engines, they accepted this cost-sharing provision.[9] The ultimate developer and producer of the plane and its engine will be selected after this design competition.

It is not within the province of the author to provide a rationalization for government support of commercial plane development. However, it should be noted that the originally highly competitive commercial sector of the aviation industry was slated for government subsidy.

Appendix B: The Importance of Aerospace Research and Development Expenditures

Since a large percentage of the nation's research and development effort is carried on by the aerospace industry, questions have been raised

---

[5] *Ibid.*, June 6, 1963, p. 6; June 7, 1963, p. 2; and June 17, 1963, p. 2. There was a suggestion that airplanes with a top cruising speed of 1,600 instead of the maximum 2,000 miles per hour be developed. It was argued that this step would reduce the initial development cost to $300 million. These planes would be designed so that they could later be modified into the speedier type. *Ibid.*, August 2, 1963, p. 8.

[6] *Ibid.*, September 11, 1963, p. 4.

[7] Douglas pleaded that it wanted to work on the DC-8 and DC-9. It had sold 208 of the former although it needed 250 sales to recoup its $300 million development costs. *Ibid.*, August 5, 1963, p. 7, and September 10, 1963, p. 5. The company also devised an unusual cost-sharing plan with its subcontractors for the development of the DC-9. See *Aviation Week*, April 15, 1963, p. 40. General Dynamics declined to bid despite its extensive experience with the B-58.

[8] *The Wall Street Journal*, October 28, 1963, p. 14; October 30, 1963, p. 17, and May 21, 1964, p. 2.

[9] *Ibid.*, May 21, 1964, p. 2 and June 3, 1964, p. 18.

pertaining to the appropriateness of the allocation of these resources among industries. It is not within the province of this book to answer this question, but any research purporting to measure the impact and importance of this industry must at least indicate the magnitude of the research and development effort centered within it.

Table 35 indicates that both the absolute level and the percentage of the nation's research and development effort concerning aircraft and missiles are increasing. The nation's share given over to the aircraft and

TABLE 35

TOTAL U. S., FEDERAL GOVERNMENT, AND AIRCRAFT-INDUSTRY EXPENDITURES
FOR RESEARCH AND DEVELOPMENT, 1953-1962

Research and development expenditures (in millions of dollars)

Year	Total U. S.	Federal government	Aircraft industry[a]		Aircraft industry total as percentage of U. S. total
			Private funds	Government funds	
	(1)	(2)	(3)	(4)	
1953	3,630	1,430	118	640	20.9
1954	4,070	1,750	...	...	...
1955	4,640	2,180	...		...
1956	6,598	3,328	266	1,812	31.5
1957	7,725	4,336	361	2,266	34.0
1958	8,363	4,759	386	2,276	31.8
1959	9,609	5,610	405	2,769	33.0
1960	10,507	6,125	451	3,180	34.6
1961	10,872	6,436	420	3,537	36.4
1962	11,560	6,729	412	3,787	36.3

SOURCES:

A: National Science Foundation, *Funds for Research and Development,* 1959, NSF 62-3

B: National Science Foundation, *Review of Data on Research and Development,* "Funds for Performance of Research and Development in American Industry," No. 30, NSF 61-51, September 1961.

C: *Ibid.,* No. 39, NSF 63-19, May 1963.

D: *Ibid.,* No. 40, NSF 63-37, September 1963.

E: U. S. Department of Labor, Bureau of Labor Statistics, *Science and Engineering in American Industry,* Final Report on a 1953-1954 Survey, NSF, 65-16, 1956.

F: *Ibid.,* Final Report on a 1956 Survey, NSF 59-50, 1959.

Col. 1:   1953-1955, A, p. 6.
             1956-1962, D, pp. 8, 10.

Col. 2:   1953-1959, A, p. 6.
             1960, B, p. 5.
             1961-1962, D, p. 8.

Cols. 3-4: 1953, E, p. 66.
             1956, F, p. 48. NSF 63-19 represents a slightly different figure, yielding a ratio of 33 percent.
             1957-1961, C, p. 4.
             1962, D, pp. 8, 10.

a According to Source A, pp. 10, 70, the data include both missile and aircraft expenditure.

missile industry has risen from 20.9 percent in 1953 to more than 36 percent in 1962. Moreover, the data are obtained by classifying companies in each industry according to the 1958 SIC.[1] But these data refer only to the aircraft and missile industries; if data for the aerospace operations as a whole were available for consideration, they would show an even sharper uptrend.

Finally, these data do not contain all expenditures for research and development. The data presented in Table 35 refer only to the direct operating costs incurred in the performance of research and development and do not include expenditures for the requisite facilities.[2] If these outlays were included, the percentage of the nation's scientific efforts which center upon the aerospace industry would be even larger.

Though the only available data impress one with the percentage of the nation's scientific resources accounted for by the aerospace industry, it must be remembered that even these data understate its impact.

Appendix C: Technological Change and Competition

In analyzing the entry of electronics firms into the aerospace industry, there was a discussion of some technological changes which affected the structure of the industry. These changes include the development of microelectronic components and integrated circuits.[1] The development of these miniaturized electronic products may cause a scientific revolution which may equal that of the development of the transistor.

The competitive effects resulting from this development are ana-

---

[1] Moreover, an individual company is assigned to a single industry even though it may have plants and research and development activities in many areas. This practice differs from the Census method of assigning plants to an industry. See National Science Foundation, "Research and Development in American Industry, 1961," *Reviews of Data on Research and Development,* No. 32, NSF 62-33, September 1962, p. 12.

[2] U.S., Bureau of Labor Statistics, *Science and Engineering in American Industry, Report on a 1956 Survey,* NSF 59-50, 1959, p. ix. It is for this reason that the figures presented in Table 35 are lower than those in Table 19 of Chapter 1.

---

[1] Integrated circuits are electronic packages which combine the functions of several electronic components. For instance, one such circuit could handle amplification, frequency conversion, and switching. *Business Week,* April 14, 1962, p. 160. There are two ways to integrate a circuit: thin metallic films are deposited through a mask to form a cluster of components, or transistor techniques are used to produce a complete circuit on a small piece of semiconductor material. *Ibid.,* December 8, 1962. The second approach was originated by the manufacturers of components and equipment systems. *Aviation Week,* March 19, 1962, p. 55.

lyzed.[2] Essentially, microcircuits of all types are useful in space applications where components of high reliability, small size, and low weight are required. The emphasis on miniaturization stemmed from the need to reduce the weight and size of electronic components designed for missiles.[3] Since this program was successful, miniaturized components are now also used in most space systems.[4]

There are numerous difficulties associated with the manufacture of microminiaturized electronic components. To achieve mass production at a relatively low cost, circuits have to be standardized,[5] but at present the problems presented by required tolerances and temperature sensitivity preclude attainment of this dual goal.[6] Moreover, semiconductor circuits would cost less than transistors alone only if firms could achieve a production rate of 65,000 circuits per month *and* if these new products replaced existing circuits using four or more transistors.[7] However, the mentioned production level requires large-scale production with somewhat large entry costs.[8] These problems led observers to believe that much time would elapse before the miniaturized components took a large share of the component market.[9] The Arthur D. Little forecast indicated that sales of microcircuits would total $600 million by 1972 and would account for 12 percent of the market for electronic compo-

---

[2] The changing structure of the electronic industry caused by the introduction of the transistor is beyond the scope of this research, for only the electronic-component manufacturers were affected.

[3] *Aviation Week,* June 16, 1958, p. 215; and February 8, 1960, p. 81. On the other hand, IBM has argued that multiple transistor packages (that is, redundant circuitry) offer equipment designers many of the advantages of microcircuits without the constraints imposed by circuit standardization. This standardization would be required for mass production. *Ibid.,* May 28, 1962, pp. 55-56.

[4] U.S., House, Subcommittee on Manned Space Flight of the Committee on Science and Astronautics, *Hearings, 1963 NASA Authorization,* Pt. 5, 87th Cong., 2d Sess., 1962, p. 2095. They have also been adopted for other than aerospace applications. See *Aviation Week,* July 8, 1963, p. 68.

[5] *Business Week,* December 8, 1962, p. 84.

[6] *Aviation Week,* May 14, 1962, p. 28.

[7] Most of the subsequent data on integrated circuits come from a report by Arthur D. Little which was abstracted in *ibid.,* February 25, 1963, pp. 87 ff.

[8] The Little study indicated that entry at this level would require about $2 million for capital and $1.4 million annual expenditures. This would enable the firm to produce 60,000 units per month and maintain a major competitive position. If the firm wanted only to keep abreast of the state of the art, and make designs or wished to have a limited innovation capability, entry would be possible at lower costs. *Ibid.,* pp. 95-97. The estimate of $1.4 million annual research and development expenditures for a major contribution may actually be on the low side. Some observers believe that $2 to $5 million would be required annually. *Missiles and Rockets,* February 3, 1964, p. 27.

[9] *Business Week,* December 8, 1962, p. 84.

nents.[10] This would be a sharp rise from the $85-million sales of 1962.[11]

The development of microcircuits was spurred by the NASA and Defense Department decision to investigate the properties both of the thin film and the semiconductor types of integrated circuits.[12] The development of these circuits has caused structural changes affecting relationships between the electronic component manufacturers, the electronic systems subcontractors, and the prime weapon system contractor. This structural change is the focal point of our analysis.

The traditional relationship has been for the prime contractor to subcontract a particular electronic item to firms which have been called the equipment or subsystem manufacturers. These firms designed circuits using discrete electronic components, which in turn were purchased from the component manufacturers.[13] Since an integrated circuit incorporates the functions of these discrete components, the use of such circuits eliminates the need for individual components such as transistors and diodes. If the firms which produced the electronic subsystems designed and produced these integrated circuits, they would be making a product competitive with electronic components.

The traditional demarcation between component manufacturers and electronic-systems manufacturers would consequently disappear. While the component manufacturers were among the firms which studied and developed alternative microelectronic approaches,[14] it was stated as unlikely that the component manufacturers would have the resources to manufacture integrated circuits.[15] The equipment manufacturers be-

---

10 *Aviation Week*, February 25, 1963, p. 87. An earlier forecast indicated that sales might reach $1 billion and account for 15 percent of the component market. *Ibid.*, May 14, 1962, p. 28. Another forecast indicated that in 1970 microelectronic sales would be between $200 and $500 million. *Missiles and Rockets*, February 3, 1964, p. 23.

11 These sales accounted for about 3 percent of the electronic component market in 1962. U.S., Department of Commerce, Business and Defense Services Administration, "The U.S. Industrial Outlook for 1963," ER-63, 1963, p. 9. Another source indicated that microelectronics sales in 1964 were not as high as the ADL estimate for 1962, *Missiles and Rockets*, February 3, 1964, p. 23.

12 *Aviation Week*, May 28, 1962, p. 36. For other discussions of the growing importance of semiconductor circuits see *ibid.*, October 29, 1962, p. 69; December 10, 1962, p. 95; and January 14, 1963, p. 83. Further discussions of their films are presented in *ibid.*, February 4, 1963, pp. 68 ff., February 25, 1963, pp. 84 ff., and July 1, 1963, pp. 89 ff.

13 *Ibid.*, January 8, 1962, pp. 85 ff.

14 *Ibid.*, March 13, 1961, p. 239; *Missiles and Rockets*, February 3, 1964, pp. 31-44.

15 *Aviation Week*, June 12, 1961, pp. 73 ff. International Resistance entered this area in 1959. *Ibid.*, November 2, 1959, p. 79. Texas Instruments, which is both a component and equipment manufacturer, had also entered this area. Varo and Fairchild semiconductors, two component manufacturers, arranged a joint venture to produce electronic products. *Ibid.*, July 20, 1959, p. 27. Similarly, Lear Siegler, an equipment manufacturer, and National Semiconductor reached an informal agreement to develop hybrid microcircuits. *Ibid.*, April 8, 1963, p. 78.

came the principal firms in the manufacture of semiconductor microcircuits. Moreover, the smaller avionic equipment manufacturers were warned by the Armed Forces against establishing in-house microcircuit capabilities.[16] Thus, it would seem that the area of integrated circuit production would be left to the larger equipment manufacturers.[17]

Another development occurred which further complicated the traditional relationships within the aerospace industry—that between the prime manager and his electronic subcontractors. Some of the major prime contractors have added in-house semiconductor manufacturing capabilities.[18] It is thus possible that any advantage gained by the equipment manufacturers from the component manufacturers may be lost to the prime contractors, if the latter decided to develop more electronic equipment.

It is still unclear what the future trend will be in this sector of the economy. It should be watched closely, for the innovations that have occurred in microelectronics came from the larger firms.[19] It may mean that entry into the electronics sectors of the industry will become increasingly more difficult. This, of course, may reduce competitiveness.

APPENDIX D: RENEGOTIATION

Renegotiation is an additional burden usually not borne by firms operating in commercial ventures. Renegotiation of profits at the end of

---

[16] *Ibid.*, March 19, 1962, p. 69. However, Radiation, Inc., which is a small avionic-equipment manufacturer with annual sales of $30 million set up its own in-house facility. This step was felt to be necessary when a major supplier was unwilling to modify some particular circuits to meet the company's needs. *Ibid.*, March 9, 1964, p. 66.

[17] *Ibid.*, March 19, 1962, p. 69 and March 11, 1963, p. 244.

[18] The Convair division of General Dynamics, Lockheed, Martin, Douglas, and Boeing were studying alternative approaches in microelectronics. *Ibid.*, March 13, 1961, p. 239. North American Aviation, Martin, and Lockheed were all actively establishing semiconductor capabilities. *Ibid.*, February 19, 1962, p. 83; October 17, 1960, pp. 54 ff.; January 8, 1962, p. 95; March 19, 1962, p. 57; and July 8, 1963, p. 68, *Missiles and Rockets*, November 12, 1962, p. 39.

[19] Among the firms developing microcircuitry are General Electric, Motorola, Westinghouse, Texas Instruments, Fairchild Camera, and Signetics. The latter two, however, cannot be classified as large firms. See *Business Week*, December 8, 1962, pp. 86-88; *Aviation Week*, January 8, 1962, pp. 85 ff., and August 27, 1962, p. 69. Other companies which have entered include RCA, General Telephone and Electric, the Philco division of Ford, Bendix Aviation, Sprague Electric, Litton Industries, Hughes Aircraft, IBM, Raytheon, Thompson-Ramo-Wooldridge, Honeywell, Ling-Temco-Vought, Aerojet, General Precision, United Aircraft, and Burroughs. Some smaller companies which also entered include Amelco, Electro-Optical Systems, General Micro-Electronics, Intellux, and Teledyne. *Missiles and Rockets*, February 3, 1964, pp. 31-46.

each fiscal year is a process of redetermination of the "fairness" of profits. All firms with annual receipts in excess of $1 million from government agencies, such as the General Services Administration, Defense Department, and NASA are subject to this provision. The firms in the aerospace industry are thus included in this category.

A renegotiation act is in essence an anomaly, for it provides for the redetermination of a company's profits after the contract has been completed. It is unusual for one party to a contract to be able to renegotiate its outcome if the provisions proved too profitable to the other party. However, the preoccupation with profits earned on government contracts, especially in times of war, has led Congress to enact a series of laws designed to prevent retention of these excessive profits.

Since an excellent history of the background and development of the renegotiation concept has already been written,[1] only the highlights of the form in which the current situation developed will be considered. After World War I, investigations revealed that there had been profiteering. Bills were introduced in Congress to control the level of profits, but nothing was accomplished until 1934 when the Vinson-Trammell Act was passed. This law limited allowable profits on naval contracts to a specified percentage of sales. Through subsequent amendments this law was extended to the Maritime Commission and to Army aircraft. The profit limitation was not on each contract, but on all contracts completed within a year. The high profits associated with war production and a Supreme Court decision which ruled against cancellation of a particular CPFF contract, holding that its 22 percent rate of return on sales was not excessive,[2] led to further reform of the renegotiation concept.

The Renegotiation Act of 1942 did not include precise percentage limitations on profits.[3] It did provide for the recovery of those profits on War and Navy Department and Maritime Commission contracts which were considered excessive. There were subsequent wartime amendments to the law, and although the renegotiation principle lapsed at the end of 1945, it was reapplied to aircraft procurement in 1948. The Renegotiation Act of 1951, which is still in existence, extended this procedure from aircraft only to most other military procurement contracts.

---

[1] Richards C. Osborn, "Background and Evolution of the Renegotiation Concept" in J. Fred Weston, ed., *Procurement and Profit Renegotiation*, (Belmont, Calif. Wadsworth, 1960), pp. 13-42. Much of the material of this section was obtained from Osborn's work.

[2] *United States* vs. *Bethlehem Steel Corporation*, 315 U.S. 289 (1942).

[3] These percentage limitations had been suspended for all companies subject to the excess profits tax by the Second Revenue Act of 1940. This act also established the excess-profits tax itself.

Each contractor subject to renegotiation files with the Renegotiation Board at the end of each fiscal year a report of the total value of sales subject to renegotiation and the total profits earned. The sales and profits of all contracts in a particular fiscal year are lumped together. From these data the Renegotiation Board then attempts to determine the fairness of profits.[4] If the board considers the profits excessive, it can order the company to return the overage to the government. These rulings can be appealed to the United States Tax Court, but the burden of proof is on the company to prove that the board's findings are incorrect.[5]

Moore has suggested that combining a full year's worth of contracts may hide a great deal of information. He suggested that contracts differ in size, risk, technical difficulty, and efficiency of performance.[6] To give each contract equal weight and to presuppose that the diversities cancel out is, in fact, making a big assumption. Combining contracts in this way may lead to inefficiencies. A firm, knowing that it already has earned substantial profits which may be adjudged excessive, may not be quite as eager to minimize costs as it would be otherwise. This again is a conjecture which cannot be verified.

Notable is the arbitrariness by which the board can make its determinations. According to law[7] it must take six statutory factors into account in making its findings. They are:

Reasonableness of costs and profits, with particular regard to volume of production, normal earnings, and comparison of war and peacetime products;

The net worth, with particular regard to the amount and source of public and private capital employed;

Extent of risk assumed, including the risk incident to reasonable pricing policies;

Nature and extent of contribution to the defense effort, including inventive and developmental contribution and cooperation with the government and other contractors in supplying technical assistance;

Character of business, including source and nature of materials, com-

---

4 The administrative steps involved in reaching such a decision are not detailed here, but can be found in Weston, *op. cit.* Other information about renegotiations is contained in Senate Document No. 126, *Report of the Joint Committee on Internal Revenue Taxation, Relating to Renegotiation.* Printed Pursuant to Public Law 216, Section 6, 84th Cong., 1st Sess., approved August 3, 1955 (May 31, 1956); U.S., House, Committee on Ways and Means, *Hearings, Extension of the Renegotiation Act,* 85th Cong., 2d Sess., July 29, 1958. `

5 Moore, *op. cit.,* p. 126.

6 *Ibid.,* p. 124.

7 Section 103 (E) of the Renegotiation Act of 1951.

plexity of manufacturing technique, character and extent of subcontracting, and rate of turnover;

Such other factors whose consideration the public interest and fair and equitable dealing may require, which factors shall be published in the regulations of the board from time to time as adopted.

The vagueness of these standards is apparent and the board itself has not published the actual tests used to meet these criteria. The possibility of disparate treatment between firms should not be ignored. Table 36 shows the rate of return on sales that the Renegotiation Board has determined to be reasonable for several companies for several years.

TABLE 36
ALLOWABLE PROFIT AS A PERCENTAGE OF SALES AFTER RENEGOTIATION FOR
SEVERAL AIRFRAME COMPANIES, 1952-1954

Company	Year	Allowable rate of return
Boeing	1952	6.30
	1953	6.30
	1954	6.31
North American	1953	6.46
	1954	6.56
	1955	6.63
Lockheed	1953	6.17
	1954	6.30
Douglas	1953	5.65
	1954	5.64
Martin	1953	6.20
	1954	6.30

SOURCE: William T. Darden, "Business Experience with Renegotiation," in J. Fred Weston, ed., *Procurement and Profit Renegotiation*, p. 61.

The interesting aspect is the differential rate of return that is allowed. There may be reasons which would justify the differential treatment of rates of return on sales. The statutory factors such as the risks which the contractors accepted and the capital committed to the business may account for these differences, but the weights placed on these factors are not explained explicitly by the Renegotiation Board. A consideration of these factors is, however, beyond the scope of this appendix. Our interest was merely to demonstrate the workings of the renegotiation principle.

INDEX

219